# Lecture Notes in Computer Science 9066

Commenced Publication in 1973
Founding and Former Series Editors:
Gerhard Goos, Juris Hartmanis, and Jan van Leeuwen

More information about this series at http://www.springer.com/series/7411

Mohamed Kassab · Marion Berbineau
Alexey Vinel · Magnus Jonsson
Fabien Garcia · José Soler (Eds.)

# Communication Technologies for Vehicles

8th International Workshop
Nets4Cars/Nets4Trains/Nets4Aircraft 2015
Sousse, Tunisia, May 6–8, 2015
Proceedings

 Springer

*Editors*

Mohamed Kassab
HANA Laboratory
Manouba
Tunisia

Marion Berbineau
IFSTTAR
Villeneuve d'Ascq
France

Alexey Vinel
Halmstad University
Halmstad
Sweden

Magnus Jonsson
Halmstad University
Halmstad
Sweden

Fabien Garcia
ENAC
Toulouse Cedex 4
France

José Soler
Technical University of Denmark
Kgs. Lyngby
Denmark

ISSN 0302-9743                    ISSN 1611-3349    (electronic)
Lecture Notes in Computer Science
ISBN 978-3-319-17764-9            ISBN 978-3-319-17765-6    (eBook)
DOI 10.1007/978-3-319-17765-6

Library of Congress Control Number: 2015935944

LNCS Sublibrary: SL5 – Computer Communication Networks and Telecommunications

Springer Cham Heidelberg New York Dordrecht London
© Springer International Publishing Switzerland 2015

Printed on acid-free paper

Springer International Publishing AG Switzerland is part of Springer Science+Business Media
(www.springer.com)

# Preface

The International Workshop on Communication Technologies for Vehicles provides an international forum on the latest technologies and research in the field of In-Vehicle, Vehicle-to-Vehicle, and Vehicle-to-Infrastructure communications. This workshop is organized annually to present original research results in areas related to physical layer, communication protocols and standards, mobility and traffic models, experimental and field operational testing, and performance analysis.

First launched by Tsutomu Tsuboi, Alexey Vinel, and Fei Liu in Saint Petersburg, Russia (2009), Communication Technologies for Vehicles workshops were then held in Newcastle-upon-Tyne, UK (2010), Oberpfaffenhofen, Germany (2011), Vilnius, Lithuania (2012), Lille, France (2013), Offenburg, Germany (2014-Spring), Saint Petersburg, Russia (2014-Fall).

These proceedings gather the papers presented at the 8th edition of the workshop (Nets4Cars-Nets4Trains-Nets4Aircarft 2015) which took place in Sousse, Tunisia on May 2015. This event was hosted by HANA Laboratory, University of Manouba, Tunisia and coorganized with ENISO, University of Sousse, Tunisia and IFSTTAR, France.

This 8th edition had dedicated tracks for Road-, Rail-, and Air-based approaches. The call for papers resulted in 27 submissions. Each of them was assigned to the Technical Program Committee members and 20 submissions were accepted for publication (10 for the road track, 6 for the rail track, and 4 for the air track). Each accepted paper got at least two independent reviews. The order of the papers in these proceedings is aligned with the workshop program.

We extend a sincere "thank you" to all the authors who submitted the results of their recent work, to our Technical Program Committee, as well as the thoughtful external reviewers.

May 2015

Mohamed Kassab
Marion Berbineau
Alexey Vinel
Magnus Jonsson
Fabien Garcia
José Soler

# Organization

## Workshop Organizers

### General Co-chairs

| | |
|---|---|
| Marion Berbineau | IFSTTAR, France |
| Abdelfettah Belghith | HANA Laboratory, Tunisia |
| Alexey Vinel | Halmstad University, Sweden |

### Organization Co-chair

| | |
|---|---|
| Mohamed Kassab | HANA Laboratory, Tunisia |
| Aref Meddeb | ENISO, Tunisia |

### TPC Co-chairs

| | |
|---|---|
| Nets4cars: Magnus Jonsson | Halmstad University, Sweden |
| Nets4trains: José Soler | Technical University of Denmark, Denmark |
| Nets4aircraft: Fabien Garcia | École Nationale D'Aviation Civile, France |

### Steering Committee

| | |
|---|---|
| Marion Berbineau | IFSTTAR, France |
| Alexey Vinel | Halmstad University, Sweden |
| Robil Daher | German University in Cairo, Egypt |
| Xu Li | State University of New York, USA |
| Antonella Molinaro | UNIRC, Italy |
| Joel Rodrigues | University of Beira Interior, Portugal |
| Thomas Strang | DLR, Germany |
| Tsutomu Tsuboi | Hamamatsu Agency for Innovation, Japan |
| Kishor Trivedi | Duke University, USA |
| Yan Zhang | Simula Research Laboratory, Norway |

### Technical Program Committee

| | |
|---|---|
| Mohamed Amine Abid | HANA Laboratory, Tunisia |
| Iñigo Adín | CEIT, Spain |
| Marina Aguado | University of the Basque Country, Spain |
| Onur Altintas | Toyota InfoTechnology Center, Japan |

| Simon Plass | German Aerospace Center (DLR), Germany |
| Joachim Posegga | Institute of IT-Security and Security Law, Germany |
| Paolo Santi | IIT-CNR, Italy |
| Lars Schnieder | Deutsches Zentrum für Luft-und Raumfahrt, Germany |
| Sidi-Mohammed Senouci | University of Bourgogne, France |
| Sébastien Simoens | Alstom, France |
| Vasco Soares | Polytechnic Institute of Castelo Branco, Portugal |
| Patrick Sondi | Université du Littoral et Côte d'Opale, France |
| Jouni Tervonen | University of Oulu, Finland |
| Alexey Vinel | Halmstad University, Sweden |

## Additional Reviewers

| Lotfi Abdi | ENIT, Tunisia |
| Ahmad Al-Khalil | University of Northampton, UK |
| Mohamed Belhassen | HANA Laboratory, Tunisia |
| Sebastian Bittl | Fraunhofer ESK, Germany |
| Ghofrane Fersi | National School of Engineers of Sfax, Tunisia |
| Paula Fraga-Lamas | University of A Coruña, Spain |
| Chong Han | University of Surrey, UK |
| Vincent Hilaire | UTBM, France |
| Arnaud Lanoix | University of Nantes, France |
| Nicolas Larrieu | ENAC, France |
| Nikita Lyamin | Halmstad University, Sweden |
| Eswaran Subha P. | International Institute of Information Technology, India |
| Dorian Petit | University of Valenciennes and Hainaut-Cambresis, France |
| Ibrahim Rashdan | German Aerospace Center (DLR), Germany |
| Zhongliang Zhao | University of Bern, Switzerland |

## Hosting Institution

HANA Laboratory, University of Manouba, Tunisia

## Organization Committee

| Sofiene Jelassi | ISIMM, Tunisia |
| Abdelwahed Berguiga | ISIMM, Tunisia |
| Amine Dhraief | HANA Laboratory, Tunisia |
| Mohamed Amine Abid | HANA Laboratory, Tunisia |
| Nour Houda Dougui | HANA Laboratory, Tunisia |

## Co-organizer and Sponsor Institutions

ENISO, University of Sousse, Tunisia
IFSTTAR, France
Halmstad University, Sweden

# Contents

## Road

# Rail

# Air

# Road

# Utilising SCM – MIMO Channel Model Based on V-BLAST Channel Coding in V2V Communication

Ahmad Baheej Al-Khalil, Scott Turner, and Ali Al-Sherbaz

The University of Northampton, School of Science and Technology, St. Georg Avenue,
Northampton NN2 6JD, UK
{ahmad.al-khalil,scott.turner,ali.al-sherbaz}@northampton.ac.uk

**Abstract.** Vehicular ad hoc networks VANETs has recently received significant attention in intelligent transport systems (ITS) research. It provides the driver with information regarding traffic and road conditions which is needed to reduce accidents, which will save many people's lives. In Vehicle-to-vehicle V2V communication the high-speed mobility of the nodes is the challenge, which significantly affects the reliability of communication. In this paper the utilising of SCM-MIMO channel model, (which is based on V-BLAST channel coding) is present to evaluate the performance of the PHY layer in V2V communication. The simulation results observed that the SCM model can overcome the propagation issues such as path loss, multipath fading and shadowing loss. The simulation considered three different environments, high, medium and low disruptions in urban traffic.

**Keywords:** VANETs, V2V, MIMO, SCM, V-BLAST.

## 1 Introduction

In the recent years the advent of Vehicular Ad-hoc Networks VANETs considers one of the most important developments in the wireless communications systems. In a recent United Nation UN road safety report around the world, it was documented that road safety deaths made up 2.2% of the leading causes of death in 2004. It has been predicted that this will rise to 3.6% by 2030. There have been recommendations made by the Global Status Report regarding the poor collaboration between the sectors made responsible for collecting and reporting data on road traffic incidents. These recommendations have also included communication between the police, health and transport services and their ability to man such operations [1]. There is therefore a need to provide the driver with information regarding traffic and road conditions to reduce these incidents, thus will keep many people's lives. VANETs is a technology which uses the moving vehicles as nodes in the wireless network, which also considers as a special case of the Mobile Ad-hoc Networks MANETs [2]. VANETs is dedicated to exchange the messages between the vehicles in two forms: vehicle to vehicle V2V and vehicle to infrastructure V2I [3]. The aim of the use of VANETs technology is to produce a full wireless communication solution among vehicles, to satisfy the

© Springer International Publishing Switzerland 2015
M. Kassab et al. (Eds.): Nets4Cars/Nets4Trains/Nets4Aircraft 2015, LNCS 9066, pp. 3–11, 2015.
DOI: 10.1007/978-3-319-17765-6_1

safety and the comfortable applications requirements such as less congestion, accident warning, road exploration, etc. An important advantage of VANETs is battery power is generated during the journey, providing an extended battery life.

The paper is organized as follows. In Section 2, important general background information on VANETs standards, MIMO technology with VANETs and V-BLAST coding are provided. The SCM channel model is explained in section 3. Next, the parameters and environments settings are presented in section 4. Section 5 is the discussion of the simulation results. Finally Section 6 is concluding this paper.

## 2     Background

### 2.1     VANETs Standard

Dedicated Short Range Communication DSRC is the wireless communication protocol for the Vehicular Ad-hoc Networks, it was approved by the United State Federal Communication Commission FCC in 1992 [4]. DSRC is allocated to support the Intelligent Transport System ITS applications in the licensed band of 5.9 GHz. In 2004, the DSRC joined the IEEE (Institute of Engineering Electrical and Electronics) and classified as a part of the IEEE 802.11 family known as IEEE 802.11p [5]. The IEEE 802.11p standard uses the same physical layer as the IEEE 802.11a standard. However, the only difference is the bandwidth channel which is 10MHz instead of the 20MHz [6]. The purpose of the IEEE 802.11p standard is to provide the minimum specification, ensuring that the devices are able to communicate in rapidly changing environment [7].

### 2.2     MIMO Technology with VANETs

In VANETs communications the advantages of having unlimited battery life and multiple antennas positions are strong factors in using Multiple-Input-Multiple-Output MIMO systems with VANETs [8]. MIMO systems perform higher capacities compared to single antenna systems. However, there are significant challenges which need to be taken in the consideration like: channel modeling, processing of space time signals in VANETs and channel coding. MIMO provides considerable advantages including having wider coverage area, enhancing the multi fading environments and improving higher data throughputs [9]. Providing high data rate at high QoS in VANETs communication system, is considered as the greatest challenges in this research area [10] [11]. Due to the factors that could affect to the signal strength such as scattering, reflection and interference, the bandwidth is needed to improve the QoS. To improve the bandwidth there are two methods in general [8], in the first approach the diversity technique is used to improve link reliability in term of improving the transmit diversity and/or the receive diversity. The use of higher modulations and efficient codes will increase the data rate which consequently leads to improving the reliability of the link [8]. In the second approach MIMO systems are used in both transmitter and receiver, while each transmitting antenna transmits a separate stream of data. However, MIMO technology seems to meet these issues in term of increasing the inbound and outbound data traffic [12].

## 2.3    Vertical Bell Labs Layered Space Time V-BLAST

V-BLAST is non – linear MIMO receiver detection algorithm to the receipt of multi antenna MIMO systems. The principle of this algorithm: V-BLAST employs successive interference cancellation SIC. At the beginning, the algorithm identifies the most powerful signal which has a highest SNR, next step it regenerates the received signal from this user from available decision. The impact of each estimated symbol is cancelled from the received symbol vector so what does SIC roughly means. One symbol is estimates from the vector $x_1x_2x_3x_4$ , for example $x_1$ then the impact of $x_1$ will be removed from the receive vector y and the rest of the symbols are decodes similarly. After decoding every symbol the effect of it will be remove progressively in the receive symbol vector and so on to decode the other receive symbol [13].

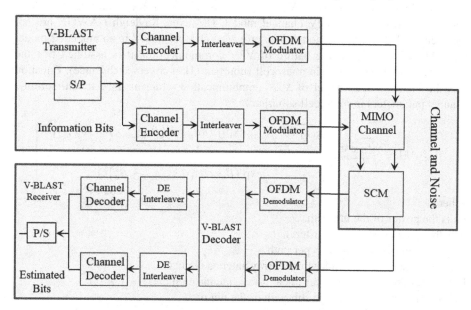

**Fig. 1.** 2x2 V-BLAST MIMO System

# 3    Spatial Channel Model SCM

## 3.1    SCM Overview

The MIMO – SCM was established in 2003 by the Partnership Project standards body, 3GPP [14]. SCM is a wireless propagation channel based on stochastic modelling, or the ray-based model, which is specified to outdoor antennas in terms of mobility. It is commonly used in a dynamic MIMO channel as it can take account of the temporal correlation parameters of the communication channel. However, an SCM is dedicated for a Code Division Multiple Access (CDMA) system with 5MHz band and 2GHz frequency [15]. The 3GPP simulated the SCM-MIMO wireless propagation channel in various cases: urban Macrocell environment, suburban Macrocell environment and urban microcell environment. They apply the concept of spatial and polarization diversity assuming multiple antennas at both the transmitter and receiver [16].The SCM distributes the positions of the scatters randomly instead of using the direct signal representation in the environment [17]. In V2V communication, the obstacles objects present in the environment (e.g. buildings, trees and vehicles) makes the signals overlap. If the overlapping does not exist, the signal will propagate as a line of sight (LOS) path, or as a non LOS (NLOS) path [18] Figure 2.

### 3.2    The Proposed Channel Model

The proposed model is built upon the 3GPP model. It mainly follows the approach of the SCM model to utilise it as a V2V channel model. In [4], Rayleigh / AWGN channel model are used as a V2V channel model. However, Rayleigh / AWGN are not representing V2V channel model. The proposed channel model is an amended model of SCM-MIMO. Due to the nature of V2V communication, it is assumed that the AoD and AoA is (180 ± 5) in microcell suburban (1km coverage distance). Equation 1 is the mathematical model of V2V communication which is used to estimate the channel parameters in microcell suburban.

$$h_{r,s,n}^{(I)}(t) = \sqrt{\frac{P_n}{M}} \sum_{m=1}^{M} \begin{bmatrix} \sqrt{V_1} \left(\theta_{m,n,AoD} \exp[j \left(kd_s \sin \left(\theta_{m,n,AoD}\right) + \Phi_{n,m}\right)] \times \\ \sqrt{V_2} \left(\theta_{n,m,AoA} \exp[j \left(kd_r \sin\left(\theta_{n,m,AoA}\right)\right)] \times \\ \exp \left(jkv \cos\left(\theta_{n,m,AoA} - \theta_v\right)t\right) \end{bmatrix} \quad (1)$$

Whereas:
Pn is the power of the nth path.
N is the number of paths (clusters).
M is the number of sub-paths per path.
S is the number of the sender linear array antenna elements.
R is the number of the receiver linear array antenna elements.
Φn, m is the phase of the mth sub-path of the nth path.
θn, m, AoD is the AoD for the mth subpath of the nth path.
θn, m, AoA is the AoA for the mth subpath of the nth path.
V1 is vehicle1 antenna gains of each array element.
V2 is vehicle2 antenna gains of each array element.
j is the square root of -1.
k is the wave number $2\pi / \lambda$, where $\lambda$ is carrier wavelength in meters.
ds is the distance in meters from the sender antenna elements.
dr is the distance in meters from the receiver antenna elements.
v is the magnitude of the sender velocity vector.
θv is the angle of the sender velocity vector.

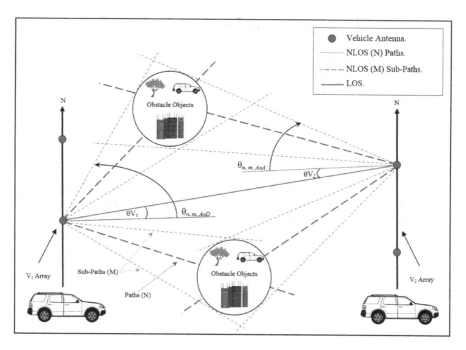

**Fig. 2.** SCM Modeling Approach in V2V

## 4    Parameters and Environment Settings

In order to estimate channel fading, channel capacity and the power delay for the V2V communication, three different speeds are considered with three environments at 5.9GHz carrier frequency: Figure 3 for the slow speed (20km\h), Figure 4 for the medium speed (60km\h) and Figure 5 for the high speed (100km\h). The three different environments have been tested according to their disruption levels: low level, medium level and high level disruptions environments. The number of clusters (Multi-path) = 2 and sub-path clusters = 5 allocated for the low level disruption environment while the number of clusters = 4 and sub-path clusters = 10 allocated for the medium level disruption environment and the number of clusters = 6 and sub-path clusters = 20 allocated for the high level disruption environment. In these environments two modulation scheme have been used 4-QAM and 16-QAM.

## 5    Simulation Results and Discussion

Different Scenarios and tests have been run using SCM-MIMO-2x2 based on the V-BLAST coding system in high dynamic disruption environment. In Equ 1, H is the instant channel parameter for 10 sec period in MIMO 2X2 matrix ($h_{11}$, $h_{12}$, $h_{21}$, $h_{22}$) generated by the SCM [3], as it's ˙ periodically change over the time to generate new H.

$$Y = H.X + N \tag{2}$$

$$\begin{bmatrix} y_1(t) \\ y_2(t) \end{bmatrix} = \begin{bmatrix} h_{11} & h_{12} \\ h_{21} & h_{22} \end{bmatrix} \cdot \begin{bmatrix} x_1(t) \\ x_2(t) \end{bmatrix} + \begin{bmatrix} n_1(t) \\ n_2(t) \end{bmatrix} \tag{3}$$

Whereas,
x is the transmitted symbol vector.
y is the received symbol vector.
h is the channel characteristics matrix.
n is the noise.

The simulation results in Figures 3, 4 and 5 show the BER vs. SNR for three different speeds (20km\h, 60km\h and 100km\h) and two different modulations 4-QAM and 16-QAM. Table 1 compares the SNRs results at BER $10^{-2}$ considerably and the simulation results seems to be consistent when the V-BLAST coding is used.

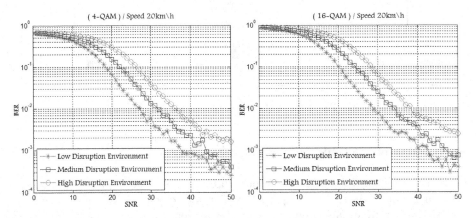

**Fig. 3.** Vehicle Speed 20 km\h (4-QAM and 16-QAM)

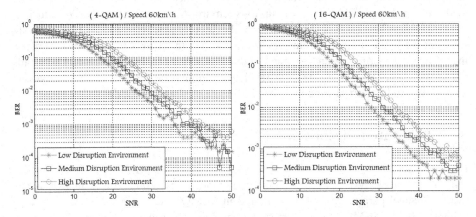

**Fig. 4.** Vehicle Speed 60 km\h (4-QAM and 16-QAM)

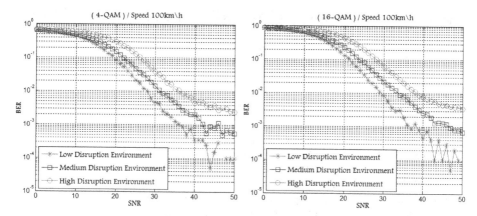

**Fig. 5.** Vehicle Speed 100 km\h (4-QAM and 16-QAM)

**Table 1.** The SNRs at BER $10^{-2}$ Gained from Figuers 3, 4 and 5 for 4-QAM and 16-QAM Modulation

| Speeds | Disruption Level Environment | | | | | |
|---|---|---|---|---|---|---|
| | *Low Disruption* | | *Medium Disruption* | | *High    Disruption* | |
| | 4QAM | 16QAM | 4QAM | 16QAM | 4QAM | 16QAM |
| 20km\h | 27 | 29 | 33 | 34 | 37 | 38 |
| 60km\h | 26 | 28 | 29 | 31 | 33 | 34 |
| 100km\h | 28 | 29 | 32 | 34 | 37 | 38 |

As shown in table 1, as a vehicle is traveling at slow speed 20km\h the results for the 16-QAM modulation are 29, 34, and 38. These results are considered consistent according to the disruption levels low, medium and high, while comparing with our previous work in [19] the obtained result were 37, 34 and 37 with the same environment settings which are inconsistent. The results in table 1 indicate that the performance of the PHY in V2V communication improves considerably and the simulation results seems to be consistent when the V-BLAST coding is used.

# 6    Conclusion and Future Work

In this paper, SCM-MIMO channel model with V-BLAST coding system is used to evaluate V2V physical layer performance. The amounts of the considered parameters in SCM-MIMO channel model attempt to mimic the highly dynamic disruption environment in V2V. The channel model with V-BLAST has improved the bit error rate for the nodes moving at different speeds, compared to the previous work [19] with Alamouti coding. On the other hand, the Rayleigh / AWGN channel model has been also used in [4] as a V2V channel model. However, Rayleigh / AWGN are a general channel model and not specifically designed to represent V2V channel model. For higher modulation rate such as 64-QAM, it is recommended to choose a more reliable/robust coding system such as T-BLAST, Spatial Modulation SM and Spatial Multiplexing.

# References

1. W. H. Organization, Global status report on road safety: time for action. WHO Library Cataloguing-in-Publication Data, Geneva (2009)
2. Prasanth, K., Duraiswamy, K., Jayasudha, K., Chandrasekar, C.: Improved Packet Forwarding Approach in Vehicular Ad Hoc Networks Using RDGR Algorithm. International Journal of Next Generation Network (IJNGN) 2, 1 (2010)
3. Kumar, R., Dave, M.: A Comparative Study of Various Routing Protocols in VANET. IJCSI International Journal of Computer Science 8, 1 (2011)
4. Al-Khalil, A., Al-Sherbaz, A., Turner, S.: Enhancing the Physical Layer in V2V Communication Using OFDM-MIMO Techniques. In: PGNet, Liverpool (2013)
5. Miao, L., Djouani, K., Wyk, B., Hamam, Y.: Evaluation and Enhancement of IEEE 802.11p Standard: A Survey. Mobile Computing 1(1) (2012)
6. Han, C., Dianati, M., Tafazolli, R., Kernchen, R.: Throughput Analysis of the IEEE 802.11p Enhanced Distributed Channel Access Function in Vehicular Environment. IEEE (2012)
7. IEEE, IEEE Draft P802.11-REVmb™/D12, Institute of Electrical and Electronics Engineers, New York, (2011)
8. Abdalla, G.: Physical and Link Layers of Vehicle Ad Hoc Networks: Investigating the performance of MIMO-OFDM and IEEE 802.11 in VANET, LAP LAMBERT. Academic Publishing (2011)
9. Nguyen, D., Garcia-Luna-Aceves, J.: A Practical Approach to Rate Adaptation for Multi-Antenna Systems. In: 19th IEEE International Conference on Network Protocols, Vancouver (2011)
10. Xue, Q., Ganz, A.: Ad hoc QoS on-demand routing (AQOR) in mobile ad hoc networks (2002)
11. Dok, H., Fu, H., Echevarria, R., Weerasi, H.: Privacy Issues of Vehicular Ad-Hoc Networks 3 (2010)
12. Bolcskei, H., Zurich, E.: MIMO-OFDM Wireless Systems: Basics, Perspectives, and Challenges. IEEE (2006)
13. Wu, Y., Peng, X., Song, Y.: A Symbol-wise Ordered Successive Interference Cancellation Detector for Layered Space-Time Block Codes. International Journal of Digital Content Technology and its Applications 5, 4 (2011)
14. Shichuan, M., Deborah, D., Hamid, S., Yaoqing, Y.: An Extension of the 3GPP Spatial Channel Model in outdoor-to-indoor environments. In: 3rd European Conference on Antennas and Propagation, EuCAP 2009, EU (2009)
15. Baum, D.S., Hansen, J., Galdo, G.D., Milojevic, M., Salo, J., Kyösti, P.: An Interim Channel Model for Beyond-3G Systems: Extending the 3GPP Spatial Channel Model (SCM). In: 2005 IEEE 61st Vehicular Technology Conference, VTC 2005-Spring (2005)
16. Xirouchakis, I.: Mathworks (July 31, 2008), http://www.mathworks.co.uk, http://www.mathworks.co.uk/matlabcentral/fileexchange/20911-spatial-channel-model-for-mimo-simulations-a-ray-based-simulator-based-on-3gpp-tr-25-996-v-6-1-0 (accessed July 02 2013)

17. Jaeckel, S., Börner, K., Thiele, L., Jungnickel, V.: A Geometric Polarization Rotation Model for the 3-D Spatial Channel Model. IEEE Transactions on Antennas and Propagation 60(12), 12 (2012)
18. Zhang, L., Chen, F.: A Channel Model for VANET Simulation System. International Journal of Automation and Power Engineering (IJAPE) 2(4), 7 (2013)
19. Al-Khalil, A.B., Turner, S., Al-Sherbaz, A.: Feasibility Study of Utilising SCM – MIMO Channel Model in V2V Communication. In: 7th International Workshop on Communication Technologies for Vehicles, Saint-Petersburg (2014)

# Service Driven Dynamic Hashing Based Radio Resource Management for Intelligent Transport Systems

Subha P. Eswaran[1], Jyotsna Bapat[1], and V. Ariharan [2]

[1]International Institute of Information Technology, Bengaluru, India
subhape@bel.co.in, jbapat@iiitb.ac.in
[2]Central Research Laboratory, Bharat Electronics Limited, Bengaluru, India
ariharanv@bel.co.in

**Abstract.** Intelligent Transport Systems (ITS) aim to improve transport safety, productivity and reliability by interconnecting different transport entities and providing real-time instantaneous transport information to various transport system users. Communication systems play an important role in achieving this mission. Heterogeneous technologies/protocols such as WLAN, DSRC, RFID, GSM, WiMAX etc. currently constitute the communication system of ITS. ITS comprises of various services (monitoring, navigation, value-added services etc.) with diverse Quality of Service (QoS), latency & throughput requirements. Large number of aperiodic and sporadic service requests from heterogeneous radio communication devices are expected to result in another type of congestion; the spectral congestion. In this paper, we propose an efficient radio resource management scheme using Complex Event Processing (CEP) based Service-Prioritized Opportunistic Communication (SPOC) architecture to address this spectral congestion. Based on CEP, SPOC processes the simple events such as information about spectrum usage patterns, radio device abilities, geo-locations, spectrum needs and derives complex spectrum allocation decisions. Spectrum allocation and management decisions are governed by policy engine of SPOC. Volume of spectrum request is predicted by Time of the Day based Dynamic Hashing algorithm that reduces computation complexities and achieves faster spectrum allocation decision. This infrastructure based spectrum management technique is shown to improve service completion rate for all devices while satisfying dynamic QoS needs of emergency/high priority services of ITS. Compared to existing scheduling schemes such as Greedy, Max-Min and Early Dead-Line First algorithms, SPOC is shown to be more suitable for ITS paradigm due to its ability to coordinate several hundreds of spectrum demands in real-time, while maintaining fairness.

**Keywords:** ITS, CEP, Dynamic Hashing, Spectrum Management.

## 1    Introduction

Intelligent Transport Systems (ITS) can be defined as the application of advanced Information & Communication Technology (ICT) to vehicles and infrastructures in order to achieve enhanced safety and mobility while reducing the environmental impacts of transportation [1]. The vision of ITS is accomplished by means of information exchange

© Springer International Publishing Switzerland 2015
M. Kassab et al. (Eds.): Nets4Cars/Nets4Trains/Nets4Aircraft 2015, LNCS 9066, pp. 12–23, 2015.
DOI: 10.1007/978-3-319-17765-6 _2

among many diverse ITS entities from road side communication infrastructures (traffic signals, sensors, message boards), transportation and management systems, to the end users - their vehicles. The information exchange in ITS should be capable of detecting and reporting various traffic events in real time and should generate useful, reliable and instantaneous traffic information to support the travelers, freight managers, system operators and other transport system users.

Communication technology entities of ITS encompass fixed devices and mobile devices fitted to vehicles and other moving objects [2]. On-board vehicle devices should have the instantaneous information exchange through which speed and nearness of the surrounded vehicles can be sensed and act accordingly to have an accident free drive. Within the vehicle there may be devices that communicate with the infrastructure entities to get traffic updates that help to avoid traffic jam or to avoid foggy and slippery roads which need to happen on the move. Some on-board devices need to communicate with infrastructure entities such as Road Side Units (RSU), message boards to get route update, map download, toll or parking information. ITS can be visualized as a coordinated and co-operative real-time information system composite of various time bounded data exchange at different service level criticalities such as ambulance, police, incident-driven, monitoring, warning and alarm services. Different services of ITS have different latency & throughput requirements and require different communication channel access requirements. For example, emergency services like incident response requires high priority channel access with less data throughput whereas data base services like route-map download requires more data throughput but low priority can be given for accessing the channel. If the spectrum sharing is not coordinated it may lead to a situation that emergency information exchanges could starve of channel congestion while high bandwidth demanding low-priority applications such as media-download occupies the channel. This requires a service driven QoS policy based spectrum sharing mechanism for future ITS.

If all ITS communication systems were to use same communication standard, it would have been easy to achieve shared communication access. But currently information exchange for ITS takes place through various forms of communication technologies (GSM, WLAN, etc.) constituting a heterogeneous network scenario. Heterogeneous communication technologies must act cooperatively to provide various services for ITS. It is also worth noting that different services of ITS demands different Quality-of-Service, end-to-end delays and bandwidth requirements [3]. In addition each ITS entity will experience different wireless channel state conditions depending upon their mobility or geo-locations. However since different ITS entities need to share the same spectral bandwidth there is a need to define spectrum sharing mechanism for ITS depending upon the services offered and channel conditions to meet the QoS requirements.

The challenges associated with the spectrum management of ITS are very close to the concerns seen in that of heterogeneous networks (HetNets) [4, 5, 6] listed in table 1. Compared to Home-Net or Health-Net scenario ITS must deal with rapidly changing complex scenario with large number of players. In addition, mobile scenario requires quick spectrum decisions compared to other HetNets and low computation capacity of the participating devices limits the use of complex distributive spectrum management solutions. This mandates the need for a centralized opportunistic spectrum management solutions for ITS. Considering these requirements, Service Prioritized Opportunistic Communication (SPOC) architecture is proposed in this paper. Our contributions are in three fold:

- Service type classification and Complex Event Processing (CEP) Engine based Service driven communication architecture proposed for ITS.
- Time of the Day (ToD) based Dynamic Hashing methodology is introduced to map the spectrum demands and spectrum availability.
- Service driven spectrum sharing algorithm based on service priorities, time-criticalities and QoS.

The rest of the paper is organized as follows: Related works are presented in Section-2. System model of SPOC-ITS is described in Section-3. Dynamic hashing and Service driven spectrum sharing algorithm are detailed in Section-4. CEP based prototype implementation and performance comparisons with Greedy/EDF/Max-Min are presented in Section-5. Conclusions and future work can be found in Section-6.

Table 1. Comparison of Heterogeneous networks

| Sl. No. | Parameter | ITS | Home Net | Health Network | Cognitive Radio Network |
|---|---|---|---|---|---|
| 1 | Heterogeneous Technologies GSM, WiFi etc. | ✓ | ✓ | ✓ | ✓ |
| 2 | High Density of nodes/sq.km >500 | ✓ | ✗ | ✗ | ✗ |
| 3 | Various service Priorities | ✓ | ✗ | ✗ | ✗ |
| 4 | Mixed & multiple time critical (Ambulance, police, fire, VIP) nodes | ✓ | ✗ | ✓ | ✗ |
| 5 | Power constraints/low battery device | ✓ | ✗ | ✗ | ✗ |
| 6 | Almost 80% of device has low capacity | ✓ | ✗ | Partial ✗ | ✗ |
| 7 | Rapid Radio environment/Channel state variation due to mobility | ✓ | ✗ | ✗ | ✗ |
| 8 | User Mobility (high speed vehicles) | ✓ | ✗ | ✗ | ✓ |

## 2  Related Work

Centralized spectrum allocation schemes for Multi-Radio Access Technology environment and for Cognitive Radio Network is introduced in [7, 8] have high latency and not scalable; making them unsuitable for ITS, where several hundreds of requests must be processed per second. Centralized solutions provided for cellular networks [9] are not suitable for ITS either, as they don't consider the service priorities or the time criticality of the spectrum needs.

Spectrum resource allocation problem is similar to any resource allocation problem and well established algorithms such as Max-Min/Back Pressure, Greedy, and Early Dead Function (EDF) can be applied. Each algorithm has its pros and cons such as

Greedy algorithm provides high throughput, but lacks in fair scheduling [10], while Max-Min Fair algorithm [11] achieves fairness at average throughput and critical jobs are not prioritized. To manage time critical jobs, EDF/mixed-critical algorithms [12] can be considered. While employing these methods time critical jobs will get served but achieves average throughput. In [13], EDF/FIFO based spectrum scheduling for voice and data processing of ITS is introduced that satisfies the QoS needs but there is no provision of improving spectrum utilization or fairness and it lacks in scalability. In [14], vehicle-mounted communication gateway for ITS is presented, for managing the on-board communication with the back-office, which doesn't include other entities like road-side infrastructures and other sensor communications. New spectrum management architecture is essential for ITS that can satisfy diverse latency needs, QoS requirements, time criticality and multiple service priorities of various entities of ITS network, while managing the multitudinous spectrum demands in a fairway. One such architecture is proposed in this paper.

# 3   System Model

## 3.1   Proposed Architectural Framework of SPOC

The architecture of the Service Prioritized Opportunistic Communication (SPOC) for ITS is depicted in Fig. 1. SPOC kind of architecture is used for spectrum management of IoT proposed in [15].The functional modules of the proposed system are described below.

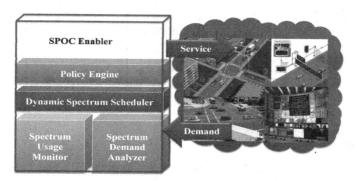

**Fig. 1.** SPOC architecture

- <u>Spectrum Usage Monitor</u>: It has spectrum sensing and interference analysis module. Information about spectrum availability of different frequency bands and their interference measures are archived by these modules. A location awareness module is used to enforce the geo-location based rules for spectrum sharing.
- <u>Spectrum Demand Analyzer:</u> Collects the spectrum demands from various players. It classifies the type of service requested and analyzes the capacities of the devices like protocol supported, latency limits and operable frequencies.

- Policy Engine: Has a set of spectrum allocation rules based on the operating spectrum band, type of service, type of player and device capabilities. These rules are dynamic depending upon geo-locations subject to local policies.
- Dynamic Spectrum Scheduler (DSS): The DSS makes spectrum allocation decisions in conform to the conditions of the Policy engine.

## 3.2  Deployment Overview of SPOC

The area of the city under ITS can be partitioned into multiple zones, based on the coverage area of the central entity. SPOC will be located in every zone that facilities the spectrum demand needs of ITS. Radio devices in each ITS zone are categorized into three major group of players: (a) Static communication devices placed across the entire zone; (b) Mobile nodes (pass by vehicles) which enter into the zone and move around the zone for limited time; (c) Moderator nodes (interceptors) which are semi-mobile and move within the zone and stays in the zone for long time (few hours). Every radio device that enters SPOC zone will be given spectrum suggestions as per the sequence flow depicted in Fig. 2.

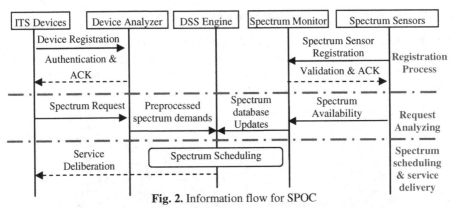

**Fig. 2.** Information flow for SPOC

## 3.3  Proposed Service Classification of SPOC

**Table 2.** Proposed Service Classification of ITS

| Type of Service | Characteristics | ITS application |
|---|---|---|
| **Type-I** - (database service) | Lowest priority/more spectrum usage time & high bandwidth > 1Mbps | Map / Media downloading, Field Vehicles, Static Infrastructures |
| **Type-II**- (Environment aware service) | Low spectrum usage time and low bandwidth <1Mbps | Inter-vehicle communication, parking and toll functionalities |
| **Type-III** - (alarm & warning service) | Low spectrum usage time and low bandwidth <100Kbps | Traffic jam/ weather warnings |
| **Type-IV**-(Incident driven services) | Highest priority / less spectrum usage time and low bandwidth <50Kbps | Ambulance/ Emergency vehicle/ road accident notification |

# 4    System Design

Spectrum decisions are processed by DSS in three phases as given below:

**Phase 1: Dynamic Hashing.** Time of the Day based Dynamic Hashing technique is introduced to categorize the requests based on bandwidth demands. Each bandwidth bucket is applied with second level hashing to obtain service classified buckets.

**Phase 2: Prioritized Scheduling.** Service classified buckets are enforced with prioritized scheduling scheme dictated from policy engine. As the scheduling algorithm is applied separately on different service buckets and not on the large set of requests, it reduces the spectrum decision making time.

**Phase 3: Spectrum Mapping.** Available Spectrum dataset is hashed with ToD based dynamic hashing using bandwidth as key. Prioritized scheduled requests of different service buckets will be mapped to the spectrum availability buckets.

## 4.1    Dynamic Hashing

The main idea of hashing is to divide the dataset 'B' into a number of 'N' disjoint subsets or buckets $B_1$, $B_2$,..$B_N$. They are useful for lookup of information since the hash indexing makes the process very efficient. In ITS, it can be noted that the requested bandwidth varies from minimum of few Kbps (alerts/warnings) to maximum of few Gbps (video surveillance/media download) [2]; accordingly it is proposed to have a hashing function that categorizes the large set of spectrum demands to smaller subsets based on requested bandwidth. By hashing the spectrum demands based on requested bandwidth, it will form 'N' different bandwidth buckets. Each bucket represents a certain range of bandwidth say bucket '1' ($B_1$) can have spectrum demands that falls between 1k to 10kbps and bucket '2'($B_2$) will have requests range from 20k to 100kbps and so on. Static hashing assumes a static number of buckets and static bucket size. However the dynamic scenario in ITS demands, variable bucket size and variable bucket numbers, i.e. dynamic hashing.

Dynamic hashing offers the flexibility of variable bucket number/size by the concept of extendable bucket or bucket spilt methods. Dynamic hashing suffers the problem of bucket re-assignment even for a small flow change which is unnecessary and increases computation burden [16]. So if the volume of requests for a bucket can be predictable, re-assignment of buckets can be done in a more efficient manner. In ITS the interesting factor is that the spectrum demand is in general proportional to the vehicle traffic. And also vehicle traffic varies according to the Time of the Day (ToD). It is also understood that as the traffic is low, the bucket numbers/size can be reduced and as the traffic is high it can be increased. Dynamic hashing with flow volume is introduced in [17], for managing data traffic in Internet where flow volume is determined using best-flow and largest-flow fit algorithms. In this paper, ToD based dynamic hashing is introduced exclusively for ITS spectrum management.

**First Level Bandwidth Hashing - ToD Based Dynamic Hashing.** Hash function is chosen to map the incoming spectrum demands into bandwidth buckets $B_1$, $B_2$,...$B_N$. Hash value is generated as following :

→  Hash value: H(bandwidth, duration of usage) mod K
→  K= N - number of bandwidth buckets.

The number of buckets and their size can be decided dynamically depending upon the incoming volume of the spectrum demand requests. Generally the bucket re-assignment is determined by policy. Here Time of the Day based policy set is adopted. Accordingly, three hash functions ($H_H$, $H_M$, $H_L$) are used to give three different bucket re-assignment strategies. $H_H$ is applied at the Time of the Day when there will be heavy road vehicle traffic. $H_L$ represents the scenario where spectrum demand requests are sporadic and minimal for most of the buckets. $H_L$ is assumed to occur at the Time of the Day when there will be low road vehicle traffic. $H_M$ is a moderate scenario of $H_L$ and $H_H$. For the $H_L$ and $H_M$ cases, the number of buckets will be less than $H_H$. Bucket assignment of ToD based dynamic hashing is shown in Fig.3.

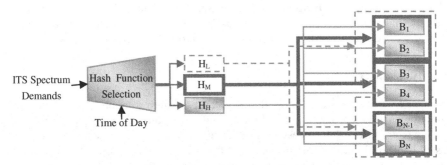

**Fig. 3.** ToD based Dynamic Hashing

**Second Level Service Hashing-Static.** Following the bandwidth dynamic hashing, a second level static hashing is carried to sub categorizes the bandwidth buckets. The second level hashing divides each bandwidth buckets into four service buckets according to class of service as discussed in section-3.3. Accordingly, four service buckets ($S_1B_i$, $S_2B_i$, $S_3B_i$, $S_4B_i$) for each bandwidth hash bucket ($B_i$) is obtained; i varies from 1,2,...N. Each bandwidth requests are scheduled depending upon the latency, QoS and device capacity which is described in the following section. Prioritized requests will be mapped to the requested bandwidth of the available spectrum. The flow of hashing, scheduling and mapping to the available spectrum is illustrated in Fig. 4 that depicts the functional overview of the spectrum decision framework of DSS.

### 4.2    Prioritized Scheduling Algorithm

Policy engine of SPOC calculates the service priority of 'i$^{th}$' spectrum demand, requesting class 'j' service of 'k' type player according to the following expression

$$S(i,j,k) = e^{\delta_j \Omega_{jk}} \times \left( \gamma_j \times \left[ \frac{q_i(t)}{M_i} \right] \right) \qquad (1)$$

where $\delta_j$ is the fairness coefficient, $\gamma_j$ is the value assignedas per the service type (shown in Table 3), $\Omega_{jk}$ is the balancing factor for player type 'k' of the traffic class 'j', $M_i$ is the tolerable latency measure of request 'i', $q_i(t)$ is the queuing time of the spectrum demand request 'i'   since its arrival until being served at time t. The priority function in equation (1) has three parts; latency term, fairness term and player term.

*Latency Term (q/M)*: The demands whose queuing time is nearing its maximum delay limit will be served at high priority. Type-4 is given high gain factor ($\gamma_j$).

*Fairness Term ($\delta_j$)*: Fairness is ensured by $\delta_j$ term. $\delta_j = \frac{n_j}{N}$, where $n_j$ is the total number of service demands waiting for $j^{th}$ service type and N is the sum of service demands in all type of services. As $n_j$ increases the chances of getting served also will increase and hence maintain the fairness.

*Player Term ($\Omega_{jk}$)*: It helps to assign additional preferences based on the type of players (vigilant/VIP vehicles) in ITS. The priority order of ITS players and their weight allocations are shown in Table-4.

This priority calculation is applied on the service buckets of each bandwidth hash buckets separately that forms prioritized FIFO queue as shown in Fig.4.

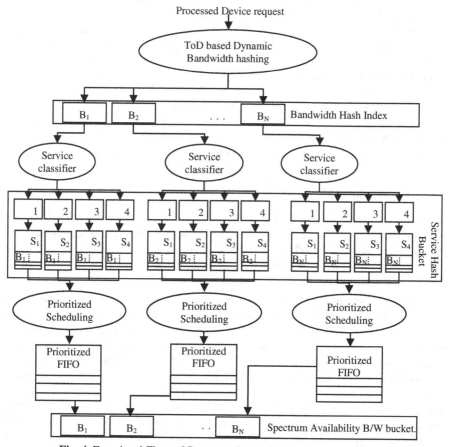

**Fig. 4.** Functional Flow of Spectrum Decision framework of DSS

**Table 3.** Service Type Prioritization

| Service Type | Priority Order | $\gamma_j$ |
|---|---|---|
| TYPE –I | 1 (Lowest ) | 0.2 |
| TYPE -II | 2 | 0.4 |
| TYPE -III | 3 | 0.6 |
| TYPE -IV | 4 (Highest) | 0.8 |

**Table 4.** ITS player Prioritization

| ITS Players | Priority ($\Omega$) |
|---|---|
| Emergency/VIP Vehicles | 1.7 |
| Interceptors | 1.6 |
| Alarm service (VMS/HAR) | 1.5 |
| Vehicles (route requester) | 1.4 |
| Field Vehicles | 1.3 |
| Static Infrastructures | 1.2 |
| Commercial Vehicles | 1.1 |

# 5      Prototype Implementation and Performance Measures

The proposed SPOC architecture is implemented in Complex Event Processing (CEP) engine. In practice, a CEP engine is used to aggregate simple events and derive a complex decision from it. CEP provides intelligence into event-driven systems by deriving higher-level knowledge from vast amount of lower-level data [18]. Spectrum decision framework for ITS is visualized as event-driven system and hence CEP is chosen to implement the same. One of the advantages of using CEP for SPOC is that it can serve hundreds of events per second with minimal latency. SPOC is implemented in JAVA 1.7 and Esper 5.0.0. SPOC and spectrum demand events from ITS scenario are simulated with two different machines having the configurations of: Intel core i3 – 2120 @ 3.3 GHz processor with 4GB RAM running Windows 7 OS.

Simulated spectrum demands are passed to SPOC using UDP socket. A packet handler at SPOC captures spectrum demand as Plain Old Java Object (POJO) and passes it to Esper engine for event processing.

## 5.1    Performance Measures

SPOC performance is compared with the three algorithms (Greedy, Max-Min, EDF) implemented with JAVA 1.7 and MySQL Server 5.0. MySQL is an Event Stream Processing (ESP) tool based on Structured Querying Language (SQL) that processes the homogenous data streams whereas CEP can handle heterogeneous data streams. The performance measures for comparison are listed below.

*Spectrum Utilization*: It is a measure for utilization of available spectrum among the requesting players such that spectrum wastage is avoided or minimal. Assuming constant spectrum availability at the start of simulation and increasing spectrum demands, percentage of spectrum utilization is calculated for EDF, Max-Min, Greedy and SPOC. Spectrum utilization improvement depends upon efficiently mapping the requirements of spectrum demand (in terms of requested bandwidth, usage time, tolerable latency) with the characteristics of available spectrum band (in terms of interference, bandwidth and idle time) and number of request served. Greedy algorithm does the mapping based on bandwidth while Max-min algorithm maps based on serving many demands and EDF allocates to highest latency prone requests. Whereas the proposed algorithm considers usage time, idle time, bandwidth, latency and type of service and achieves improved spectrum utilization factor than other three algorithms, as shown in Fig.5.

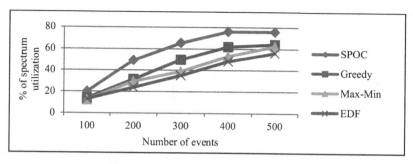

**Fig. 5.** Spectrum Utilization Comparison

<u>Fairness Measure (impact of $\delta$ term):</u> The special feature of the SPOC system is that in spite of the priority based servicing, it maintains fairness among all types of services. It can be observed from Fig. 6 that SPOC offers almost equal service completion ratio (for 500 uniformly distributed events of all types of service) whereas greedy and EDF fails to achieve fairness. It also out performs Max-Min.

Servicing – Rate of emergency request: Type-IV events are highly time-critical events having deadline in terms of few milliseconds, failing which they will get discarded. As the demands of such requests increases, meeting the time constraints of all such events will be not possible leading to service blocking. The service percentage of Type-IV demands is taken as a measure to evaluate the algorithms shown in Fig.7.

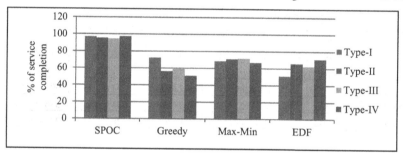

**Fig. 6.** Fairness Measure Comparison

## 5.2    Observations and Discussion

Hashing reduces the number of search in mapping 'm' bandwidths to 'n' demands. The referenced algorithms (Greedy/EDF/Max-Min), for every spectrum allocation, all 'm' resources and 'n' requests have to be processed and compared to derive the best solution that leads to $m \times n$ computations. Whereas with hashing mechanism, search is limited by the number of buckets (N) that reduces the input space by explicitly eliminating known mismatches. Hence computation complexity is approximately equivalent to $\frac{m \times n}{N^2}$. When the number of bucket is approximately equal to $\frac{n}{\log n}$, the computation is as minimal as $max(\log m, \log n)$. Along with this, the use of CEP significantly improves the service time than SQL based implementation. The events serving percentage of the referenced algorithms in comparison with SPOC is shown in Table 5.

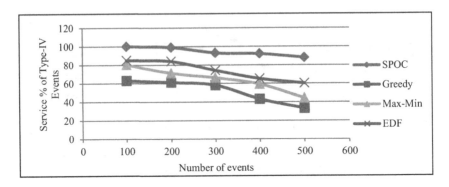

**Fig. 7.** Emergency – Requests Serving Rate Comparison

At heavy traffic, SPOC could accommodate many requests as compared to other algorithms as noted from table 5. From Fig. 5 to 7, it can be observed that Greedy offers better spectrum utilization but fails to handle emergency cases. EDF may perform better for handling emergency service but fails to offer fairness and spectrum utilization. Max-Min offers fairness but throughput is less compared to SPOC. Proposed algorithm achieves all the three measures while reducing number of computations using hashing. In addition CEP based proposed solutions can handle hundreds of requests per second providing real-time services.

**Table 5.** Servicing percentage of various algorithms compared with SPOC

| Traffic Type | Service demands (all types) | SPOC | EDF | Max-Min | Greedy |
|---|---|---|---|---|---|
| Peak ($H_H$) | 1200 | 1078 (89.8%) | 607 (50%) | 634 (53%) | 598 (49%) |
| Medium($H_M$) | 670 | 639 (95.5%) | 398 (59%) | 404 (60%) | 386 (57%) |
| Low($H_L$) | 300 | 300(100%) | 211 (70%) | 228 (76%) | 224 (74%) |

# 6    Conclusions

In this paper, zone-based service-driven opportunistic communication enabler has been proposed for ITS which consists of Dynamic Spectrum Scheduler (DSS) and policy engine. Based on the current spectrum occupancy, type of spectrum demands from ITS players and the capabilities of the radio devices, DSS allocates the spectrum in real time. The policy engine considers the different functional requirements of ITS objects while deciding the priorities for spectrum access. Time of the Day based Dynamic Hashing is introduced to handle the dynamic volume of spectrum demands and reduce computation complexities. The advantages of ITS-SPOC enabler are that it is flexible, adaptive and has low service denials. It can support multitude service demands with improved spectrum utilization as compared to well established scheduling algorithms such as Greedy, Max-Min or Early Dead-Line First. Dynamic nature of SPOC allows it to adopt varying priority measures to match with the different city traffic needs. SPOC enabler can act as a gateway for ITS-communication system to support instantaneous real-time traffic information exchange which is the prerequisite to manage the city-wide traffic efficiently. Security measures for SPOC will be considered for future scope of the work.

**Acknowledgements.** The authors are thankful to DeitY, Government of India, for sponsoring the project no. 14(1)/2013-CC&BT for the research in these areas.

# References

[1] Katiyar, V., Prashat, K., et al.: An Intelligent Transport Systems Architecture using Wireless Sensor Networks. IJCA (2011)
[2] Report from USDOT- Research and Innovative Technology Administration (RITA) - Intelligent Transportation Systems (ITS)-Standards Program and strategic plans (2011), http://www.its.dot.gov
[3] Papadimitratos, P., La Fortelle, A., et al.: Vehicular communication systems: Enabling technologies, applications, and future outlook on intelligent transportation. IEEE Communications Magazine 47(11), 84–95 (2009)
[4] Fitch, M.: Perspectives and problems of opportunistic and dynamic spectrum management. In: IEEE General assembly and Scientific Symposium (2011)
[5] Torabi, N.: Cross-Layer Design for prompt and Reliable Transmission Over Body Area Networks. IEEE Journal of Biomedical and Health Informatics (2014)
[6] Akyildiz, I.F., et al.: Spectrum management in cognitive radio adhoc networks. IEEE Network (2009)
[7] Bahrak, B., Park, J.M.: Ontology-based Spectrum Access Policies for Policy-based Cognitive Radios. IEEE DYSPAN (2012)
[8] Tesanovic, M., Bucknell, P., et al.: Service-domain solutions to radio interference for M2M communications and networking. IEEE GlobeCom (December 2012)
[9] Zhai, C., et al.: Cooperative Spectrum Sharing between Cellular and Ad-Hoc Networks. IEEE Transactions on Wireless Communications (2014)
[10] Driouch, E., et al.: A greedy spectrum sharing algorithm for cognitive radio networks. In: IEEE International Conference on Computing, Networking, and Communication (2012)
[11] Le, L.B.: Fair resource allocation for device-to-device communication in wireless cellular networks. IEEE Globecom (2012)
[12] Mollison, M.S., et al.: Mixed criticality real-time scheduling for multi-core systems. In: IEEE International Conference Computer and Information Technology, CIT (2010)
[13] Wang, X., et al.: The Service modeling and scheduling for wireless access network oriented intelligent transport systems. IEEE ISAP (2013)
[14] Sciandra, V., et al.: A Smart Communication gateway for V2I applications in Public Transport. IEEE COLCOM (2012)
[15] Eswaran, S.P., Ariharan, V., Bapat, J.: Event Driven Opportunistic Communica-tion for Smart City. In: IEEE Next Generation Mobile Apps, Services and Technologies (NGMAST), -ITASC, Oxford, UK (September 2014)
[16] Chang, Y.-I., et al.: A Dynamic Hashing Approach to supporting load balance in P2P systems. IEEE ICDCS (2008)
[17] Jo, J.-Y., et al.: Internet traffic load balancing using dynamic hashing with flow volume. Proceedings of the SPIE 4865 (2002)
[18] Luckam, D.: The Power of Events: An Introduction to Complex Event Processing in Distributed Enterprise Systems. Addison-Wisley (2007)

# Cross-Layer Design Based Transmit Antenna Selection for Vehicular Ad-hoc Networks

Basma Bouraoui[1,2], Marie Zwingelstein-Colin[1], Mohamed Gharbi[1],
Iyad Dayoub[1], and Rabah Attia[2]

[1] IEMN/DOAE, University of Valenciennes and Hainaut-Cambresis,
59313 Valenciennes Cedex 9, France
[2] SERCOM Laboratory, Tunisian Polytechnic School,
Carthage University, 8.p.743, 2078 La Marsa, Tunisia
`basma.bouraoui@etu.univ-valenciennes.fr`
{`marie.zwingelstein-colin,mohamed.gharbi,iyad.dayoub`}`@univ-valenciennes.fr`
`rabah.attia@enit.rnu.tn`

**Abstract.** The wide range of applications in Vehicular Ad-hoc NETworks (VANETs) make vehicles connected all along the trip. For reasons of security or leisure, the connected vehicles ask frequently to establish connection in the network. Due to the high request for access to the channel, some vehicles could be temporarily blocked from sending or receiving data. In this paper, we are interested in minimizing the vehicles blocking effect and in improving the throughput in VANET by implementing a cross-layer design (PHY/MAC) based on transmit antenna selection jointly with a dedicated MAC protocol. We show a significant performance improvement of the throughput in the network.

**Keywords:** Cross-layer design, multiple-input multiple-output (MIMO), ZF-BLAST detector, transmit antenna selection, Vehicular Ad hoc NETworks (VANETs), throughput.

## 1 Introduction

In recent years, Vehicular Ad-hoc NETwork (VANET) is an emerging field of research for its importance in daily life. The researchers focused on a number of applications such as security to ensure a safe trip for the driver and passengers in the vehicle as well as entertainment to make the trip more enjoyable [1]. However, it is necessary, for better reliability that these various applications do not interfere with each other. Consequently, many users could be temporarily blocked under the medium access control (MAC) layer to avoid interference and collision.

Cross-layer approaches are a suitable solution to achieve better performance in vehicular environment [2]. Several cross-layer designs (PHY/MAC) have been proposed for VANETs [3–6], where one or several parameters of the physical layer are adapted to improve the output of the MAC layer and/or vice versa. In [3], authors proposed a cross-layer design based on modulation rate adaptation

© Springer International Publishing Switzerland 2015
M. Kassab et al. (Eds.): Nets4Cars/Nets4Trains/Nets4Aircraft 2015, LNCS 9066, pp. 24–34, 2015.
DOI: 10.1007/978-3-319-17765-6_3

for vehicular networks in urban and downtown environments. In [4], a bit rate adaptation protocol that is responsive to rapidly varying channel conditions is proposed. Caizzone et al. proposed in [5] a mechanism that increases or decreases the transmission power based on the number of neighbors. In [6], Rawat et al. proposed another mechanism that focuses on adapting the transmit power based on the network density and the time during which a sender must wait to avoid a collision before reattempting to access the channel (contention window size).

On another point, multiple-input multiple-output (MIMO) systems have been proposed in VANETs to provide reliable transmission using space-time coding or spatial multiplexing techniques [7]. In particular, many algorithms of antenna selections have been proposed in the literature to improve the performance of VANETs [8,9]. In [8], authors proposed an antenna selection approach in vehicle-to-road (V2R) communications, where the road side uses all available antennas but the vehicle side chooses a subset of available antennas such that the link capacity becomes maximized. In [9], an antenna selection procedure for vehicle to vehicle communication systems in highways is proposed to achieve better capacity performance.

The cross-layer (PHY/MAC) approach has been associated with antenna selection in [10] with the aim to maximize the network throughput under the Automatic Repeat Request reQuest (ARQ) protocol as well as to solve the node blocking problem associated with the IEEE 802.11 MAC protocol. In this paper, we adapt the idea proposed in [10] to the VANETs environment, where vehicle-to-vehicle (V2V) data transmissions are carried out over time-varying channels due to vehicles mobility. We show, through simulations, that a significant improvement of the network throughput can be achieved compared to the case of no antenna selection and the conventional MAC protocol.

This paper is organized as follows. In Section 2, a cross-layer design based on transmit antenna selection as well as the proposed MAC protocol for V2V communications are introduced. The VANET simulation environment and the performance analysis of the proposed design are given in Section 3. Finally, some conclusions are drawn in Section 4.

Some notations are used in the following: matrices are represented as bold uppercase, vectors as bold lowercase and complex scalars as italic lowercase,$(.)^H$ is the conjugate transpose (Hermitian), $Q(.)$ is the complementary error function under Gaussian statistic, $r_{i,j}$ is the $(i,j)^{th}$ entry of the matrix $\mathbf{R}$, $q(.)$ is the modulation dependent quantizing function.

## 2   Cross-Layer Design and MAC Protocol for V2V Communications

In this Section, we first present a cross-layer design based on transmit antenna selection that maximizes the throughput by selecting the optimum subset of transmit antennas for each transmitter (Section 2.1). This cross-layer scheme is then jointly proposed with a MAC protocol that minimizes the transmission blocking effect inherent to the frequent request for connection in the network

(Section 2.2). The adaptation of the cross-layer scheme and the MAC protocol to the context of V2V communications in VANETs where the channel changes over time due to the vehicles mobility, is presented in Section 2.3.

## 2.1   Transmit Antenna Selection Approach

We consider spatial multiplexing (V-BLAST) over MIMO time-varying flat-fading channel with $N_T$ transmit and $N_R$ receive antennas ($N_R \geqslant N_T$). The $\ell^{th}$ received MIMO symbol is expressed by:

$$\mathbf{y}[\ell] = \mathbf{H}[\ell]\,\mathbf{\Pi}[\ell]\,\mathbf{x}[\ell] + \mathbf{n}[\ell], \tag{1}$$

where $\ell$ is the symbol time index, $\mathbf{y}[\ell] \in \mathbb{C}^{N_R \times 1}$ is the received signal vector, $\mathbf{H}[\ell] \in \mathbb{C}^{N_R \times N_T}$ is channel matrix, $\mathbf{x}[\ell] \in \mathbb{C}^{N_T \times 1}$ is the transmitted signal vector with $E[\mathbf{x}^H\mathbf{x}] = P_t$, $\mathbf{\Pi}[\ell] \in \mathbb{R}^{N_T \times N_T}$ is a permutation matrix corresponding to the detection ordering [11] and $\mathbf{n}[\ell] \sim \mathcal{CN}(0, \sigma^2 I_{N_R})$ is the circularly symmetric complex Gaussian noise vector. In order to simplify the presentation, the time index $\ell$ is removed in the following equations.

We assume the Zero-forcing decoding scheme at the receiver [12] through QR decomposition, and that the channel matrix is perfectly known at the receiver. The greedy QR-decomposition of the channel matrix is written as $\mathbf{H}\mathbf{\Pi} = \mathbf{Q}\mathbf{R}$ where $\mathbf{Q} \in \mathbb{C}^{N_R \times N_T}$ is a unitary matrix and $\mathbf{R} \in \mathbb{C}^{N_T \times N_T}$ is an upper triangular matrix. The received signal is first multiplied by $\mathbf{Q}^H$, yielding $\tilde{\mathbf{y}} = \mathbf{Q}^H\mathbf{y} = \mathbf{R}\mathbf{x} + \tilde{\mathbf{n}}$. Hence, the $i^{th}$ element of $\tilde{\mathbf{y}}$ is given by:

$$\tilde{y}_i = r_{i,i}\,x_i + \sum_{j=i+1}^{N_T} r_{i,j}\,x_j + \tilde{n}_i, \qquad i = 1, 2, ..., N_R. \tag{2}$$

The interference nulling and cancellation is done as follows: first, the symbol from the last antenna is detected and quantized to the nearest transmitted symbol $\hat{x}_{N_T} = q(\frac{\tilde{y}_{N_T}}{r_{N_T, N_T}})$. Then, the contribution of $\hat{x}_{N_T}$ is removed from $\tilde{\mathbf{y}}$ before the detection of $x_{N_T - 1}$ and so on. So we get:

$$\hat{x}_i = q\left(\frac{\tilde{y}_i - \sum_{j=i+1}^{N_T} r_{i,j}\,\hat{x}_j}{r_{i,i}}\right), \qquad i = 1, 2, ..., N_T - 1. \tag{3}$$

Considering packets of $L$ MIMO symbols and the BPSK modulation scheme, as well as ignoring error propagation in the cancellation process, the packet error rate is:

$$PER = 1 - [\prod_{i=1}^{N_T}(1 - SER_i)]^{L/N_T}, \tag{4}$$

where $SER_i$ and $\gamma_i$ are the symbol error rate and the instantaneous signal-to-noise ratio at the $i^{th}$ received antenna given by (5) and (6), respectively.

$$SER_i = Q(\sqrt{2\,\gamma_i}), \qquad i = 1, 2, ..., N_T. \tag{5}$$

$$\gamma_i = \frac{r_{i,i}^2 P_t}{N_T \sigma^2}, \qquad i = 1, 2, ..., N_T. \qquad (6)$$

For all possible subsets of $K \leq N_T$ transmit antennas, $K \in \{1, 2, ..., N_T\}$, the associated throughput, which is given by (7) and (8) for the Go-Back-N protocol with a window size $W$ and the Selective-Repeat protocol [13] respectively, is first evaluated by the receiver based on the knowledge of $\mathbf{H}$. Then, the receiver informs the transmitter about the antennas subset which provides the highest throughput (for this purpose, we assume an error-free feedback channel).

$$\eta(GBN) = K \times (1 - PER)/[1 + (W - 1) \times PER], \qquad (7)$$

$$\eta(SR) = K \times (1 - PER). \qquad (8)$$

### 2.2 MAC Protocol

In this section, we provide a quick presentation of the MAC protocol originally proposed in [10], adapted to our V2V context. This protocol aims at reducing the blocking effect which appears in IEEE 802.11p MAC protocol when two (or more) transmitters want to transmit simultaneously while being in the same transmission range: simultaneous transmissions have to be forbidden in order to prevent the vehicles from interfering with each other.

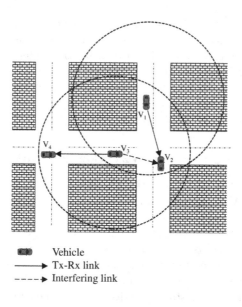

＊＊＊ Vehicle
⟶ Tx-Rx link
---→ Interfering link

**Fig. 1.** An example of a four vehicles topology

We consider a typical V2V network topology as depicted in Fig. 1, where the vehicles $V_1$ and $V_3$ want to transmit data to the vehicles $V_2$ and $V_4$ respectively. Circles around $V_1$ and $V_3$ represent their radio range. Supposing that $V_1$ is the first to access the channel, it sends a transmission request to $V_2$. When $V_2$ receives the transmission request, it calculates the throughput over different subsets of transmit antennas and saves this information in a sorted list AS[1] with the identity of the corresponding antennas (this list is created for each transmission request and updated only by the receiver). Then, $V_2$ sends its AS list to $V_1$ which informs all neighboring vehicles (i.e., $V_2$ and $V_3$ in this case) about the identification of the antennas chosen for transmission, noting that when a transmitter receives an AS list from its neighbors, it transmits the list to its receiver. The antenna selection process is also repeated between $V_3$ and $V_4$. At this stage, the handshake between the vehicles $V_1$, $V_3$ and $V_2$, $V_4$, respectively is finished.

As seen in the scenario, $V_3$ is a potential interferer to $V_2$, which would result in a blocking effect under the classical 802.11 MAC layer. In order to avoid this effect, the MAC protocol in this paper leverages the interference cancellation ZF-BLAST procedure described in Section 2.1. However, to make the interference cancellation possible, the sum of the number of transmit antennas selected by each receiver should not exceed the number of receive antennas $N_R$. We will refer to this assumption as the *Antenna quantity restriction hypothesis*. In order to ensure this hypothesis, $V_2$ checks whether the number of selected antennas by itself and by the neighboring vehicle $V_4$ does not exceed $N_R$. If the hypothesis is not satisfied, $V_2$ selects another antennas combination from its AS list by taking into account the AS lists of the neighboring vehicles (i.e. $V_4$). When the *Antenna quantity restriction hypothesis* is reached, $V_2$ apprises $V_1$ of the final list of transmit antennas chosen for the transmission between them. Finally, $V_1$ updates its AS list and informs its neighboring vehicles.

At this time, all vehicles are ready to transmit their data through the adequate subsets of transmit antennas. Each transmitting vehicle starts transmitting its data and each receiving vehicle extracts the desired packet using the ZF-BLAST detector. Note that when packets do not reach the receiver they are re-transmitted using the GBN protocol or the SR protocol, otherwise a reception confirmation acknowledgment is sent to the transmitter.

### 2.3    Cross-Layer Design Steps in V2V Communications

In this section, we explain how the technique developed in section 2.1 and 2.2 can be adapted to a V2V communication context where the channel changes over time. Note that we limit ourselves to single-hop V2V communications. The time-varying character of the channel is expressed by the maximum Doppler shift, which is proportional to the vehicles speed. It is given by $f_D = \frac{V_r}{\lambda}$, where $V_r$ is the relative velocity between the transmitter and the receiver and $\lambda = \frac{c}{f}$ is the wavelength, where $c$ is the speed of light and $f$ is the wave's frequency. Note that the channel remains stationary for a coherence time $T_c \approx \frac{1}{f_D}$ [14].

---

[1] Antenna Selection.

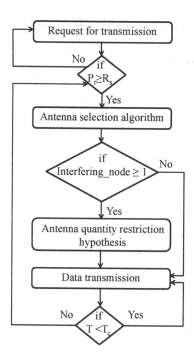

**Fig. 2.** Organizational structure of the cross-layer design

The different stages of the proposed cross-layer scheme are depicted in Fig. 2. To explain how the algorithm works, let us denote $(V_T, V_R)$ a pair of transmitting and receiving vehicles. When $V_T$ requests to establish a connection with $V_R$, then if $V_R$ is not in $V_T$'s transmission range, the power at the reception is not sufficient to receive the request for packet transmission. In this case, if $V_T$ does not receive any response from $V_R$, it considers that the connection between them is impossible and it seeks for another potential receiver. However, if $V_T$ and $V_R$ are within the same radio range, $V_R$ applies the antenna selection approach and ensures that the *Antenna quantity restriction hypothesis* is verified, knowing that $V_R$ can find its neighbors which also ask to transmit data, from the AS lists received (from $V_T$ and its neighbors). When $V_R$ chooses its final list AS, it forwards it to $V_T$ and its neighbors.

Finally, $V_T$ is ready to transmit data during a coherence period $T_c$. After that, the receiver $V_R$ should look for a new subset of transmit antennas according to a new channel estimation. Furthermore, $V_R$ must verify whether it is still in $V_T$'s radio range; if yes, it selects a new antennas subset; if not, the transmission between $V_T$ and $V_R$ is stopped (note that after each $T_c$ the distance between the transmitter and the receiver does not change significantly).

# 3    Performance Analysis of the Cross-Layer Design

## 3.1    Simulation Environment

In order to evaluate the performance of the proposed approach in a VANET environment, we consider 20 vehicles which are randomly distributed in a $100m \times 100m$ area (i.g. downtown) and which drive at a constant speed (40 km/h) in predictable roads as shown in Fig. 3. In addition, we assume that all the vehicles have the same transmit power $P_t$ and the same receiver sensitivity $R_s$. The signal propagation follows a path-loss model given by :

$$P_L = \frac{(4\pi)^2 d^\alpha}{\lambda^2}, \tag{9}$$

where $d$ is the distance between the transmitter and the receiver and $\alpha$ is the path loss exponent. The average received power can be expressed as:

$$P_r = P_t + G_t + G_r - 10 \log_{10}(P_L), \tag{10}$$

where $G_t$ and $G_r$ are the antenna gains of the transmitting and receiving antennas, respectively. The radio range, $R$, depends on the environment between the transmitter and receiver, as well as the receiver sensitivity $R_s$. It is defined as the distance at which $P_r = R_s$, that is:

$$R = \left( \frac{P_t \, G_t \, G_r \, \lambda^2}{(4\pi)^2 R_s} \right)^{1/\alpha}. \tag{11}$$

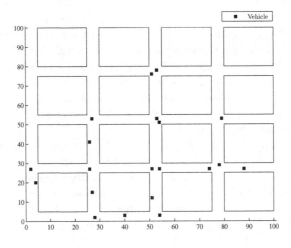

**Fig. 3.** Vehicle mobility scenario

We assumed that all vehicles in the simulated area will emit or receive information over Rayleigh fading channels during a simulation time $T_s$, as long as the power at the reception is sufficient to properly receive data. During $T_s$, some vehicles may leave the simulated area. In this case, we suppose that the transmission between the receiver and the transmitter is stopped.

In [10], authors neglect the interference radiated at a distance greater than $R$ from the transmitter (for such a distance the cross-layer scheme is not realized). The focus of this work is more realistic since we also evaluate the effect of the interference form vehicles outside the radio range. The instantaneous signal-to-interference-plus-noise ratio (SINR) is expressed by:

$$\xi_i = \frac{r_{i,i}^2 \, P_{r_i}}{\sum_{j=1}^{N} P_{ij} + \sigma^2},$$ (12)

where $P_{r_i}$ is the received power at the $i^{th}$ antenna and $N$ is the number of interfering vehicles outside the radio range of $i$ and $P_{ij}$ is the strength of the received interference from $j$ to $i$.

## 3.2  Simulation Results

We studied the network performance in terms of throughput vs. input signal-to-noise ratio $P_t/\sigma^2$. The simulation parameters used in this paper are shown in Table 1. The simulation is run 30 times with each time a new random topology realization, and the throughput is averaged over the number of simulation and the number of V2V-links. Fig. 4 shows the average throughput per single-link (V2V) according to the proposed approach. In order to evaluate the results, we also plot the throughput for SR without antenna selection using the classical IEEE 802.11p MAC protocol. The throughput given without antenna selection is lower than those given by the cross-layer scheme for SR and GBN. We can also note that the throughput for SR is slightly higher than for GBN due to the frequent packet error when employing GBN.

At low SNRs the antenna selection approach tends to choose the minimum number of transmit antennas. However, at high SNRs, the optimal subset consists in all available transmit antennas. But to satisfy the *Antenna quantity restriction hypothesis* and allow more nearby transmissions, vehicles are forced to use a less than optimal number of antennas. This fact reduces the throughput of a single-link (V2V), but increases the average throughput of the network by giving the opportunity to other vehicles to communicate.

It should be noted that various factor affect the overall throughput of the network including the number of antennas $N_T$, the radio range area and the network density. The latter is due to the *Antenna quantity restriction hypothesis* which limit the maximum number of simultaneously transmitting vehicles within the same radio range to be $N_R$. The proposed cross-layer scheme associated with MAC protocol solves partially the problem, and is more efficient in low density networks. Nevertheless, the proposed protocol remains more efficient than the conventional IEEE 802.11p MAC protocol also in dense networks.

**Table 1.** Simulation Parameters

| Frequency | $f$ | 5.9 GHz |
|---|---|---|
| Simulation Time | $T_s$ | 50 s |
| Number of Simulations | | 30 |
| Number of Nodes | | 20 |
| Transmitter Power | $P_t$ | 30 dBm |
| Receiver Sensitivity | $R_s$ | -90 dBm |
| Transmitting Antennas Gain | $G_t$ | 0 dBi |
| Receiving Antennas Gain | $G_r$ | 0 dBi |
| Path Loss Exponent | $\alpha$ | 3 |
| Area | | 10 km$^2$ |
| Velocity | $\mathcal{V}$ | 40 km/h |
| Symbol Duration | | 8 $\mu s$ |
| Frame Length | $L$ | 180 BPSK symbols |
| Coherence Time | $T_c$ | 20 ms |
| Network Configuration | | Single hop |
| ARQ Protocol | | GBN or SR |
| Go-Back-N window size | $W$ | 4 |

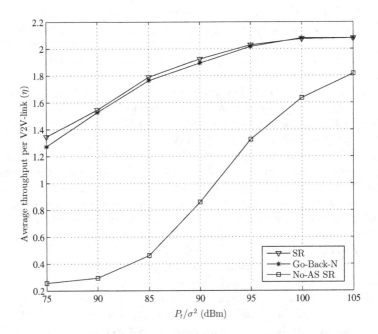

**Fig. 4.** Throughput performance in $4 \times 4$ - MIMO Rayleigh fading channel, ignoring interference

The results of Fig. 4 do not consider the residual interference of the equation (12). Fig. 5 shows the performance of the proposed cross-layer approach, in terms of throughput, in both cases: without considering the interference (without Int.) and with taking into account the interference (with Int.). As depicted, the curves are almost superimposed indicating low power interference coming from distant neighboring in this environment. One might say that, despite the interference that was ignored in the first simulations, the throughput gain remains quasi-identical. The results can only strengthen the conclusions drawn previously.

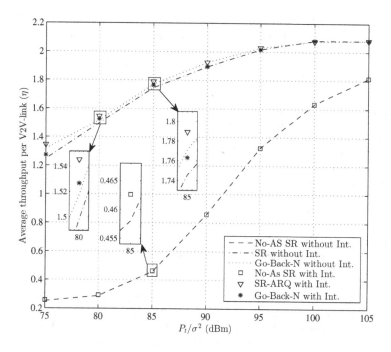

**Fig. 5.** Throughput comparison with and without taking into account the interference form vehicles outside the transmitter radio range, in a 4×4-MIMO Rayleigh fading channel

## 4    Conclusion

In this paper, we investigated the performance of a cross-layer design based on a transmit antenna selection at the receiver side and an associated MAC protocol in VANETs. We showed a large throughput gain using the mixture between the antenna selection approach and the proposed MAC protocol compared to the case of no antenna selection jointly with the classical IEEE 802.11p MAC protocol which is not resilient against the node blocking problem. Similarly, we showed that despite the interference that a receiver may suffer from neighboring outside its radio range, this approach is effective in terms of throughput.

**Acknowledgments.** This work was supported by the regional CISIT program funded by the North Region and the FEDER.

# References

1. Hartenstein, H., Laberteaux, K.: Vanet vehicular applications and inter-networking technologies. John Wiley & Sons Wiley-Blackwell (2009)
2. Jarupan, B., Ekici, E.: A survey of cross-layer design for VANETs. Journal Ad Hoc Networks 9, 966–983 (2011)
3. Camp, J., Kinightly, E.: Modulation Rate Adaptation in Urban and Vehicular Environments: Cross-Layer Implementation and Experimental Evaluation. IEEE/ACM Transactions on Networking 18, 315–326 (2008)
4. Vutukuru, M., Balakrishnan, H., Jaleson, K.: Cross-Layer Wireless Bit Adaptation. ACM SIGCOMM Computer Communication Review 4, 3–14 (2009)
5. Caizzone, G., Giacomazzi, P., Verticale, L.M.G.: A Power Control Algorithm with High Channel Availibility for Vehicle Ad hoc Networks. In: IEEE International Conference on Communications, vol. 5, pp. 3171–3176 (2005)
6. Rawat, D., Yan, G., Popoescu, D., Weigle, M., Olariu, S.: Dynamic Adaptation of Joint Transmission Power and Contention Window in VANET. In: IEEE 70th Vehicular Technology Conference Fall(VTC 2009-Fall), pp. 1–5 (2009)
7. Attia, A., ElMoslimany, A.A., El-Keyi, A., ElBatt, T., Bai, F., Saraydar, C.: MIMO Vehicular Networks: Research Challenges and Opportunities. Journal of communications 7, 500–513 (2012)
8. Mousavia, H.S., Khalighinejad, B., Khalj, B.H.: Capacity maximization in MIMO vehicular communication using a novel antenna selection algorithm. In: 9th International Wireless Communications and Mobile Computing Conference (IWCMC), pp. 1246–1251 (2013)
9. Jedari, E., Atlasbaf, Z., Noghanian, S.: Effects of Antenna Selection on the Capacity of Vehicle to Vehicle Communications in Highways. In: IEEE APS/URSI International Symposium, Florida, USA, pp. 2109–2110 (2013)
10. Mao, W.F., Hamouda, W., Dayoub, I.: MIMO Cross-Layer Design for Ad-hoc Networks. In: IEEE Global Telecommunications Conference, pp. 652–660 (2010)
11. Jiang, Y., Varanasi, M.K.: The effect of ordered detection and antenna selection on diversity gain of decision feedback detecor. In: 9th International Wireless Communications and Mobile Computing Conference (IWCMC), pp. 5383–5388 (2007)
12. Shiu, D., Kahn, J.M.: Layered Space-Time Codes for Wireless Communications using Multiple Transmit Antennas. In: IEEE International Conference onC ommunications ICC 1999, pp. 436–440 (1999)
13. Garcia, A.L., Widjaja, I.: Communications Networks. McGraw-Hill (2000)
14. Proakis, J., Salehi, M.: Digital Communications (2007)

# F-ETX: An Enhancement of ETX Metric for Wireless Mobile Networks

Sebastien Bindel[1,*], Serge Chaumette[1], and Benoit Hilt[2]

[1] LaBRI, University of Bordeaux, France
[2] MIPS, University of Haute Alsace, France

**Abstract.** The accuracy and the reactivity of link quality estimators are key concepts in Mobile Ad hoc networks (MANETs) and especially in Vehicular Ad hoc Networks (VANETs), since routing process uses link quality related metrics based on neighbour information for making routing decisions. The Expected Transmission Count (ETX) is the most salient metric that assesses the link quality for wireless ad hoc and mesh networks. Its estimation varies according to the link changes like disruption and bidirectional to unidirectional switching. Such changes occur more often in highly mobile networks like VANETs. In order to be efficient routing protocols have to deal with these events. It has been observed that current implementation of ETX leads to a limited accuracy and cannot be efficient in VANETs. In this paper is presented an algorithm which makes the ETX metric more adapted for VANETs. Our contribution significantly improves the reactivity and the accuracy of the metric. In addition, our metric is not limited to the link quality estimation but also brings a link stability information. This results a new metric called Fast-ETX (F-ETX). This metric has been tested under realistic physical layer and mobility patterns to evaluate its reactivity, accuracy and stability properties.

**Keywords:** VANET, ETX, local link quality, routing metric, dynamic window.

## 1  Introduction

A wireless ad hoc network results from the cooperation of independent entities to form a decentralized network without Access Points (AP). MANETs are a subset of ad hoc networks consisting of mobile nodes moving arbitrarily. RFC 2501 [4] describes the MANET features and reveals four salient characteristics: dynamic topology, variable link capacity (bandwidth, jitter, error rate, ...), energy constraints and limited physical security. Among the set of current challenges for MANETs, routing is still an important one wherein a dynamic topology implies many rapid path changes. MANET routing protocols attempt to hide the effects of the mobility to higher layers by determining virtual stable paths to transport data. For this, routing processes use values called metric to select the best route.

* This research was supported by a DGA-MRIS scholarship.

M. Kassab et al. (Eds.): Nets4Cars/Nets4Trains/Nets4Aircraft 2015, LNCS 9066, pp. 35–46, 2015.
DOI: 10.1007/978-3-319-17765-6_4

Historically only the number of hops was taking into account, without considering the link quality. That is why in wireless environments, metrics like ETX based on link observation give better performances, especially about the packet delivery ratio [5].

Some routing protocols for VANETs (subset of MANETs) such as OLSR (Optimized Link State Routing Protocol) [9] maintain a global topology view to compute the best path. This strategy becomes inefficient if the environment changes rapidly. Other routing protocols such as BATMAN (Better Approach To Mobile Ad hoc Networking) [8] have another philosophy. They maintain both a local and global vision of the network. The local view is based on the local links quality with direct neighbours and the path selection is made from a global point of view. For example, BATMAN uses the ETX metric to estimate the local link quality and determine an end to end path by a computation taking into account the succession of the local link quality estimations through the route.

De Couto et al. proposed the ETX metric in [5] and implemented it in DSDV (Destination Sequenced Distance Vector) and DSR (Dynamic Source Routing) to compare its performances with the "classical" hop count metric. Javaid et al. [6] studied ETX and its variants. They observed that most of metrics were designed for Wireless Mesh Networks (WMNs) and use some techniques to improve performances (i.e. the channel selection to have less interferences). Liu et al. [7] made a proposition to adapt the ETX metric to MANETs. The contribution is based on a novel computation method but requires also a modification of the routing messages. This work is the only one to adapt the metric for MANETs but any propositions explored its reactivity when events occur (e.g. links disruption and links becoming unidirectional). Nodes in VANETs should be quickly aware about link state changes. This is a key issue for a better efficiency in VANET routing protocols and applications [2]. To this end we suggest in this paper a new algorithm with two features. The first one improves the metric reactivity when specific events induced by mobility occur (i.e. link disruptions and bidirectional link becoming unidirectional). The second one deals with the link stability.

The remainder of this paper is divided into four parts. Section 2 reviews the ETX metric and presents an analysis on its behaviour when specific events occur. Section 3 presents the algorithm of the F-ETX and a performance analysis. In section 4 the enhanced metric is tested under realistic physical layers in the ns-3 simulator. Section 5 concludes on the paper and open future works.

## 2   ETX Metric

The hop count metric is the historical technique used by routing protocols to select the best path to route end-to-end traffic. It has the benefit to be simple and requires low computation. But if a destination can be reached via two paths with the same hop count value, the routing process chooses one arbitrarily. It is therefore essential to take into account the link or the path quality, especially when nodes are mobile and the environment disturbs the wave propagation like in urban setting.

## 2.1   Basic ETX

The ETX of the link aims to predict the number of retransmissions required to send a packet over this link. ETX is an additive metric. It means that the ETX of a route is the sum of the ETX of each link composing the route. Its computation is based on the delivery ratio $d_f$ which is the probability of a data to be delivered. And the reverse delivery ratio $d_r$ represents the probability that the ACK packet is successfully received back. The expected probability that a message is successfully received and acquitted is $d_f \times d_r$. If we consider a packet transmission as a Bernoulli trial (success or fail), ETX is calculated as following:

$$ETX = \frac{1}{d_f \times d_r} \tag{1}$$

Accordingly, the expected loss estimation is:

$$ETX_l = \frac{1}{(1 - d_f) \times (1 - d_r)} \tag{2}$$

ETX provides information on the link loss ratio in each direction, on the link quality and the presence of asymmetric links when $d_r$ is null.

## 2.2   $d_f$ and $d_r$ Computation

These ratios are computed by sending broadcast probe packets at an average period $\tau$. A jittered parameter is added up to $\pm 0.1\tau$ per probe to avoid synchronization. A node receiving a probe must rebroadcast it and allows for the originator of a probe to compute the $d_r$ probability. This feature is native for wireless mesh nodes but must be implemented for ad hoc nodes. Besides, a mechanism to avoid a broadcast storm due to the rebroadcasting of probe packets is mandatory. Finally, nodes are using a windowing mechanism to compute the $d_f$ and $d_r$ probabilities. Two types of window are currently used.

- **Temporal windows:** De Couto and all. [5] suggested the use of timers to count probe packets. To compute $d_r$ each node remembers the packet probe sent and triggers a timer. If this probe is received back within a period (i.e. the window size) it is considered as received, otherwise it is considered as lost. The $d_f$ is computed by counting incoming probes native from neighbours every $\pm 0.1\tau$ time. The main benefit of this method is the feedback about the delay set with timers maintained after each probe packet that has been sent, until its reception. However, a mechanism (e.g. a garbage collector) must be implemented to delete too old timers in order to not overload nodes with expired timers.
- **Sequence Number (SN) windows:** Another method for computing $d_r$ and $d_f$ is based on SN. In order to determine the freshness of the carried information, current routing protocols include a SN field. The last version of BATMAN algorithm (i.e. BATMAN IV) uses this information to maintain windows for computing delivery and reverse delivery ratios [8]. Each node

sends periodical probe packets that contain a SN representing its freshness and marks the packet received in the current window according to its SN. After each sending, if the maximum size is not reached, the window is increased. Otherwise it is shifted by one to maintain a fresh window. Algorithm 1 describes the basic method to fill up a window when a probe packet is received.

---

**Algorithm 1.** Management algorithm for a SN window

---
**INPUT:** SN value extracted from the probe packet
1: **function** MARK RECEIVED PACKET(window, SN value, MAX_WINDOW_SIZE)
2:     **if** SN value < window.first_value **then**
3:         drop information
4:     **else**
5:         **if** SN value < window.at(window.size−1) **then**
6:             window.at(SN value-window.at(0)) ← marked as received
7:         **else**
8:             counter ← (SN value-1)-window.at(window.size-1)
9:             **while** counter > 0 **do**
10:                 slide window
11:                 −−counter
12:             **end while**
13:             **if** window.size < MAX_WINDOW_SIZE **then**
14:                 window ← increase by one
15:             **else**
16:                 window ← slide by one
17:             **end if**
18:             window.at(window.size-1) ← marked as received
19:         **end if**
20:     **end if**
21: **end function**

---

Nodes compute ETX by maintaining a window for each probability ($d_f$ and $d_r$). Each probability is computed by counting all packets marked as received in the associated window $F$ having the window's size $\varsigma$. In the following equation, $F_i$ is the value stored at the $i^{th}$ cell of $F$.

$$probability = \frac{\sum_{i=1}^{\varsigma} F_i}{\varsigma} \tag{3}$$

Temporal windows have the advantage to provide information on delays. However, in order to determine if an incoming packet is expected, it must be identified (commonly by a sequence number). A node must extract from the packet the sender's address, the packet ID and its transmission time. Because only one timer is required to maintain the window freshness, methods based on sequence numbers are less complex than the temporal solutions. To determine if an incoming packet is expected, a node inspects only the sender's address and the sequence number fields in the packet. As a result, the computation task is reduced, increasing the node's capabilities and reducing its energy consumption.

## 2.3   Analysis of ETX

To improve the time detection of ETX, two approaches are possible. The first one is to reduce the sending interval. But this method leads to increase the number of probe packets per second, overloading the network. In addition, this method is limited by the media access technique and the number of nodes in the network. Another method is to use different window sizes, which is believed as more interesting. The impact of different window sizes for link events like the emergence, the disruption and a bidirectional link becoming unidirectional have been analyzed and tested. For each case, a theoretical analysis is presented with a plot to support our demonstration.

We choose to study the $ETX_l$ for a local link evaluation. Simulations have been performed under JbotSim [3] offering a simulation environment for prototyping distributed algorithms in dynamic networks. It makes a perfect sense here because we test only the behaviour of $ETX_l$ for a link without taking into account any additional information. In our scenarios a periodic interval of one second for sending probe packets has been defined. These packets contain three fields; the current sequence number, the node ID that initiated the message and the previous sender ID. A node originates a probe packet by fixing its current sequence number and populating the second and third fields with its ID. When a neighbour rebroadcasts a probe packet it updates only the previous sender field with his own ID. A node drops a packet if it is not the originator of the incoming rebroadcasted packet. This feature guarantees a local link evaluation only.

**Link Emergence**   A link is discovered as soon as a window marks a packet as received (see algorithm 1). According to the equation 4, a packet sent has a 100% chance to be lost if the value of $ETX_l$ converges to 1. At the opposite, a packet has a 100% chance to be delivered if the value of $ETX_l$ converges to $+\infty$.

$$\lim_{\substack{d_f \to 0 \\ d_r \to 0}} ETX_l = 1 \qquad\qquad \lim_{\substack{d_f \to 1 \\ d_r \to 1}} ETX_l = +\infty \qquad (4)$$

The maximum value of ETX is reached when the windows of $d_r$ and $d_f$ get to their maximum size. However, because packets are returned after a RTT (Round Trip Time), the growth of $d_r$ window is slower than the one of $d_f$ window. Therefore results a time offset between the $d_f$ and the $d_r$ window. Whereas all nodes send periodically probe packets over an interval noted $P$ and the RTT (Round Trip Time) of their packet is $RTT_b$. Since windows have a maximum size $n$, the maximum ETX value is reached after a $nP + RTT_b$ period. Figure 1(a) shows the impact of the window size on the convergence time to reach the

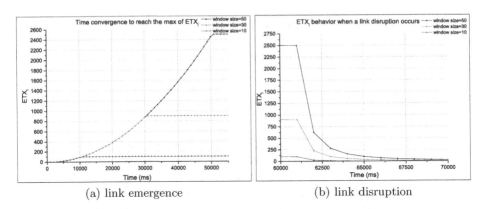

(a) link emergence                    (b) link disruption

**Fig. 1.** Emergence and disruption

maximum value of ETX. Note that we limited the max ETX value to the sum of the $d_f$ and the $d_r$ windows size $+ 1$.

**Link Disruption.** All packets lost or dropped are marked by a null value in the window. Packet losses under JBotSim have been simulated thought link disruptions because it does not support error probability models. A link is declared as disrupted by ETX when windows have marked all expected packets as lost (i.e. as null). This behaviour is different from the emergence case because a disruption can occurs when a node did not receive either or both its own and neighbour's probe packet. The time to detect a link disruption varies from the previous case. As a result, the time to declare a link as disrupted is in the interval $[nP, nP + P]$. We have simulated several window sizes and triggered a link disruption even when the maximum value of ETX has been reached. The result is shown in figure 1(b).

**Unidirectional Link Detection.** The reverse delivery probability $(d_r)$ measures the capability of neighbours to send back a probe packet. If a link is unidirectional, a node only receives probe packets originated by its neighbours $(d_f)$ but does not receive back its own probe packet from its neighbours $(d_r$ is null). Therefore the detection of bidirectional links becoming unidirectional depends on the window size maintained for $d_r$. We have simulated a bidirectional link becoming unidirectional and traced the behaviour of $d_r$ with different window sizes in figure 2.

**Discussion.** It is observed that the window size has an impact on the convergence time and the granularity of ETX values. With a small window size, the ETX reaches its maximum and minimum quickly because the windows are filled up faster. However, the convergence with larger windows is significantly slower. The resulting granularity is improved (i.e. more different ETX values are available). For example, a window with a size of 5 is efficient to declare quickly a

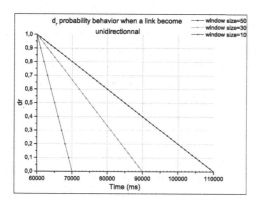

**Fig. 2.** unidirectional link

disruption. This is especially adapted to evaluate link quality in highly mobile networks. But it provides a poor granularity to estimate the link quality (only 5 values). A window with a size of 60 has a better granularity (i.e. 60 values) but has a slower convergence time to declare for example a link disrupted. This type of window is more adapted for estimating the quality of static of semi-static links. Therefore, the classical ETX version implies a trade-off between the convergence time and granularity and it becomes difficult to give an efficient link estimation for both volatile and static links.

## 3   Computation of F-ETX

We have profited from the experience of TCP congestion-avoidance algorithm to design an algorithm which improves the reactivity and the accuracy of ETX. Our goal here is to find a trade-off between a fast convergence and a good accuracy. We suggest here a new algorithm with two features; one dealing with the convergence time and another one, with the metric accuracy. This algorithm has been tested with the JbotSim simulator where we have simulated a direct communication between two nodes. We present each improvement independently from each other although they are gathered into the same algorithm.

### 3.1   Convergence Time Improvement

The moving average is an analysis technique used in statistics to calculate an average over a certain period of time. Unlike the simple average method, where the calculation is made with the full data set. Its moving version calculates the average over a last period of time. This approach has the main benefit to give more importance to the newest values in the data set ensuring a higher freshness of the analysis. Even if this method is used in the current implementation of ETX, its limitations have been demonstrated in the previous section. To deal with this problem the use of the weighted moving average method is suggested.

We choose to weight data according to the number of detected losses. This strategy penalizes probabilities when the last packet expected is lost and increases as the number of losses grows. Let the binary weight called $w^{nth}$ weighting n-day values $x_n...., x_1$ (i.e consecutive expected SN), $\alpha$ is the number of consecutive packets marked as lost in the window and $F_n$ the window size at the $n$ day moment. The number of data weighted with a non null weight is determined by the equation 5.

$$\theta = \frac{F_n}{2^\alpha} \tag{5}$$

Until losses are detected, probabilities are computed following the equation 6 wherein each data in the window is weighted with a binary value determined by the equation 5.

$$probability = \frac{w^n x_n + w^{n-1} x_{n-1} + ... + w^1 x_1}{\sum_{i=1}^{n} w^n} \tag{6}$$

This process maintains the same weight when $\theta$ is one and takes over as soon as the last expected packet is received. This approach can be presented in a different way to provide a simpler implementation for nodes. Our weighting method puts a positive weight on data according to the half of window size and leaves the others with a null weight. In doing so, our algorithm can be also seen as successive reductions. For each expected packet detected as lost, the window size is halved to keep the newest values. The algorithm has been tested both when a disruption occurs and when a bidirectional link becomes unidirectional. Table 1 sets out the convergence time of the classical ETX and our enhanced version.

**Table 1.** Detection time comparison

| Maximum window's size | Time for detection (classical ETX) | Time for detection (Enhanced ETX) |
|:---:|:---:|:---:|
| 50 | 50s | 5s |
| 30 | 30s | 4s |
| 10 | 10s | 3s |

Theses results show a improvement of the detection time with our algorithm.

## 3.2   Accuracy Improvement and Link Stability Estimation

As indicated earlier, as soon as an expected packet is lost, the size of the window is halved. Sporadic losses have a low impact on the window size but, a link disruption which implies continuous losses, reduces significantly its size. We suggest an algorithm that uses the window size to adjust the link quality estimation, also called the link stability evaluation. Figure 3 shows the decision logic scheme of this algorithm. It uses two variables; the $Threshold that contains the window size when a loss occurs and the $Counter that counts received packets when the current window size is equal or higher than $Threshold.

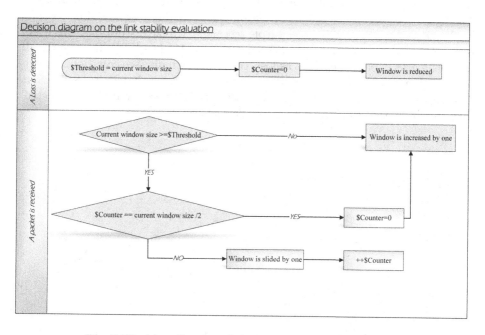

**Fig. 3.** Decision diagram of the link stability computation

When a loss appears, the algorithm saves the current window size (also called the threshold) before being halved. Until the current window size is lower than the threshold, for each new received packet the window size is incremented by one. If the window size reaches the threshold, the algorithm switches to another strategy. For each new incoming packet, the window is shifted by one and a counter ($Counter) is incremented. If counter value reaches the half of the current window size, the window is incremented by one and the counter is reset. The algorithm restarts this process until the maximum window size is reached. As a result, the growth of the window follows a stepwise according to the reception of successive packets. This achievement results from a link stabilization and a correlation between the window size and the link stability (bigger is the window size, higher is the stability) can be observed.

To show its efficiency the algorithm has been simulated under JBotSim in two situations. The first one is the disruption of a link and the second one is when a bidirectional link becomes unidirectional. Our study is based on the behavior of a static window with a maximum size of 30 SN (classical ETX case) and a dynamic window (its maximum size is also fixed at 30 SN) managed by our suggested algorithm. Results shown in figure 4 represent the values of $ETX_l$ normalized to [0,255]. Red rectangles indicate the occurrences of link disruption. A better detection of the link disruptions with a metric based on the dynamic window size (step falling edge) is observed. It is also observed that the metric takes 4 seconds to declare the link as disrupted. Besides the classical ETX metric is not enough reactive to adapt its estimation to the dynamic of the link (see figure 4(a)). The figure 4(b) shows the second situation where the bidirectional link becomes unidirectional as indicated in the purple rectangle. Unlike disruptions, this event is not detected by the static window used by the classical ETX. Despite the $d_r$ window marks expected packets as lost, the $\mathrm{ETX}_l$ formula (see equation 2) needs to have significantly losses in windows for $d_f$ and $d_r$ to change its estimation. But with the dynamic window the changing to an unidirectional link is detected. Like the disruption case the detection takes 4 seconds.

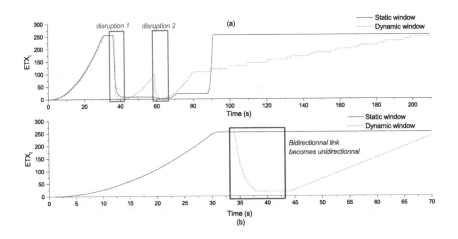

**Fig. 4.** Classical and enhanced $\mathrm{ETX}_l$ comparison

Our enhanced metric based on dynamic window size is clearly more reactive and sensitive. It is explained by the reduction process that highly regresses the metric value by removing old values in the windows. Unlike the static window size has to wait to be filled up with a null value, representing the loss of all expected packets. If the link reappears the dynamic window has the best performance with a link evaluation process adapted faster to a link upcoming. However a static window keeps for a long time too old expected packets. Therefore a disrupted link is considered as a persistent during all the time of convergence. It can be also observed the stair effect introduced by our algorithm when the windows (for $d_r$ and $d_f$) reach their thresholds (right part of figure 4). This is the result of the link stability process that gradually increases the metric value.

To conclude, our algorithm improves the behaviour of the classical ETX metric by making it more reactive, sensitive and gives information about the link stability. These new features make the metric more responsive to link volatility like in VANETs. Therefore, we call this enhanced metric F-ETX for Fast-ETX.

## 4  F-ETX Experimentation Under Realistic Condition

This experimentation aims to make a statistical evaluation on the granularity of F-ETX and classical $ETX_l$ with three static windows sizes (5, 25 and 64 packets). We have implemented these metrics into the BATMAN routing protocol that we have added into ns-3 [1]. Our evaluation scenario places 20 mobile nodes on a 2D grid. A realistic physical propagation model is used. It is based on a Three-LogDistance attenuation model (d1=39m, d2=120m, exp0=2, exp1=2,076) and a Rayleigh fading model (Nakagami model with m=1). Communications use the 802.11p standard. The gain of the antennas are set to zero meanwhile the Tx power level is set to 1dBm and the Tx power start and the Tx power end values are set to zero. Figure 5 summarizes with the box-and-whiskers the ability of metrics to estimate the link quality. The results below show the estimations given on all links during the simulation by the $ETX_l$ metric, including three static window sizes fixed at 64, 30 and 5 SN. And the F-ETX (dynamic window) with a maximum window size fixed at 30 SN.

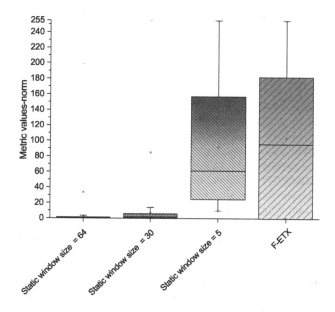

**Fig. 5.** Ability of ETX $_l$ and F-ETX to estimate link qualities

It is observed on the static window sizes, the influence of window size on the distribution of values taken by $ETX_l$. With a larger window size, the values taken by $ETX_l$ are more present in the minimum bound. This observation is explained by the fading and the disruption effects which drop a lot of expected packets conducting to low metric values. Besides, a shortest window size shows a better distribution on the metric values (cf. fig 5). The F-ETX metric appears as the most relevant. Firstly, the box-and-whisker of the F-ETX metric covers more values than other metrics. Secondly, F-ETX has an higher median value than the best static window size (cf. 5 SN). This means that the fading has a lower impact on the F-ETX metric values than done by $ETX_l$ with static window sizes. In addition F-ETX has the best distribution set with a median value close to the mean. This is the result of the use of a dynamic window whose size is self adapted by the link stability process described in section 3.2.

## 5   Conclusion and Future Works

In this paper we have presented the F-ETX metric, an enhancement of the classical ETX metric adapted to the fast changing environment like in VANETs. The metric uses dynamic windows and a process based on the link stability. The results from tests under JBotSim and ns-3 have supported our approach. The F-ETX metric appears to be more reactive, accurate as the classical ETX metric. This makes F-ETX a very good candidate for a routing protocol metric. Future works will lead to integrate F-ETX in routing protocols in order to make intensive tests. This should confirm that F-ETX is a new efficient routing metric adapted to MANETs and VANETs.

## References

1. The ns-3 network simulator, http://www.nsnam.org/
2. Belyaev, E., Vinel, A., Egiazarian, K., Koucheryavy, Y.: Power control in see-through overtaking assistance system. IEEE Communication Letters 17(3), 612–615 (2013)
3. Casteigts, A.: The jbotsim library. CoRR abs/1001.1435 (2013), http://arxiv.org/abs/1001.1435
4. Corson, S., Macker, J.: Mobile ad hoc networking (manet): Routing protocol performance issues and evaluation considerations. RFC 2501 (January 1999), https://www.ietf.org/rfc/rfc2501.txt
5. De Couto, D.S.J., Aguayo, D., Bicket, J., Morris, R.: A high-throughput path metric for multi-hop wireless routing. In: Proceedings of the 9th Annual International Conference on Mobile Computing and Networking, pp. 134–146. ACM, New York (2003), http://doi.acm.org/10.1145/938985.939000
6. Javaid, N., Javaid, A., Khan, I.A., Djouani, K.: Performance study of etx based wireless routing metrics. In: 2nd International Conference on Computer, Control and Communication, IC4 2009, pp. 1–7 (February 2009)
7. Liu, Y., Mi, Z.-C., Zhang, J.-F., Qu, X.: Improvement of etx metric base on olsr. In: 2010 International Conference on Wireless Communications and Signal Processing (WCSP), pp. 1–4 (October 2010)
8. Quartulli, A., Cigno, R.: Client announcement and fast roaming in a layer-2 mesh network. Tech. rep., University of Trento (October 2011), http://eprints.biblio.unitn.it/2269/1/report.pdf
9. Clausen, T., Jacquet, E.P., Optimized, E.: link state routing protocol (olsr). RFC 3626 (October 2003), https://www.ietf.org/rfc/rfc3626.txt

# City-Obstacles Impact on OLSR-Based Routing Protocols

Mohamed Belhassen[1], Amine Dhraief[1], and Abdelfettah Belghith[2]

[1] HANA Lab, University of Manouba,Tunisia
[2] College of Computer and Information Sciences, King Saud University, Saudi Arabia
{mohamed.belhassen,amine.dhraief}@hanalab.org abelghith@ksu.eda.sa

**Abstract.** Vehicle mobility in presence of obstructing obstacle is one of the main problems limiting the deployment of vehicular ad hoc networks. Indeed, in such a highly dynamic network, underlying routing protocols struggle to find valid routes towards destination nodes. In this paper, we evaluate the performance of Cartography Enhanced OLSR with obstacle awareness protocol (CE-OLSR-OA) as well as Position based OLSR (P-OLSR) and OLSR with movement prediction (OLSR-MOPR) routing protocols in the context of an urban VANET with obstructing obstacles. In these three OLSR-based routing protocols, the awareness about nodes locations is differently utilized in order to sustain the stability of selected routes. Conducted simulations show the superiority of CE-OLSR compared to OLSR-MOPR and P-OLSR in terms of routes validity, throughput and end-to-end delay metrics. Furthermore, we show that CE-OLSR is more suitable to real time applications than OLSR-MOPR.

**Keywords:** Routing, VANET, OLSR based protocols, position based routing, movement prediction.

## 1 Introduction

It is worth pointing out that vehicular ad hoc networks (VANETs) have a wide range of applications such as road traffic regulation, road safety, driver assistance and entertainment. Although the clear usefulness of vehicular multi-hop ad hoc networks (VANETs), their real deployment stills limited by the inefficiency of underlying routing protocols[1]. Indeed, the scarcity of the radio resources, the highly mobility of the nodes and the obstructing obstacles side effects represent the three major problems that harm the operation of these protocols in the context of urban VANETs. Moreover, mobilily cannot be simply resolved by increasing the routing traffic since it consumes further valuable network resources. Therefore, the mobility problem has to be treated otherwise.

Several research works have attracted the community attention towards the usefulness of utilizing the nodes positions to assist routing protocols in taking more accurate routing decisions [2,3,4,5], especially in highly mobile environments such as VANETs. Some routing schemes [6,7,5] are entirely driven by nodes locations instead of link states. Other subset of position-based protocols,

M. Kassab et al. (Eds.): Nets4Cars/Nets4Trains/Nets4Aircraft 2015, LNCS 9066, pp. 47–59, 2015.
DOI: 10.1007/978-3-319-17765-6_5

such as [8,9], continues using link states during routing; while nodes locations are used to sustain the stability of selected routes. Further reading about VANETs, the existing taxonomies of their existing routing protocols, and current research challenges of routing in this class of mobile ad hoc networks could be found in these recent surveys [10] [11] [12] [2].

In this paper, we investigate the impact of obstructing obstacles on the performance of three Optimized Link State Routing (OLSR) position-based routing protocols: OLSR with MOvement PRediction (OLSR-MOPR), Position-based OLSR (P-OLSR) and Cartography Enhanced OLSR with Obstacle Awareness (CE-OLSR-OA). To the best of our knowledge, these routing protocols did not previously been evaluated in such a context. We implement all of these protocols in the same framework: OMNET++ V4.1 simulator coupled to SUMO traffic simulator. The obtained results show the superiority of CE-OLSR compared to OLSR-MOPR and P-OLSR in terms of routes validity, throughput and end-to-end delay metrics. Furthermore, we show that CE-OLSR is more suitable to real time applications than OLSR-MOPR.

The reminder of this paper is organized as follows. In section 2, we describe the basic concepts of OLSR protocol [13]. Then, in section 3, we summarize the modifications proposed in OLSR-MOPR protocol [9] to sustain the stability of selected routes. In section 4, we detail the functioning of P-OLSR protocol [8]. In section 5, we overview the core concepts of CE-OLSR-OA protocol [14]. In section 6, we evaluate OLSR, OLSR-MOPR, P-OLSR and CE-OLSR-OA in the context of an urban VANET with obstructing obstacles. Section 7 concludes the paper.

## 2   Optimized Link State Routing Protocol (OLSR)

OLSR [13] is the adaptation of the well-known link state routing paradigm to mobile ad hoc multi-hop networks. In this context, the overhead induced by the routing has to be reduced to its minimum as these networks suffers form the scarcity of the available radio resource. To do so, OLSR relies on two fundamental concepts: (i) a two levels link-state routing strategy and (ii) the multi-point relay (MPR) nodes. In the following, we briefly overview these two concepts.

### 2.1   Two Levels Link-State Routing Strategy

OLSR relies on a two levels link-state routing strategy: the first level focuses on the two-hop neighbourhood of the node, while the second one on more distant nodes. For this purpose, OLSR defines two different control messages: (i) HELLO and Topology Control (TC) messages. Each node periodically broadcasts to its two-hop neighbourhood a HELLO message to declare its local topological changes. Distant nodes become aware of these topological changes through TC messages which are less frequent than HELLO messages. OLSR sets the periodicity of TC messages longer than that of HELLO messages as distant nodes do not require a timely tracking of distant topological changes. It is sufficient for distant nodes to be roughly informed about the distant topology to be able to reach it. More precisely, when a data packet is sent to a distant node, the topology disseminated through TC message is used to reach its two hop neighbourhood. If the data packet succeed in reaching the two hop neighbourhood of the destination node, it is more likely able to reach this destination. In fact, the two hop neighbourhood of the destination node is more informed by the local topological changes of the destination node through its generated HELLO messages. This property of OLSR is commonly known as the fish eye property.

## 2.2   The Multi-Point Relay Concept

OLSR introduced the multi-point relay (MPR) nodes to reduce the routing signalling overhead. MPR nodes of a given node N is a subset of its immediate neighbours that covers all its two hop neighbours. Whatever the considered heuristic of MPR computation, the MPR concept targets to reduce the overhead of routing traffic that need to be forwarded to distant nodes such as TC messages. MPR concept benefits is two folds. Firstly, it limits the number of nodes that generate or relay routing traffic destined to the entire network. Secondly, it reduces the size of link state information which is included in TC messages. Actually, only a subset of the neighbours called MPR selectors are by default included into TC messages. That way, each node of the network perceives a sub-topology (but covering) of the distant areas of the network.

OLSR success comes from the fact that the mechanisms adopted to reduce the routing overhead. However, in network with high dynamics such as VANETs, OLSR performance is highly deteriorated because of nodes mobility. In order to overcome this deficiency several derivative of OLSR have been proposed in the last decade. In the following, we further detail three OLSR-based protocols: P-OLSR, OLSR-MOPR and CE-OLSR. In these protocols, the network cartography (nodes locations) is utilized in various ways to alleviate the mobility problem.

# 3   OLSR with Movement Prediction Protocol (OLSR-MOPR)

In a mobile environment, the selected MPR graph may rapidly change. Thus, to enhance the stability of this graph, the OLSR with movement prediction protocol (OLSR-MOPR) [9] enhances OLSR with the awareness of nodes movements (nodes locations and their velocity components: $V_x$ and $V_y$). During the routing table calculation, instead of selecting the shortest path as it is done in OLSR, OLSR-MOPR selects the most stable route towards each destination node in the network. In addition, during MPR computation, instead of using the coverage degree of one-hop neighbours, OLSR-MOPR privileges the use of a link stability metric called Global Link Stability (GLS). Thus, the most stable one-hop neighbours, in terms of GLS, are firstly selected as MPR independently of their coverage degree. Authors of OLSR-MOPR proposed two strategies of MPR calculation called respectively (i) "MOPR one-hop-based MPRs" selection and (ii) "MOPR two-hops-based MPRs selection". Each of these strategies uses a specific GLS calculation scheme.

In the first MPR selection strategy ("MOPR one-hop-based MPRs"), the GLS is calculated according to Eq. 1. In this formula, $i$ is the node making the MPR calculation, $j \in$ one-hop neighbours set of $i$, $LS(i, j)$ is the link stability of the link $[i, j]$ which is calculated according to Eq.3, $r(i)$ is the number of one-hop neighbours of node $i$. In this MPR selection strategy, the GLS of a given one-hop neighbour $j$ is calculated based on the link stability (LS) of $j$ coupled with its coverage degree.

$$GLS(i,j) = LS(i,j)\frac{r(j)}{\sum_k r(k)} \tag{1}$$

In the second MPR selection strategy ("MOPR two-hops-based MPRs selection"), the GLS is calculated according to Eq. 2. In this strategy, both one-hop and two-hop link stability information is invoked when calculating the GLS of a given node link. In this equation (Eq.2), $k \in$ one-hop neighbours of $j$, $l \in$ one-hop neighbours of $i$ and $m \in$ one-hop neighbours of $l$.

$$GLS(i,j) = LS(i,j)\frac{\sum_k LS(j,k)}{\sum_{l,m} LS(l,m)} \tag{2}$$

Note that, the link stability of a given node, whose formula is given in Eq.3, is proportional to its expected link lifetime. In this formula the "MaxLifeTime" term is used for normalization purpose.

$$LS(i,j) = \begin{cases} \frac{Lifetime(i,j)}{MaxLifeTime} & if Lifetime(i,j) < MaxLifeTime \\ 1 & otherwise \end{cases} \tag{3}$$

The current implementation of OLSR-MOPR is not sufficiently detailed in [9]. For this reason, in order to evaluate this protocol in a VANET context, we took some implementation decisions that we detail as following.

In OLSR-MOPR, each node is supposed to be aware about its neighbours positions by the means of an underlying layer. Although the fact that such an assumption could be true in a particular VANET, it is not guaranteed to be available in all mobile ad hoc networks. In addition, to make a fair comparison with remaining routing protocols, each node has to declare its position to neighbouring node through its own routing messages (such as HELLO). For this reason, in our implementation of OLSR-MOPR, each node include its position in its generated HELLO messages. That way, its neighbours become aware about its position. Furthermore, each node can infer the velocity of its immediate neighbours by monitoring its two last positions. So, when receiving a HELLO message, the receiver node stores the included position and its reception time in its repository. If it has already an old position about the HELLO sender node, it calculates the velocity of this sender node which will be stored locally for a later usage.

The second implementation decision taken relates to the calculation of the link lifetime of a neighbouring node. In fact, authors of OLSR-MOPR did not mentioned precisely when the node calculates the link lifetime of its neighbouring nodes. In our implementation, the link lifetime about a given one-hop neighbour N is calculated by the receiver node (R) at the reception of the HELLO message sent by N. Then, each time the node R needs to know the remaining link lifetime of N, R updates this link lifetime using the associated reception time-stamp before using it.

The third implementation decision is about the LS of two-hop neighbours. Indeed, the OLSR-MOPR paper did not mentioned how this information is communicated to two-hop neighbours. In our implementation, each node include the LS of its neighbours in its generated HELLO when using the second MPR calculation scheme ("MOPR two-hops-based MPRs selection").

The last implementation decision that we took in our OLSR-MOPR implementation is about the routing table calculation. In fact, OLSR-MOPR assumes the availability of an underlying multipath routing algorithm which delivers some routes towards each destination node. Then, OLSR-MOPR selects the most stable route, in terms of GLS, among these routes. Theoretically, if we do not fix a clear strategy to limit the length of the selected routes, the most stable routes will be longer than the shortest one. So, we will uselessly consume the precious radio spectrum. To avoid such a situation (selection of long routes), in our implementation of OLSR-MOPR, we have willingly chosen the following routing table calculation (RTC) scheme. The implemented RTC scheme operates almost similarly to the basic OLSR RTC scheme but with some modification to insure finding the most stable route while limiting the length of selected routes. In OLSR, when calculating the routing table, the node starts by adding its one-hop neighbours using its one-hop neighbour set. Then, it adds its two-hop neighbours located in its two-hop neighbours set. Finally, it iterates several times though its Topology Set to add farther nodes.

In our OLSR-MOPR implementation, we start by adding one-hop neighbours that have a GLS>0. Then, we iterate through the two-hop neighbours set. But, instead of selecting the gateway mentioned in the two-hop tuple as it is done in OLSR, we try to find the best gateway that leads to this two-hop neighbour. That is, we select the gateway that leads to the most stable route toward this two-hop neighbours. Similarly, for farther nodes known through the topology tuples, before adding a route toward a N-hop node the node C calculating the routing table acts as following. It (node C) iterates through accessible "N-1" hop nodes (i.e. nodes existing in the routing table) while testing if there is a topology tuple leading to the N hop node and having as gateway the current "N-1" hop node. If so, it selects as gateway to the current N hop node, the "N-1" hop node that leads to the stablest route. Hence, in our implementation we insure the finding of the most stable route towards each node of the network while limiting the route length.

# 4   Position-Based OLSR Protocol (P-OLSR)

Because of the proactive nature of OLSR, collected link states have to be stored and used for a given period of time. During the link states hold time, some of them may become invalid due to nodes mobility. So, a given node N may select as MPR or as a gateway an unreachable node that leaves its (N) transmission range. To avoid such a situation, the Position-Based OLSR Protocol (P-OLSR) [8] avoids the slection of these moving nodes by adding the awareness about nodes movement to OLSR. In terms of routing signalling, P-OLSR is very similar to OLSR. Indeed, the unique difference consists in appending into HELLO messages the position as well as the velocity components ($V_x$ and $V_y$) of sender nodes. Upon receiving a HELLO message, the receiver node stores the position, the velocity components as well as the HELLO reception time in its local OLSR repository. Thus, each node can easily determine wether its neighbour nodes remain in its transmission range or not. Note that, in P-OLSR, the transmission range is supposed to be known by every node in the network. In P-OLSR, the avoidance of unreachble nodes from being selected as gateways or MPR is performed proactively and reactively. Actually, when calculating the routing table or the MPR set, the node uses on the information about its neighbours locations and movements to filter out proactively unreachable nodes. In addition, when the node is invoked to forward a data packet, it verifies the reachability of the corresponding gateway. If the gateway is assessed as unreachble (based on its position and its movement information), it recalculates the routing table as well as the MPR set. If the newly calculated routing table contains a gateway G leading to the data packet destination, the data packet is forwarded toward G, otherwise the data packet is dropped.

# 5   Cartography Enhanced OLSR Protocol with Obstacle Awareness (CE-OLSR-OA)

In order to adapt OLSR to mobile networks, in a previous work [6], we proposed the Cartography Enhanced OLSR Protocol (CE-OLSR). In CE-OLSR, the network cartography (awareness about nodes positions) is used in various ways to alleviates the problems resulting from nodes mobility. The main building blocks of CE-OLSR consist in a cartography gathering and a stability routing schemes. These two schemes cooperate together to empower the routing efficiency in the context of highly mobile ad hoc networks while keeping its overhead as minimum as possible. Thanks to the collected network cartography, CE-OLSR builds a more accurate and complete network topology than that of OLSR. On the other hand, CE-OLSR performs a judicious stability routing approach permitting to tolerate some nodes movement during the unavoidable waiting time required to receive subsequent locations updates of different nodes of the MANET. Note that in the first version of CE-OLSR [6], since nodes build the network topology only based on nodes positions and their transmission range, they are unable to avoid obstructing obstacles standing in the network area. For this reason, in a subsequent work [14], we proposed CE-OLSR with obstacle awareness (CE-OLSR-OA). In CE-OLSR-OA, mobile nodes are endued with awareness about the map of obstructing obstacles standing in the network area in order to become able to avoid them during routing. In the following sub-sections, we briefly overview the core concepts of cartography gathering and stability routing with obstacle avoidance schemes adopted in CE-OLSR.

## 5.1   Cartography Gathering in CE-OLSR

Instead of building the network topology based on link states as it is done in OLSR, in CE-OSLR nodes build the network topology based on nodes locations (network cartography) and their transmission range. So, nodes must have their own mechanism permitting to collect the network cartography. To preserve the valuable network resources, CE-OLSR embeds the nodes locations in basic OLSR messages. In CE-OLSR both HELLO and TC messages are modified in order to disseminate the nodes locations jointly to corresponding nodes links. More precisely, when sending a HELLO message, sender node joins its position as well as the positions of its heard neighbours to its generated HELLO. When generating a TC message, MPR nodes include the positions of published neighbours. By default, MPR nodes only declare in their TC messages the links toward their MPR selectors nodes.

In order to be able to discriminate the freshest nodes positions among available collected ones, each position is timestamped using the sequence number of the first HELLO message declaring it. So, for each node declared whether in TC or HELLO message, the timestamp (HELLO sequence number) is joined to the declared position. Using such a lightweight network cartography gathering scheme, each node becomes aware about the freshest collected network cartography.

Because of the ceaseless nodes movements, the collected cartography is unavoidably different from current network cartography. So if we build the network topology without considering the continuous nodes movements, the perceived topology may be invalid compared to real one. Subsequently, nodes have to tolerate some nodes movements when building the perceived network topology. This feature is insured using the following stability routing scheme.

## 5.2   Stability Routing Approach with Obstacle Avoidance Capability

Thanks to the adopted network cartography gathering scheme, CE-OLSR succeeds in building a more accurate and complete network topology than that of OLSR. In fact, unpublished links because of control messages collisions or because of underlying OLSR optimizations could be inferred implicitly in CE-OLSR. But, as we just stated in in the end of the last section, nodes mobility invalidates rapidly the collected network cartography (compared to real cartography). Subsequently, the perceived network topology could be invalid compared to real one. In fact, long links could be rapidly broken especially for highly mobile nodes. To overcome this limitation, CE-OLSR alleviates the side effect of nodes mobility by willingly underestimating the network connectivity. More precisely, when building the network topology based on the collected network cartography, CE-OLSR uses a stable transmission range ($STX_{Range}$) which is smaller than the real one (see Eq.4). Using such a scheme, nodes only keep links that tolerate some movements of its extremities without being broken. However, using such a stability routing scheme will make selected routes a little bit longer than shortest real paths.

$$STX_{Range} = TX_{Range} - StabilityDistance \qquad (4)$$

Contrary to OLSR, P-OLSR and OLSR-MOPR, CE-OLSR builds the network topology based on its cartography instead of the collected link states. So, it is more affected by the existence of obstructing obstacles. In order to make CE-OLSR able to avoid obstacles standing the network area, in the second version of CE-OLSR called CE-OLSR-OA, each node is assumed to be aware about the map of the obstacles standing in the network area. That way, each node can filter out links that cross obstacles from the perceived network topology.

# 6    Performance Evaluation

In this section, we first describe the simulation set-up. Then we define the used metrics. Finally, we detail and discuss the results of simulation scenarios.

## 6.1    Simulation Set-Up

We implemente all considered routing protocols (OLSR, P-OLSR, OLSR-MOPR and CE-OLSR) under INETMANET Framework within the OMNeT++ network simulator (Version 4.1). In order to build the VANET environment, we coupled the SUMO simulator to the OMNET++ simulator. The simulated VANET covers an area of 1000 m by 1000 m. Routes forming this VANET are set such as they form a square grid of 16 cells (4 X 4 grid) as depicted in Fig.1. Each route contains a single lane in each direction. In this network, we set 12 vehicle flow sources (see Fig.1). In each vehicle flow, a vehicle enters the network each 25 second in average. Vehicle departure times are randomized using "randomize-flows" sumo parameter. When a given vehicle reaches a sink edge (the network boundary), it leaves the network.

The vehicles properties are set as follow. The acceleration is set to 0.8 $m/s^2$; while the vehicle deceleration is set to 4.5 $m/s^2$. The vehicle length is set to 5 m and the minimum gap between two subsequent vehicles is set to 2 m. Since we are modelling an urban VANET environment, we set the maximum vehicle speed to 60 $km/h$. The vehicles following model is set to the collision free Krauss Following model [15]. In each junction, four traffic lights are set to regulate the vehicle priorities (one of each edge). When encountering a junction, a vehicle selects, with equal probabilities, one of the three remaining edges.

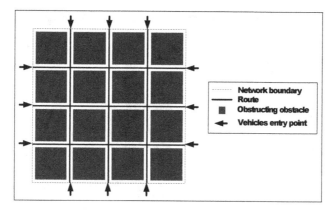

**Fig. 1.** Simulated VANET map

The nodes transmission range is fixed to 350 m. The network capacity is set to 11 Mbps. The CE-OLSR protocol parameters are set as following. "TcRedundancy" parameter is fixed to 0, which means that MPR nodes publish only their MPR selectors in their generated TC messages. The periodicity of TC messages is fixed to 8 s and that of HELLO messages is set to 2 s. The OLSR sending jitter is chosen randomly from the [0, 0.5] seconds interval. CE-OLSR stability distance parameter is fixed to 20 m. Regarding OLSR-MOPR protocol, the GLS is computed using the first proposed formula (Eq. 1) and the MaxLinkLifetime parameter is set to 200 s.

For scenarios invoking data traffic, we set-up 4 Constant Bit Rate (CBR) data flows between 4 different vehicles pairs. Each flow extremity (vehicle) in a given data flow remains far from the other extremity during the whole simulation time. This is insured by putting each one of them in a different parallel road. The size of transmitted data packets is set to 1000 B.

The selected scenarios are executed for a simulation time equal to 350 s. The first 250 s of the simulation (transient regime) is truncated from simulation results. Finally, we consider a network containing 16 square obstructing obstacles having a size of 210 m by 210 m. Each grid cell contains one of these obstacles (see Fig.1).

**Routes Validity Metric.** In addition to traditional metrics such as achieved throughput and end-to-end delay, we need another metric that evaluates the ability of underlying routing function to achieve correct routing decisions. The consistency of retained paths could be evaluated through the routes validity metric. This metric measures the consistency of the routing table of a given node compared to the real network state (topology). It is worthy to note that in all considered OLSR based protocols, each entry in the routing table points only to the next gateway leading to the ultimate destination. Subsequently, the whole route toward a given destination is retained in a distributed manner in

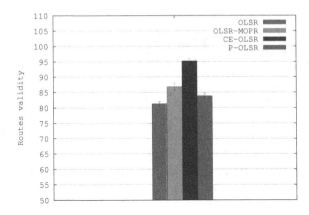

**Fig. 2.** Routes validity in the absence of data flows

the routing tables of intermediate gateways. A given route is considered as valid if it exists in the real network topology. In addition, routes that are absent in the routing table of a given node are also termed valid if they do not exist in the real network topology. Besides these two mentioned cases, the route is considered as invalid. We define the routes validity of a given node as the percentage of valid routes retained in its routing table.

## 6.2    Simulation Results

In this section, we start by evaluating the routes validity of all considered routing protocols in the context of urban VANET with obstructing obstacles. Then, we evaluate these protocols in terms of achieved throughput and end-to-end delay of received data packets.

**Routes Validity of Various Studied Protocols** In the first simulation set, we study the ability of OLSR and its considered derivatives to retain valid routes. Figure.2 portrays the routes validity obtained when we run these protocols in the absence of data traffic. As depicted in this figure, CE-OLSR outperforms all other considered protocols by more than 10%. In the second position we found OLSR-MOPR followed by P-OLSR. In this first simulation set, OLSR leads to the worst performance with a routes validity which painfully reaches 81.5%.

Now we evaluate the impact of data flows on the routes validity metric. In fact, in a real context, routing protocols strive to perform well in the presence of data flows. Indeed, data packets may collide with routing traffic which generally leads to the deterioration of routes validity. Figure 3 depicts the impact of data flows on the achieved routes validity. According this figure, CE-OLSR is less impacted by data traffic compared to remaining routing protocols. In fact, the routes validity of CE-OLSR decreases by less than 3% when we apply four data flows of 30 Packets/flow/second. In a similar data load, the performance of

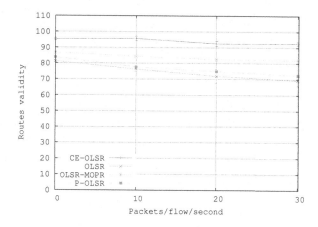

**Fig. 3.** Impact of data flows on routes validity metric

OLSR-MOPR decreases by about 5% compared its performance in data free simulations. Performed simulations (Fig.3) show that P-OLSR and OLSR are more impacted by the presence of data flows than CE-OLSR and OLSR-MOPR. Actually, their performance decreases by about 9% and 12% respectively compared their performances in a data free context.


**Achieved Throughput and En to End Delay of Received Data Packets.**
In the second simulation set, we turn to evaluate the performance of studied protocols in terms of achieved average throughput and end-to-end-delay of received data packets. For data flows less or equal to 30 Packets/flow/second, CE-OLSR and OLSR-MOPR achieve similar throughput. But for a traffic higher than 40 Packets/flow/second, CE-OLSR outperforms OLSR-MOPR by about 2.6 Packets/flow/second. In the same way, OLSR and P-OLSR perform similarly in the case of data traffic less or equal to 30 Packets/flow/second. For a higher traffic, OLSR performs better than P-OLSR by about 2 Packets/flow/second.

In terms of end-to-end-delay of received data packets, CE-OLSR leads to the best performance compared to remaining studied protocols. In the highest tested data load (40 Packets/flow/second), the end-to-end delay achieved by CE-OLSR is less than 160ms. In a similar data load, the end-to-end delay of remaining protocols ranges between 195 ms and 444 ms. Note that the end-to-end delay achieved by OLSR is smaller than that of OLSR-MOPR. This behaviour return to the stability routing scheme used in OLSR-MOPR that my increase the length routing paths. Compared to P-OLSR, OLSR achieves a comparable end-to-end-delay for data loads less or equal to 20 Packets/flow/second. But for higher data traffic, the performance of P-OLSR is affected compared to OLSR. This could be explained by the MPR computation scheme of P-OLSR that increases the broadcast overhead of P-OLSR compared to OLSR by omitting unreachable neighbours from MPR computation process. Subsequently, the overall number of MPR in the network is higher in P-OLSR than that in OLSR.

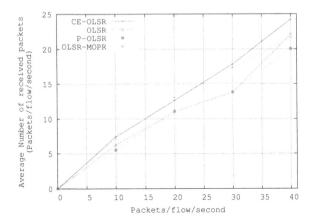

**Fig. 4.** Average throughput

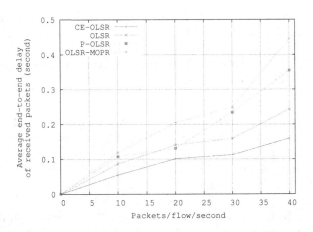

**Fig. 5.** Average end-to-end-delay of received data packets

## 7   Conclusion

In this paper, we evaluated OLSR, P-OLSR, OLSR-MOPR and CE-OLSR-OA
in the context of urban VANETs. Conducted simulations showed the superiority
of CE-OLSR compared to the remaining routing protocols in terms of route
validity metric, throughput and end-to-end delay of received data packets. In
this preliminary work, we used a simple, though representative, urban VANET
model to test the considered protocols. Further performance evaluation in the
context of real urban or highway VANETs will be investigated.

# References

1. Clausen, T., Jacquet, E.P., Optimized, E.: link state routing protocol (olsr). RFC 3626 (October 2003), https://www.ietf.org/rfc/rfc3626.txt
2. Fonseca, A., Vazo, T.: Applicability of position-based routing for {VANET} in highways and urban environment. Journal of Network and Computer Applications 36(3), 961–973 (2013),
http://dx.doi.org/http://dx.doi.org/10.1016/j.jnca.2012.03.009
3. Abid, M., Belghith, A.: Period size self tuning to enhance routing in manets. International Journal of Business Data Communications and Networking (IJB-DCN) 6(4), 21–37 (2010)
4. Belghith, A., Abid, M.: Autonomic self tunable proactive routing in mobile ad hoc networks. In: IEEE International Conference on Wireless and Mobile Computing, Networking and Communications (WIMOB 2009), pp. 276–281 (2009)
5. Abid, M., Belghith, A.: Stability routing with constrained path length for improved routability in dynamic manets. Personal and Ubiquitous Computing 15(8), 799–810 (2011)
6. Belhassen, M., Belghith, A., Abid, M.A.: Performance evaluation of a cartography enhanced olsr for mobile multi-hop ad hoc networks. In: 7th IEEE Conference on Wireless Advanced (WiAd 2011), pp. 149–155 (2011), doi:10.1109/WiAd.2011.5983303
7. Karp, B., Kung, H.T.: GPSR: Greedy perimeter stateless routing for wireless networks. In: Proceedings of the Sixth Annual ACM/IEEE International Conference on Mobile Computing and Networking (MobiCom 2000), Boston, Massachusetts, pp. 243–254 (2000)
8. Sharma, S.: P-olsr: Position-based optimized link state routing for mobile ad hoc networks. In: IEEE 34th Conference on Local Computer Networks, LCN 2009, pp. 237–240 (2009)
9. Menouar, H., Lenardi, M., Filali, F.: Improving proactive routing in vanets with the mopr movement prediction framework. In: 7th International Conference on ITS Telecommunications, ITST 2007, Sophia Antipolis, France (2007)
10. Sharef, B.T., Alsaqour, R.A., Ismail, M.: Vehicular communication ad hoc routing protocols: A survey. Journal of Network and Computer Applications 40, 363 (2014), doi:10.1016/j.jnca.2013.09.008
11. Singh, S., Agrawal, S.: Vanet routing protocols: Issues and challenges. In: 2014 Recent Advances in Engineering and Computational Sciences (RAECS), pp. 1–5 (2014), doi:10.1109/RAECS.2014.6799625
12. Aashish Kumar, M.T.: Geographical topologies of routing protocols in vehicular ad hoc networks a survey. International Journal of Computer Science and Information Technologies 5(3), 3062–3065 (2014)
13. Clausen, T., Jacquet, P.: Optimized link state routing protocol (olsr). In: EXPERIMENTAL RFC 3626 (2003)
14. Belghith, A., Belhassen, M.: Ce-olsr: a cartography and stability enhanced olsr for dynamic manets. Transactions on Internet and Information Systems, KSII 6(1), 290–306 (2012)
15. Krauss, S.: Microscopic modeling of traffic flow: investigation of collision free vehicle dynamics, Ph.D. thesis, Koeln Univ, Germany (1998)

# TCP Application Recovery Improvement After Handover in Mobile Networks

Hajer Souri[1], Amine Dhraief[1], and Abdelfettah Belghith[2]

[1] HANA Lab, University of Manouba, Tunisia
[2] College of Computer and Information Sciences, King Saud University, Saudi Arabia
{hajer.souri,amine.dhraief}@hanalab.org, abelghith@ksu.edu.sa

**Abstract.** Host and network mobility support mechanisms aim to provide a seamless access to Internet while end users are changing their point of attachment. When a mobile entity roams from a network to another, a handover occurs causing communication session discontinuity degrading real-time application performance. Assuming that such inconvenience is a congestion, TCP recovery is slow and careful. We have previously proposed a cooperation between TCP and MIPv6 and proved its efficiency through OMNeT++ simulations. In this paper, We study its efficiency in the context of mobile networks. Therefore, we implement xNEMO; a compliant implementation of NEtwork MObility Basic Support (NEMO BS) in OMNeT++. Besides, in order to enhance the performance of TCP application, we propose to modify the TCP behaviour after a recovery from a handover. Simulations show that the cooperation between TCP and NEMO BS reduces the Application Recovery Time and enhances the performance of the TCP application.

**Keywords:** Network Mobility, TCP, Application Recovery Time, OMNeT++.

## 1 Introduction

The constant reachability of mobile IP devices is no more a vision but a dominant reality. The continuous connectivity to Internet requires a good management of frequent changes from a network to another in order to guarantee the good functioning of Internet applications, especially the real time ones. Therefore, it is important to assign a unique identifier to each mobile entity which allows to maintain communication sessions with other peers. Mobile IPv6 (MIPv6)[7] and Network Mobility Basic Support (NEMO BS)[2] are the IETF proposed protocols to manage respectively host mobility and network mobility. They enable mobile entities/networks to ensure session continuity while roaming between IP networks . However, keeping the roaming seamless still a major topic of research.

Guaranteeing reliability for Internet applications is ensured through the use of TCP, a major Internet transport layer protocol. It controls data transmission and ensures the stability of Internet application. Improving the performance of TCP is a key element to guarantee the reliability of application and even the

© Springer International Publishing Switzerland 2015
M. Kassab et al. (Eds.): Nets4Cars/Nets4Trains/Nets4Aircraft 2015, LNCS 9066, pp. 60–71, 2015.
DOI: 10.1007/978-3-319-17765-6_6

transparency of network roaming. In this context, it is important to mention that TCP different algorithms confuse between movement and congestion when recovering after packet losses. This was highlighted in our previous work[4,3] when studying the impact of the mobile node's movement on TCP sessions. The reaction of TCP after the packet loss caused by devices movement is the same as its reaction at the diagnosis of a network congestion, *i.e.* TCP recovery after network switching takes a long time to occur.

In order to address such misbehaviour in the context of host mobility, we have previously proposed to establish a novel solution that enhances the Application Recovery Time (ART) of TCP applications for MIPv6 nodes[5]. We proposed a cross-layer cooperation between TCP and MIPv6 layers notifying TCP of the end of an ongoing handover. Thus, the TCP activity is recovered. Our solution was proven to efficiently reduce up to 43% of the ART.

In this paper, we extend our previous work[5] in order to deal with mobile networks. The focus of our study is the efficiency of our proposed cross-layer cooperation when it is between TCP and NEMO BS. Hence, we implement a compliant version of NEMO BS by extending xMIPv6, the framework simulating the behaviour of MIPv6 nodes in OMNeT++[10]. Besides, being aware that the reason of the transmission interruption was not a congestion but a handover,we also propose to modify the behaviour of TCP after a recovery from a handover by resettling the state of TCP as if no interruption occurred and thus the careful and slow recovery is avoided. The performance evaluation of our proposals shows that the TCP application performance is significantly improved in the context of mobile networks.

The reminder of this paper is organized as follows: an overview of Network Mobility Basic Support as well as a quick review of TCP performance in mobile environments are given in section 2. Section 3 is dedicated to describe the issue of TCP applications while moving from a network to another and present our revised solution to enhance the functioning of TCP. In section 4, we present the evaluation of the performance of our overall proposal in the framework of mobile networks after implementing the NEMO BS specification on OMNeT++. Conclusion and perspectives are presented in the section 5.

## 2   Related Works

In the following section, we first present the Mobile Network Basic Support details and then brievly prensent TCP and its performance in mobile networks.

### 2.1   Network Mobility

A mobile network, NEMO, is the association of several devices connected and moving together forming a mobile network using each the same communication medium. In NEMO, each device, a Mobile Network Node(MNN), has its own IPv6 address but the same IPv6 prefix advertised by a specific router and shall be permanently reachable and connected.

NEMO Basic Support(NEMO BS) [2] was proposed as an extension to MIPv6 in order to manage the Network Mobility. There are different scenarios of mobile networks in the current daily life. Among them, we mention:

– Personal networks: People daily carry multiple IP devices such as smart-phones, PDAs, cameras and laptops. A cell phone or a 3G key could act as a mobile router managing their connectivity and continuous reachability,
– Public transport systems are moving towards being equipped with mobile routers in order to enable passengers handheld devices to hold their connectivity,
– Car area networks: Intelligent cars are a strategic target of network mobility, as car industry is likely to equip cars with more connected IP devices. A car, hence, becomes a mobile network where different IP devices, already installed in the car or belonging to the passengers, wish to be constantly connected. Public transport vehicles where many passengers carrying their mobile devices seek Internet access, are also typical mobile networks.

A NEMO changes its point of attachment to the Internet with time. A Mobile Router (MR), a MIPv6 enabled mobile node endowed by routing capabilities, is responsible of providing Internet connection to the mobile and fixed nodes.

The home network has an assigned bloc of prefixes , Mobile Network Prefixes (MNPs), that a special entity called home agent advertises,hence, theoretically, MR may have one or few home addresses. These configured addresses are permanent and valid even when the NEMO is out of its home network but topologically correct only in the home link. Besides, MR advertises one or few prefixes in its subnet that are used by nodes on its link to configure their addresses.

When the NEMO leaves its home network and attaches to a new access point, it acquires a topologically correct address called Care-of Address (CoA) configured using its own ID combined with the prefix being advertised on the foreign link. Forthwith, MR sends a Binding Update (BU) with mobile network prefix

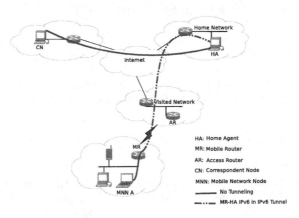

**Fig. 1.** NEMO Basic Support Protocol operation

information included to its home agent to inform about its newly configured address.

At the reception of the MR's BU, the home agent must first validate it, creates a new binding cache entry if no relevent one already exists. Then, it sends a Binding Acknowledgement (BA) to MR and establishes a bi-directional tunnel to MR for the requested MNP and starts advertising reachability to the mobile network. Hence, at the reception of a BA, MR may resume flowing data in the tunnel. Packets exchanged between the MNNs and their Correspondent Nodes (CNs) are routed through the home agent via the established tunnel (Figure 1).

## 2.2 TCP in Wireless and Mobile Networks

TCP is the major protocol that ensures Internet services reliability, congestion control, flow control and connection management. Mainly, it is able to control congestion by managing the transmission rate in order not to exhaust the available network bandwidth. Wireless and mobile networks suffers from the variability of the radio link quality and signals fluctuation so that transmission speed is lower and the Bit Error Ratio (BER) is higher.TCP performance are likely to be affected by mobility (*i.e.* handovers) and congestion that cause variable or even high delays (RTT)[9]. As a consequence, the retransmission timer expires. Hence, most TCP variations reduce their congestion window (cwnd) to 1 and enter a careful and slow transmission phase which degrades the application performance. [6], [1], [8] and others proposed solutions to improve the performance of TCP in wireless environments. Our work in [5] briefly descibes some of them.

## 3   Explicit Handover Cross-Layer Triggers and Its Implications in Mobile Networks

In [5], we defined the Application Recovery Time (ART) as the time that elapses between the last data packet received before a handover and the first data packet received after a handover. We showed that a handover usually finishes before the recovery of application as depicted in Figure 2.

This is due to the lack of communication between the IP and the transport layers. TCP continues executing its instructions waiting for the expiry of the retransmission timer that could have been doubled few times whilst the handover end had already took place. The adopted TCP algorithm keeps transmitting packets as far as needed while setting the retransmission timer (RTO) at each time. When an acknowledgment is received, RTO is canceled. But, when a handover occurs, Acks are lost and hence RTO expires triggering the detection of a problem. TCP, then, keeps retransmitting the packet that is suspected to be

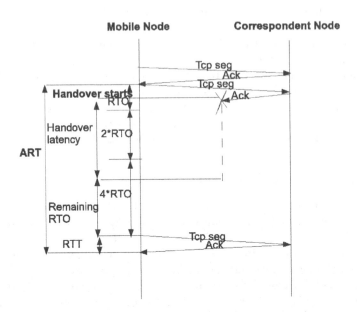

**Fig. 2.** Application Recovery Time

lost and resetting RTO to the double of its previous value at each expiry until the reception of an acknowledgment. Meanwhile, the handover may finish and a tunnel between the MR and the HA may be established but the ongoing TCP session would not notice it and keeps waiting the RTO expiry to resume retransmission.

To deal with this inconvenience, we proposed to establish a cooperative behaviour between the IP layer and TCP allowing the notification of TCP at the end of a handover and the establishment of a tunnel with the home network. Thus, TCP cancels the retransmission timer and retransmits the earliest non acknowledged segment. Our simulations showed that the proposal significantly reduces the ART in the case of MIPv6. In this paper we intend to prove its efficiency in the context of mobile networks by adopting the same cooperation mechanism.

Furthermore, canceling the retransmission timer will only speed the resumption of the TCP algorithm functioning. However, almost all of the TCP algorithms still consider the retransmission timer expiry as a congestion problem and then reduce remarkably its state variables. Most of the algorithms enter the Slow Start phase at the expiry of RTO. This implies the reduction of the cwnd and the ssthresh as follows:

$$flightSize = min(awnd, cwnd)$$
$$ssthresh \leftarrow max(flightSize/2, 2)$$
$$cwnd = 1MSS$$

where awnd is the TCP advertised window MSS is the maximum segment size. Then, TCP starts sending one single packet and waits until the reception of its acknowledgment to send two new other packets and so on until reaching the newly set ssthresh strikingly lower than the former value. Such reduction instantly degrades drastically the performance of the TCP transmission reducing significantly the rate of the mobile node's transmitted packets. Yet, the congestion estimation is completely wrong.

Indeed, as a handover lasts usually a few minutes at most, we assume that we have a quite restricted distance traveled during the movement of the mobile node/network. This assumption implies that we could consider that the density in the network that the mobile entity have just left is quite similar to the network area to which it currently belongs. Therefore, network congestion state is assumed to be relatively stable during the handover. Thereby, forcing TCP to reduce its state variables and enter Slow Start at the end of a handover is useless.

Therefore, we judged worthwhile to adapt the behaviour of TCP in mobile environments when it is running on a Mobile Node side. All the same, it is important to maintain it independent of any intermediaries. As the reception of an explicit handover cross-layer trigger informs the TCP layer about a handover taking place, it becomes simpler to amend the behaviour of TCP only when needed. So, we propose to resettle the TCP state variables after the handover to its recorded values just before the handover *i.e.* the Slow Start phase is eventually avoided and packet transmission rate would keep increasing just like the way it was increasing before the handover. At each expiry of an RTO, the RTO is doubled and the unacked TCP segment having the smallest sequence number is retransmitted. If the mobile node receives an ACK, that means that the network is congested. So, the mobile node must react conventionally by reducing the ssthresh and the cwnd and re-entering Slow Start smoothly increasing its packet transmission. However, if a handover cross-layer trigger is received, then we have a handover that has just been finished. Thus, our proposal is that the mobile node sends the unacked TCP segment having the smallest sequence number and when the ACK is received it checks whether it acknowledges some or all the data transmitted before the handover to decide data to be transmitted next. Besides, TCP resets cwnd and ssthresh to their values just before the handover and continues its normal operation. The TCP algorithm becomes as follows.

---

**while** RTO Expires **do**
   $RTO \leftarrow RTO * 2$
   Enter Slow Start
   Retransmit one segment
   **if** explicit handover cross-layer trigger **then**
      {Handover is the cause of the RTO expiry}
      Retransmit one segment
      **if** received ACK **then**
         $cwnd \leftarrow recordedCwnd$
         $ssthresh \leftarrow recordedSsthresh$
         **if** All data acknowledged **then**
            Send new data
         **else**
            Retransmit all unAcked data
         **end if**
      **end if**
   **else if** received Ack **then**
      {Congestion is the cause of the RTO expiry}
      Continue Slow Start {Congestion is the cause of the RTO expiry}
   **end if**
**end while**

---

## 4    Performance Evaluation

The performance evaluation of our proposal is the objective of this section. The influence of the cooperation between TCP and NEMO Basic Support as well as the modified TCP behaviour are investigated.

### 4.1    Simulation Setup

we perform evaluation on the OMNeT++ simulator [10] using the INET framework[1]. To achieve simulations, we use the Tahoe, Reno and NewReno implementation of TCP in INET.

Among the goals of this work, we want to test our proposed enhancements in mobile networks. However, there is no NEMO BS compliant implementation known for the OMNeT++ simulator. Therefore, we have had to design and develop our own implementation of the protocol according to the standards and specifications of the IETF. Having dissected the different features and specifications of the NEMO BS and carefully studied the xMIPv6 implementation, we have decided to be based on it to develop our NEMO BS protocol by extending its functionalities, data structures and messages. As a result, we developed the xNEMO, the extension of INET, that implements the NEMO Basic Support protocol according to the specification of the IETF[2].

To perform the simulation and evaluation, we use two mobile routers MR1 and MR2 that are roaming from their home networks to new foreign networks.

---

[1] http://inet.omnetpp.org/

Besides, we dispose of a mobile node MN that is moving between its home network and the two mobile networks related to the two mobile routers MR2 and MR1. A second scenario is also considered. It extends the first one by adding few extra nodes in order to take into consideration relatively dense networks. Nodes are scattered in the different subnetworks. Each node is communicating wirelessly with a correspondent node exchanging a UDP data flow.

The network configuration is as follows; in both scenarios we use the IEEE 802.11b for wireless communication with 2Mbps bitrate. The mobile node is moving from its home network to the visited network with a velocity of one meter per second. We use the rectangle mobility model to simulate the MN movement from the home network to the visited network. The delays separating two routers or a hub and a correspondent node are 50ms, while, the delays separating a router and a hub or an access point are $10^{-3}\mu s$. The access points beacon interval is 0.1s. The transmission range of each access point as well as the different nodes is 177m. Figure3 shows the basic simulation network without the extra nodes with the UDP flow. To observe results during the movement of the Mobile Node as well as the Mobile Routers, simulations lasts 600 seconds.

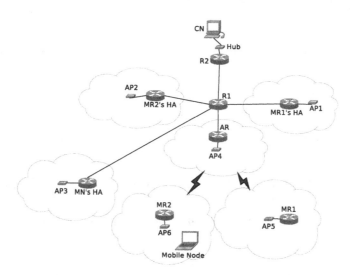

**Fig. 3.** Basic NEMO simulation network

## 4.2   Metrics

The purpose of simulations is to evaluate the impact of the explicit handover cross-layer triggers and the new behaviour of the TCP algorithm upon the reception of this cross-layer trigger on the TCP application recovery in the context of mobile networks.

TCP Application Recovery Time (ART) is an important metric we have to keep track of in order to evaluate the cross-layer trigger. We also keep track of the congestion window (cwnd) and the TCP packets sent by the mobile node during the simulations in order to evaluate the modification in the behaviour of the TCP algorithm.

Besides, the evaluation of the performance of our optimizations have been done while varying the density of our networks. Simulations are done using empty networks as well as loaded networks.

### 4.3   Simulation Results and Evaluation

Through Fig.5 and Fig.4 we can notice the difference between the round trip time (RTT) in the home network and the round trip time in the visited mobile network(Fig.5) and the round trip time in a simple foreign network (Fig.4), the difference is important regarding the number of tunnels in NEMO (nested tunnels) and then the number of subnetworks traveled by packets. And as the RTT is a component of the Application Recovery Time (ART)[5], that explains partially the importance of the ART in the Mobile Networks.

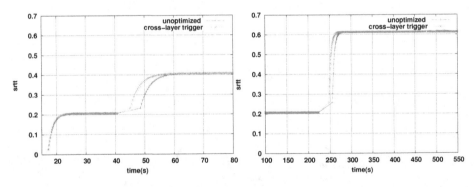

**Fig. 4.** TCP Smoothed RTT in MIPv6 (seconds)     **Fig. 5.** TCP Smoothed RTT in NEMO (seconds)

Fig.6 and Fig.7 illustrate the evolution of the TCP congestion window size with three configurations; the red line for the unoptimized TCP, the green line is for TCP enhanced by the cross-layer triggering and the blue line is for cross-layer triggering plus modified behaviour of TCP. In all the scenarios, handover between the mobile node's home network and the first mobile network is triggered approximately at the 243rd second and the second handover between the two mobile networks is triggered at roughly the 461st second.

From Fig.6 and Fig.7, we notice that the ART when roaming between the two mobile networks is less then the ART when roaming between the mobile node's home network and the first mobile network. This due to the fact that the mobile node's home agent does not perform the Duplicate Address Detection (DAD) when receiving a Binding Update from a mobile node having already a cache entry in the cache list which is the case of our scenario and thus the BU/BA phase composing the handover latency is decremented by one second.

The figures clearly show that with the cross-layer triggering the TCP application is recovered earlier *i.e* ART is reduced especially in the case of the quite loaded network (Fig.7). Besides, adopting a modified behaviour of the TCP algorithm allows a much better recovery of the application by recovering the state variables of TCP (cwnd and ssthresh).

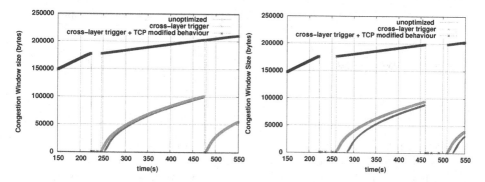

**Fig. 6.** cwnd size, empty cells          **Fig. 7.** cwnd size, 28 nodes,300kbps

Fig.8 and Fig.9 show the evolution of the number of the TCP packets sent by the mobile node. Both figures show that the number of packets sent increases faster when adopting the cross layer triggering and the TCP modified behaviour (the blue line).

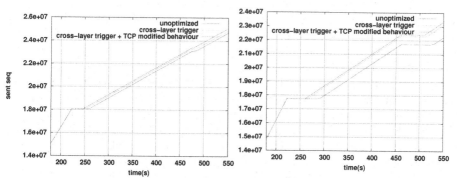

**Fig. 8.** TCP Sequence number, empty cell  **Fig. 9.** TCP Sequence number, 28nodes, 300kbps

Tab.1 presents and compares the number of TCP packets sent in each simulation, it also demonstrates that the performance of the TCP application has been improved by adopting the proposed enhancements as the number of packets sent when TCP is augmented by the cross-layer triggers and the modified behaviour is much bigger (22176 packets in empty cells and 20492 packets in loaded cells) than the number of transmitted packets in case of unoptimized TCP (21703 packets in empty cells and 19403 packets in loaded cells).

**Table 1.** Number of TCP packets sent by the mobile node during the different NEMO simulations

|                                          | empty cells | loaded cells |
|------------------------------------------|-------------|--------------|
| Standard                                 | 21703       | 19403        |
| cross-layer triggering                   | 21967       | 20279        |
| cross-layer triggering+ modified TCP     | 22176       | 20492        |

## 5 Conclusion

Wireless mobile networks present few challenges due to the nature of wireless links. They have to frequently change their points of attachment while moving around because of the relatively short range of transmission of access routers. This requires different steps to be taken before becoming reachable again. Hence, the interruption of data transmission becomes frequent and the time that an application recovery takes to recover is considerably larger than the handover latency. It is fair to say that this inconvenience is due to the lack of cooperation between mobility protocols and TCP. We have been interested in this problem previously and proposed a cross-layer cooperation between these protocols and TCP. Host Mobility case was studied in an earlier work while this paper treats the networks mobility case. We implemented the xNEMO extension to INET framework on OMNeT++ deploying the Network Mobility Basic Support protocol (NEMO Basic Support) according to the the specification of the IETF. Our proposed cooperation was tested using our new INET extension (xNEMO). Simulations showed that our proposal significantly reduced the Application Recovery Time in the mobile platforms context and the introduction of the modified behavior of TCP after recovery improved the performance of the TCP application. As a future work, we intend to consolidate the simulation results by moving to a broad-scale implementation with simulation tools and in a second time with a real test beds. The vehicular networks, indeed, would be an ideal canvas to test our work. In fact, they are typical mobile environments where it is plausible to consider a vehicle as a mobile network. Whether its a private car or a public transportation, NEMO Basic Support would be an exemplary mean of managing devices connection inside the vehicle.

# References

1. Casetti, C., Gerla, M., Mascolo, S.: Tcp westwood: End-to-end congestion control for wired / wireless networks. Wireless Networks 8(5), 467–479 (2002), http://portal.acm.org/citation.cfm?id=582460
2. Devarapalli, V., Wakikawa, R., Petrescu, A., Thubert, P.: Network Mobility (NEMO) Basic Support Protocol. RFC 3963 (Proposed Standard) (January 2005), http://www.ietf.org/rfc/rfc3963.txt
3. Dhraief, A., Belghith, A.: An experimental investigation of the impact of mobile ipv6 handover on transport protocols. The Smart Computing Revue, KAIS 2(1) (February 2012), http://www.smartcr.org/view/view.html
4. Dhraief, A., Chedly, Z., Belghith, A.: The impact of mobile ipv6 on transport protocols an experimental investigation. In: 2010 International Conference on Communication in Wireless Environments and Ubiquitous Systems: New Challenges (ICWUS), pp. 1–8 (October 2010)
5. Dhraief, A., Souri, H., Belghith, A.: Explicit mipv6 handover cross-layer triggers and its impact on tcp application recovery time. In: 2013 International Conference on Computer Applications Technology (ICCAT), pp. 1–8. IEEE (2013)
6. Fu, C.P., Liew, S.C.: TCP Veno: TCP Enhancement for Transmission Over Wireless Access Networks. IEEE Communications 21(2), 216–228 (2003), http://citeseerx.ist.psu.edu/viewdoc/summary?doi=10.1.1.2.1469
7. Johnson, D., Perkins, C., Arkko, J.: Mobility Support in IPv6. RFC 3775 (Proposed Standard) obsoleted by RFC 6275 (June 2004), http://www.ietf.org/rfc/rfc3775.txt
8. Lee, D.C., Kim, H.J., Koh, J.Y.: Enhanced algorithm of tcp performance on handover in wireless internet networks. In: NPC, pp. 684–690 (2004)
9. Tian, Y., Xu, K., Ansari, N.: TCP in wireless environments: problems and solutions. IEEE Communications Magazine 43(3), S27–S32 (2005), http://dx.doi.org/10.1109/MCOM.2005.1404595
10. Varga, A.: OMNeT++ User Manual, Version 4.1 (2010), http://www.omnetpp.org

# Effective Certificate Distribution in ETSI ITS VANETs Using Implicit and Explicit Requests

Sebastian Bittl, Berke Aydinli, and Karsten Roscher

Fraunhofer ESK, 80686 Munich, Germany
{sebastian.bittl,berke.aydinli,karsten.roscher}@esk.fraunhofer.de

**Abstract.** Security and privacy of current Car-to-X systems heavily depends on the usage of pseudonym certificates. These carry the required information for authenticating messages received from other vehicles. However, only a limited amount of detailed studies about certificate distribution strategies in VANETs as well as attack surfaces of such systems has been proposed. Therefore, a general study about possible distribution mechanisms and their parametrization is provided in this work. Thereby, the management of entries in request lists is identified as a key issue for system performance. Additionally, a design flaw in the currently standardized ETSI ITS distribution scheme is outlined leading to the possibility of an attacker significantly increasing channel load on the safety critical control channel. A solution to this problem is suggested and an evaluation of its performance is provided. Furthermore, the evaluation shows the great influence of request list management on authentication delay and thus on security inducted packet loss.

**Keywords:** Certificate distribution, VANET, ETSI ITS, security.

## 1 Introduction

Wireless Car-to-X communication systems, often called vehicular ad hoc networks (VANETs) like ETSI intelligent transport systems (ITS) in Europe [1], are in the wake of deployment in upcoming years. Thereby, security and privacy issues of such systems are a core point of concern. The main reason for this is the intended use for safety critical applications, even during so called Day 1 use cases from 2015 on. Thus, a security scheme for VANET messages has been developed and is in the still ongoing process of standardization [4,17].

Privacy of VANET users is commonly protected by a pseudonym scheme using changing pseudonym certificates to authenticate messages, e.g., Cooperative Awareness Messages (CAMs). Thereby, tracking of vehicles can be avoided or at least hindered [11]. However, usage of such authentication schemes in VANETs requires to distribute pseudonym certificates frequently alongside with data used by applications. Without the corresponding certificate received messages cannot be verified and thus are not provided to higher level applications [4].

Recent work in the area of certificate distribution in VANETs can be found in [9,10,12,13,16]. Moreover, current ETSI ITS and WAVE standards specify a

M. Kassab et al. (Eds.): Nets4Cars/Nets4Trains/Nets4Aircraft 2015, LNCS 9066, pp. 72–83, 2015.
DOI: 10.1007/978-3-319-17765-6_7

system using a combination of different mechanisms proposed in literature [2,4]. However, prior work has not studied the influence of different sub-mechanisms specified in ETSI ITS and WAVE on overall certificate distribution performance. Moreover, the design of the used explicit certificate request scheme has not been standardized in detail. Thus, we provide a proposal for how to manage explicit requests and show its suitability as well as significant influence on system performance during our simulation based evaluation.

The remaining part of this work is outlined as follows. Section 2 gives an overview about current state of the art regarding certificate distribution in VANETs and open issues in this area. Moreover, we point out a newly discovered security flaw in the mechanism of implicit certificate requests. Afterwards, Section 3 describes proposed enhancements to prior distribution strategies. Section 4 introduces the simulation environment used for further evaluation alongside with the studied traffic scenarios. Furthermore, the obtained evaluation results are discussed. Finally, Section 5 provides a conclusion about the achieved results.

## 2    Certificate Distribution in VANETs

Basically, VANET pseudonym certificates (PSCs) are distributed by embedding them into the so called security envelope of a message. In both ETSI ITS and WAVE, the security envelope is constructed at the network layer. This means that certificates can only be distributed when high layer functionalities, e.g., the CAM facility, trigger sending of a new message [2,4].

Instead of including the full PSC an ITS-station (ITS-S) can choose to just include an eight byte hash value (obtained via SHA-256) of the certificate. This is done in order to make the overall message shorter to save bandwidth on the wireless channel. The impact of this mechanism is quite significant, as the size of the security envelope is reduced to about 50% of its size compared to the case of a full certificate being included [7].

There are mainly three different kinds of certificate distribution techniques in ETSI ITS and WAVE based VANETs [2,4]. These are

1. always include the certificate,
2. cyclic certificate emission and
3. request based certificate distribution.

In regard to ETSI ITS, the first strategy is used for Decentralized Environment Notification Messages (DENMs) and all messages secured with the *generic* security profile [4]. The reason for this is the assumption that information distributed via DENMs is highly time critical. Thus, no so called authentication delay can be accepted for the corresponding use cases. An authentication delay occurs when a message is received from another ITS-S whose certificate is unknown because it is neither appended to the current message nor had it been received before.

For CAMs (or BSMs in WAVE) the second as well as third pseudonym certificate distribution strategy is used [2,4]. In both standards the cyclic PSC inclusion frequency is fixed. Additionally, a certificate request scheme, with some concepts similar to the proposals from [16], is used.

A congestion based PSC emission approach is proposed in [9,10]. However, comparison in these works is done only with the individual strategies given above, but not with the combined strategy used in current standards. Furthermore, no details on the request scheme in the systems used for comparison of the new approach is given in [9,10]. Thus, congestion based PSC distribution is not considered in this work, as it focuses on the influence of different certificate request mechanisms within the ETSI ITS framework.

For further analysis we separate the discussion of the certificate request scheme from standards [2,4] into the two cases of implicit and explicit requests.

### 2.1   Implicit Certificate Request

According to [4] each sent CAM serves as an implicit PSC request to any other ITS-S who has not received the current PSC of the sender. This means, that after receiving a message from a formerly unknown ITS-S the receiver includes its own certificate in the very next CAM. This concept is described as neighborhood aware certificate omission in [16].

The reason behind this rule is the assumption of a symmetric communication relation, i.e., a new ITS-S who just appeared in communication range is assumed to not know about the receiver as the receiver did not know about the sender. However, while this technique of certificate distribution has the potential of reducing authentication delay, it also causes a significant security issue.

The issue arises from the fact that any received CAM from a newly discovered ITS-S triggers inclusion of the full certificate in the next CAM of every receiver. This means that the sender does not need to authenticate itself to the receiver to cause the inclusion. Thus, a malicious user (attacker) can frequently send out CAMs without included certificate using a changing random hash value as his identifier and thereby cause every receiver to send its certificate in its next CAM. Thereby, the attacker causes the receivers to include the full certificate in (almost) every CAM. This will lead to increased channel utilization (in about two times the communication range of the attacker) and thus the communication conditions become more difficult for legitimate users. An attacker can try to use this mechanism to perform a denial-of-service (DOS) like attack on a VANET.

In order to analyze the DOS weakness we separate the implicit request scheme into two parts. These are

1. unsecured implicit certificate request and
2. secured implicit certificate request.

An unsecured request occurs in case a station receives a message (e.g. CAM) from another ITS-S whose PSC it does not know and the message only includes the digest of the other ITS-S's PSC. This means that the digital signature of the received message cannot be verified. Given the fact that maximum CAM emission frequency is 10 Hz and regular certificate inclusion happens with 1 Hz [4,5] in ETSI ITS (or 2 Hz in WAVE), one can assume that the majority of messages is broadcast without including a full PSC.

This means that unsecured implicit PSC requests are more likely to happen than secured ones. Therefore, the influence on system performance of skipping this kind of requests in order to avoid the above described DOS weakness can be expected to be significant.

A secured implicit certificate request occurs in case an ITS-S receives a message from a formerly unknown station which included the station's full PSC. Thus, the message can be verified using its digital signature.

An evaluation of the influence of (not) using the different kinds of implicit requests on overall system performance is provided in Section 4.

## 2.2  Explicit Certificate Request

An explicit PSC request can be performed by including a shorted version of the SHA-256 hash value of the PSC into the so called *request unrecognized certificates* header field of the security envelope. This header field includes a list of up to six entries [4]. However, the standard [4] does not specify how to manage these entries at all. Obviously, a request should not be repeated if it was successfully answered, however multiple different possibilities exist in other cases. Thereby, two main aspects can be differentiated.

First of all, it is considered how to handle new requests when there are more pending (i.e., not sent) requests than available places in the request list. Significant options are to

- drop new entries when the list is full,
- buffer new entries, but do not throw away already present entries or to
- maintain the list in a FIFO (first in first out) manner in which a new entry replaces the oldest one.

The second aspect to be studied is how to treat an entry after it was sent. Possibilities include mainly to

1. only include a request once (remove after sending) or to
2. repeat the request. Multiple possibilities exist for this strategy including
   (a) repeating for a fixed time (remove by timeout),
   (b) repeating for a fixed number of requests or
   (c) a combination of both.

It would also be possible to repeat a request until it is answered. However this is probably not a good strategy in VANETs due to the high mobility of participants. This can easily lead to a situation in which only a single packet can be exchanged between two ITS-Ss. In this case, the repeated requests just lead to unnecessary overhead.

Choices 2a and 2b differ in general due to the adaptive CAM emission frequency varying in the range from 1 Hz to 10 Hz (see [5] for CAM generation rules). This means that fixing the number of requests can only roughly control the time span for which a request is repeated. Assuming that the connectivity between vehicles is mainly time dependent (due to node mobility), we select 2a for our evaluation given in Section 4.

### 2.3  Attack on Certificate Distribution

As outlined in Section 2.1, the unsecured implicit certificate request mechanism leads to the possibility of an attacker being able to cause regular ITS-S to unnecessarily send their full certificate. Thereby, the channel load is increased and communication conditions become more difficult. In case the VANET has enough spare bandwidth the attack potential can probably be tolerated, but in case of an already highly used communication channel countermeasures are required.

A straight forward way to avoid the described weakness would be to not respond to unsecured implicit certificate requests. However, this could even make the overall situation worse. The reason being that the entire system of explicit certificate requests depends on using information from unverified messages. In case of the described attack it will flood the request lists of ITS-S with bogus entries and thereby it becomes highly unlikely that correct requests are sent out.

Given a system without support for unsecured implicit requests, the effect of the attack on used channel bandwidth will probably be small, as only three bytes are used for a single explicit certificate request [4]. However, the performance of the whole explicit request scheme can be expected to decrease significantly due to the lack of correctly sent requests. In such a situation the PSC distribution solely depends on cyclic certificate inclusion and secured implicit requests.

Section 4.5 provides an evaluation of the attacks influence on overall system performance as well as the efficiency of the outlined countermeasure.

## 3  Proposed Certificate Distribution Strategy

Based on the analysis of available PSC distribution strategies from Section 2, a new strategy is proposed in the following. It is based on the combination of methods from [4], but specifies the different strategies in greater detail.

Firstly, we keep cyclic PSC distribution with 1 Hz as in [4]. Moreover, all kinds of implicit PSC requests (secured and unsecured) are used. These are the quickest ones of all PSC distribution strategies, as they do not require any kind of interaction between stations. Additionally, they do not cause any extra overhead, like sending of extra data fields as used for explicit PSC requests.

Furthermore, our approach uses an explicit PSC request scheme with repeated requests. Thereby, we maintain the request list in a FIFO manner. This is motivated by the high mobility of ITS-S in VANETs. Thereby, stations tend to leave the communication range of the ego vehicle quite fast. This means that ITS-S whose CAMs were received lately are more likely to receive a response than those whose CAMs had been received earlier. Moreover, entries are dropped from the list after not receiving any message from an ITS-S whose PSC was requested for more than one second (remove by timeout). The one second time span was chosen to be equal to the maximum time span between sending of two CAMs by an ITS-S. As the CAM generation rate varies, entries are not removed from the request list after a fixed number of requests (see also Section 2.2).

A simulation based evaluation of the suggested certificate distribution strategy is given in the following Section 4.

# 4    Evaluation

In order to evaluate the performance of the distribution strategy proposed in Section 3 a simulation based approach is used. Thereby, the influence of the different sub-mechanisms of the combined approach is also studied. Furthermore, the influence potential of the DOS attack described in Section 2.1 on systems using implicit PSC requests is studied. Therefore, the used simulation environment, studied scenarios and achieved results are described in the following.

## 4.1    Simulation Environment

To evaluate PSC distribution strategies a simulation environment utilizing multiple tools is used. Thereby, the well known traffic flow simulator SUMO [6] provides realistic vehicle mobility. Furthermore, the wireless connections between vehicles are modeled with the network simulator ns-3 [14] with an integrated full ETSI ITS compatible C2X protocol stack. This stack is provided by the ezCar2X framework. The wireless channel modeling follows the results from [8]. A detailed description of the simulation framework can be found in [15].

## 4.2    Scenarios

To evaluate the above described PSC distribution mechanisms two different road network scenarios are used. In both full penetration of C2X technology in all vehicles is assumed.

The first scenario is a variant of the well known freeway scenario. Thereby, a deterministic traffic flow is assumed on all six lanes (three in each direction). The vehicles' intervals and speeds on different lanes are adjusted as given in [3].

For the second scenario, the road network was build up by exporting a representation of the real world roundabout found in Munich Maxvorstadt from Open Street Map (OSM). The resulting network was imported into SUMO and traffic flows were generated using the SUMO random trip generator. The simulation was run multiple times with different values for the initial random seed to achieve statistically significant results.

Both scenarios use the concept of a so called core zone [3,13] to avoid edge effects. Thereby, statistics are only collected inside a geographical subset of the whole simulation scenario, which is surrounded by an additionally simulated area.

## 4.3    System Performance Metrics

In our evaluation we use three different metrics to describe the performance of certificate distribution in VANETs. These are,

- average authentication delay,
- average number of discarded messages of ITS-S in close vicinity of the ego vehicle whose PSCs are unknown and
- average receive data rate as a metric for the channel load.

Thereby, the authentication delay is determined as the time difference between reception of the first message from an ITS-S and the reception of the ITS-S's certificate. The minimum of this time span is zero, in case the first received message contains the full certificate.

The second metric is inspired by prior work in [10]. It is assumed that it is more important to know the certificates of vehicle in close vicinity of the ego vehicle than it is to know the ones of more far away ITS-S. We chose a cyclic area with radius 200m as the core area of interest around each ITS-S. This metric is called cryptographic packet loss in [10].

### 4.4   Simulation Results Without Attacker

For both used road topologies the following certificate distribution schemes are taken into regard during the evaluation:

1. ETSI ITS based scheme from Section 3 using repeated explicit requests,
2. strategy 1 without repeated explicit certificate requests (onetime requests),
3. strategy 1 without unsecured implicit requests,
4. strategy 2 without unsecured implicit requests,
5. strategy 1 without any implicit requests,
6. strategy 2 without any implicit requests,
7. strategy 3 without any explicit requests (i.e., only secured implicit requests),
8. the always include strategy as a reference scheme.

In the following, we use the above given numbering scheme to refer to the individual strategies.

Strategy 7 is the only one which does not require to use any information from messages whose digital signature cannot be checked due to an unavailable full certificate. As the attack outlined in Section 2.3 makes the unsecured information used for explicit request almost unusable, this strategy resembles worst case system performance in case of an active attack (see also Section 4.5 below).

Firstly, results for the average authentication delay for the freeway scenario are given in Fig. 1. The x-axis is given in reverse order, as it displays the average time between two successive vehicles (as e.g., used in [13]). With decreasing time intervals between vehicles the traffic density increases.

One can see from Fig. 1 that strategy 1 clearly outperforms its alternatives. The authentication delay is much smaller, which means certificates are exchanged significantly faster. It is only outperformed by the always include strategy, which features no authentication delay at all. However, this strategy leads to excessive channel usage as illustrated in Fig. 5 and Fig. 6 later on.

Furthermore, one can clearly see the major impact of the certificate request strategy on system performance. All strategies using repeated requests clearly outperform their respective counterparts using just one-time requests.

Fig. 2 gives the authentication delay results for the roundabout scenario. As for the freeway scenario, strategy 1 outperforms its alternatives. Due to lower vehicle mobility and a smaller geographical setup absolute numbers are lower for the roundabout scenario (Fig. 2) compared to the freeway scenario (Fig. 1).

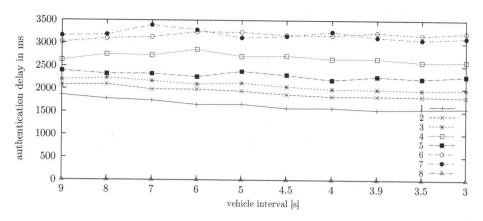

**Fig. 1.** Authentication delay in a freeway scenario with varying traffic density

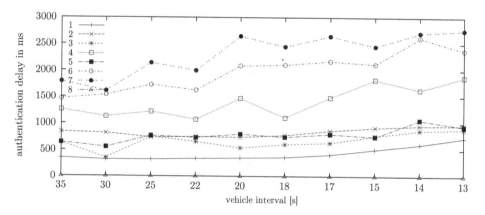

**Fig. 2.** Authentication delay in a roundabout scenario with varying traffic density

The results described above for PSC distribution strategies are clearly supported by the metric of the number of discarded messages from vehicles with unknown PSCs in a car's vicinity as illustrated in Fig. 3 and Fig. 4. Again strategy 1 clearly outperforms its alternatives except of reference scenario 8.

One can clearly see a negative impact on system performance by disabling the unsecured implicit certificate request mechanism (strategy 3) from Fig. 1, 2, 3 and 4. The authentication delay as well as the cryptographic packet loss increase significantly compared to strategy 1. This holds for strategy 2 vs. strategy 4, too. Fully disabling implicit requests further decreases system performance as exhibited by results for strategies 5 (vs. 3) and 6 (vs. 4).

From all provided simulation results, one can clearly see that strategy 7 provides a bad system performance, which is thereby shown to highly depend on using unverified information. Thus, disabling this mechanisms to guard the system from attacks is probably not a good solution in practice.

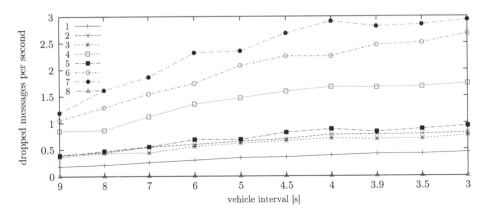

**Fig. 3.** Number of received messages from vehicles with unknown PSCs (cryptographic packet loss) in 200 m vicinity in the freeway scenario

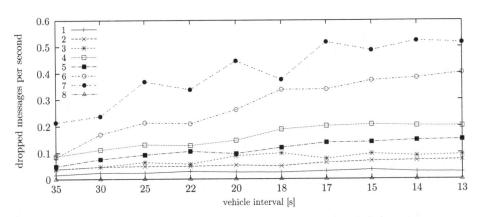

**Fig. 4.** Number of received messages from vehicles with unknown PSCs (cryptographic packet loss) in 200 m vicinity in the roundabout scenario

Figure 5 shows the average receive data rate of vehicles in the freeway scenario. One can see that the for all distribution strategies, except of the always include one (strategy 8), the results for this metric are very similar. Thus, strategy 1 also performs well in regard to the criterion of caused channel usage.

Figure 6 illustrates the obtained results for the receive data rate of vehicles in the roundabout scenario. The overall data rates are lower in this scenario compared to the ones in the freeway scenario due to significantly lower traffic density. However, the general trend of numbers as well as the relation between results for the different certificate distribution strategies is the same for the roundabout scenario as it is for the freeway scenario.

Moreover, our simulations also show that the additional requests for certificates generated by the optimistic approach do not lead to a significant increase

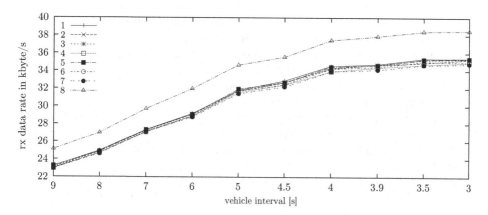

**Fig. 5.** Receive data rate in a freeway scenario with varying traffic density

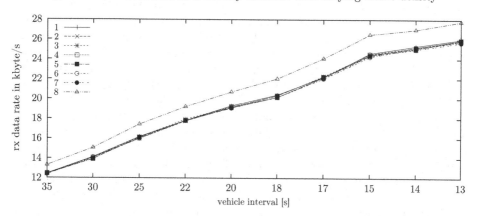

**Fig. 6.** Receive data rate in a roundabout scenario with varying traffic density

of the channel load. For all tested scenarios the increase was smaller then 1‰. Thus, one can conclude that using the optimistic approach can significantly increase certificate distribution performance of VANETs.

### 4.5   Simulation Results with Attacker

Two alternatives are considered for handling the DOS attack from Section 2. Either one accepts increased channel load and leaves its handling to other mechanisms like distributed congestion control (DCC) or one disables unsecured implicit requests. We use a single static attacker who sends out CAMs from an RSU with new identifiers at 10 Hz frequency (upper bound from regulators).

For both considered scenarios our results show that the attack cannot congest the wireless channel with certificate distribution strategy 1 (see Section 3) in use. Thus, the attack causes increased channel load but is not able to prevent ITS-S from regular communication. Thus, the attacked system works as the always send strategy in regard to metrics of authentication delay and cryptographic packet loss. Therefore, the corresponding graphs are not given here again and the reader is referred to preceding Section 4.4 instead (see Fig. 1, 3, 2 and 4).

Although the attack renders the explicit certificate request mechanism unusable, we do not see any negative effect of this aspect when using strategy 1. The reason for this is the availability of enough spare channel capacity to send all messages with embedded full certificate via the manipulated unsecured implicit request scheme. Thus, explicit requests are never required and the failure of that mechanism does not cause decreased system performance in our scenarios.

The increase in receive data rate within communication range $r$ of the RSU is significant for both considered scenarios. It even slightly exceeds the channel load generated by the reference strategy 8 sending the certificate in every message. This is caused by explicit certificate requests. The request list of attacked ITS-S is always full, while in the reference strategy 8 there is no request list at all. Outside $r$ the channel load decreases and reaches the normal value at about $2 \cdot r$.

Disabling unsecured implicit requests as a countermeasure to the attack (see Section 2.3), does not lead to acceptable results for studied scenarios. Authentication delay and cryptographic packet loss show significant performance degradation, which almost reaches the upper bound given by strategy 7. However, an increase in channel load (caused by regular ITS-S) can be avoided as expected. As the attack cannot exhaust the system's spare channel capacity in the given scenarios, we do not recommend to disable unsecured implicit certificate requests. This may change in future scenarios with higher regular channel utilization leading to a decrease in available spare channel capacity.

In both scenarios our evaluation of the DOS attack clearly shows the impact of the attack. Within the RSUs communication range the channel load increases significantly. However, the system has enough spare communication capacity to avoid serious consequences of the attack. Advanced mechanisms, like attack detection and selective disabling of certificate distribution mechanisms, to conquer the outlined attack are out of scope of this paper and are subject to future work.

## 5    Conclusion and Future Work

Securing Car-to-X communication between ITS-S in VANETs is gaining importance in the wake of mass deployment of such systems. Thereby, an acceptable trade off between fast security mechanisms and their overhead in regard to communication bandwidth has to be achieved.

The attack potential of a static single attacker on currently standardized certificate dissemination was shown. Thereby, it was found that even in quite densely populated scenarios the attack is not able to congest the wireless channel so far that a successful DOS attack would be possible. However, for future extensions of communication in VANETs the attack has to be considered as it requires the system to have a significant spare bandwidth available to avoid harmful impact of the attack on overall system performance.

Furthermore, the major influence of the explicit certificate request strategy on overall system performance is shown. A novel strategy for managing request lists is proposed and evaluated against different alternatives. Thereby, the proposed system clearly outperforms its alternatives. Thus, the proposed certificate request strategy should be regarded for usage in future VANET systems like ETSI ITS and WAVE.

Future work can study advanced mechanisms to limit the impact on used channel bandwidth caused by the outlined DOS attack on currently standardized pseudonym certificate distribution strategies.

# References

1. Memorandum of Understanding for OEMs within the CAR 2 CAR Communication Consortium on Deployment Strategy for cooperative ITS in Europe (June 2011)
2. Draft Standard for Wireless Access in Vehicular Environments - Security Services for Applications and Management Messages, P1609.2, D12 (January 2012)
3. Intelligent Transport Systems (ITS); STDMA recommended parameters and settings for cooperative ITS; Access Layer Part (2012)
4. Intelligent Transport Systems (ITS); Security; Security header and certificate formats (2013)
5. Intelligent Transport Systems (ITS); Vehicular Communications; Basic Set of Applications; Part 2: Specification of Cooperative Awareness Basic Service (August 2013)
6. Behrisch, M., Bieker, L., Erdmann, J., Krajzewicz, D.: SUMO - Simulation of Urban MObility: An Overview. In: SIMUL (2011)
7. Bittl, S., Gonzalez, A.A., Heidrich, W.: Performance Comparision of Encoding Schemes for ETSI ITS C2X Communication Systems. In: VEHICULAR, pp. 58–63 (June 2014)
8. Cheng, L., Henty, B.E., Bai, F., Stancil, D.D.: Highway and Rural Propagation Channel Modeling for Vehicle-to-Vehicle Communications at 5.9 GHz. In: IEEE Antennas and Propagation Society International Symposium, pp. 1–4 (July 2008)
9. Feiri, M., Petit, J., Kargl, F.: Evaluation of Congestion-based Certificate Omission in VANETs. In: IEEE VNC, pp. 101–108 (November 2012)
10. Feiri, M., Petit, J., Schmidt, R., Kargl, F.: The Impact of Security on Cooperative Awareness in VANET. In: IEEE VNC, pp. 127–134 (December 2013)
11. Harding, J., et al.: Vehicle-to-Vehicle Communications: Readiness of V2V Technology for Application. Tech. Rep. DOT HS 812 014, Washington, DC: National Highway Traffic Safty Administration (August 2014)
12. Kargl, F., Schoch, E., Wiedersheim, B., Leinmüller, T.: Secure and Efficient Beaconing for Vehicular Networks. In: ACM VAINET, pp. 82–83 (2008)
13. Kloiber, B., Strang, T., de Ponte-Mueller, F., et al.: An Approach for Performance Analysis of ETSI ITS-G5A MAC for Safety Applications. In: ITST (November 2010)
14. Riley, G.F., Henderson, T.R.: The ns-3 Network Simulator. In: Modeling and Tools for Network Simulation, pp. 15–34 (2010)
15. Roscher, K., Bittl, S., Gonzalez, A.A., et al.: ezCar2X: Rapid-Prototyping of Communication Technologies and Cooperative ITS Applications on Real Targets and Inside Simulation Environments. In: 11th Conference WCI (October 2014)
16. Schoch, E., Kargl, F.: On the Efficientcy of Secure Beaconing in VANETs. In: ACM WiSec, pp. 111–116 (2010)
17. Schütze, T.: Automotive Security: Cryptography for Car2X Communication. In: Embedded World Conference (March 2011)

# QoE-Driven Video Streaming System over Cloud-Based VANET

Sofiene Jelassi[1], Amna Bouzid[2], and Habib Youssef[3]

[1] ISIM of Monastir, Route Korniche - BP n 24, 5000 Monastir, Tunisia
sofiene.jelassi@infcom.rnu.tn
[2] Isitcom, GP1 - Hammam Sousse, Tunisia
amna.bouzid@isetsousse.tn
[3] CCK, University Campus of Manouba, Tunisia
habib.youssef@fsm.rnu.tn

**Abstract.** The cloud-based VANETs (Vehicular Ad-Hoc NETwork) will be deployed in the near future that is going to extend VANET applications to include multimedia services. Motivated by that fact, we build a video streaming framework over a cloud-based VANET architecture that is composed of a central cloud, roadside cloudlet and vehicular cloud. The video streaming content can be seen by in-move vehicles' passengers or static vehicles' drivers that maintain a synchronized list of available video content located inside our system facilities. A *video streaming scheduling* is created upon the reception of a video content request at the vehicle, the cloudlet or the center cloud as a function of the vehicular cloud conditions and content localization. The video streaming scheduling defines the involved nodes in a video delivery session and its perceived quality. A set of VMs are installed over the cloudlets that plays the role of roadside video streaming servers. They exchange control information about vehicles' mobility and contents using a background process in order to achieve uninterrupted streaming sessions. The vehicles include a QoE-monitor that measures end-user quality and reports it to the QoE-controller, which resides in VMs or in the vehicles.

## 1 Introduction

It is required to support video streaming over vehicular networks, VANET (Vehicular Ad-hoc NETwork), in order to extends its range of applications and enhance users' experience. This includes in addition to infotainment services, navigation, safety and maintenance applications [1]. However, providing an acceptable quality of video streaming service is a challenge given the characteristics of VANETs, such as high network topology dynamics inducing short-lived sessions, an error-prone wireless channel and a limited end-to-end bandwidth. Existing work for providing video streaming on vehicular networks use often traditional techniques in order to consider VANET features, such as light signaling protocols, predictive handovers, resources' reservation, network coding, packet header compression, efficient coding scheme and loss concealment algorithms [2] and [3]. Moreover, proposals that use

M. Kassab et al. (Eds.): Nets4Cars/Nets4Trains/Nets4Aircraft 2015, LNCS 9066, pp. 84–93, 2015.
DOI: 10.1007/978-3-319-17765-6_8

relay nodes for enabling video streaming have been thoroughly investigated in the literature [4]. However, they were concerned with emergency video dissemination rather than unicast entertainment-oriented video streaming [1] and [2].

The effective penetration of cloud technology in the supply chain of legacy services was a stimulating factor to think about integrating a cloud system and its underlying principle in a VANET environment [5] and [6]. This explains why a number of cloud-based VANET architectures have been recently proposed and developed in the literature [7], [8] and [9]. In addition to the basic cloud functionalities, namely storage and computing sharing, a cloud can host many business logics composing a given service.

This paper introduces an innovative solution in order to provide a satisfactory video streaming quality over a cloud-based VANET architecture. The improvement of video streaming delivery conditions over VANET is realized using cloudlets installed across roads and highways deployed by roadside infrastructure providers. They are connected to the roadside units using high speed connections. Each roadside cloudlet run at least one Virtual Machine (VM) that includes a video streaming server that represents a partial image of the central video streaming server installed at the central cloud. In order to prevent service interruption, a video streaming scheduling is built by the client, the cloudlet or the central cloud as a function of content availability and vehicles trajectory.

The remaining parts of this paper are organized as follows; in the section 2, we briefly describe cloud-based VANET architectures. Section 3 presents our proposed framework for providing QoE-centric video streaming service over cloud-based VANET. Section 4 outlines our strategy to prevent service interruption. Section 5 describes the workflow of video streaming components at vehicle and cloudlets. The conclusion is presented in Section 6.

## 2    The Cloud-Based VANET Architecture at a Glance

A comprehensive cloud-based VANET architecture has been proposed in [9]. The whole system is graphically illustrated in Fig. 1. As we can see, it integrates a central cloud (CC), a roadside cloud (RSC) as well as a vehicular cloud (VC). The CC is located at the root or backend of the proposed cloud-based VANET architecture. It manages Virtual Machine (VM) and dispatches tasks and content across the RSC as a function of resources availability, clients' requests and vehicles' mobility. The RSC includes a set of roadside cloudlets (RCL) that can be seen as a small-scale cloud connected directly to a given RSU (RoadSide Unit). This means that access delay to a RSU from a cloudlet is almost equal to zero. A RCL is intended to provide cloud services to vehicles located in its coverage [9]. A cloudlet is able, similar to a CC, to virtualize physical resources, such as CPU, memory and hard disk. Moreover, it acts as a local cloud provider that offers essential cloud services, such as storage and computing. The geographical proximity of RSC and vehicles enables a reduced last-hop access and transfer

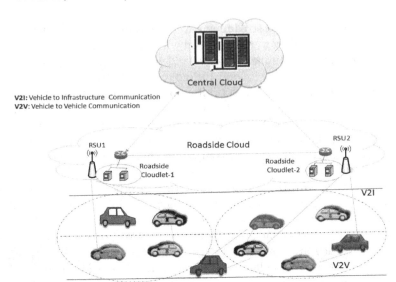

**Fig. 1.** The global architecture of a typical cloud-based VANET

delays. A vehicle can select a nearby roadside cloudlet in order to use virtualizable resources defined in the term of a VM. In order to assure an uninterrupted cloud service, the customized VM should be synchronously transferred between the roadside cloudlets as a function of vehicle mobility. This is widely known as VM migration that is a fundamental functionality in cloud environment.

A Vehicular Cloud (VC) is located at the bottom of the cloud-based VANET architecture. It is defined as a transient mobile cloud composed by a collection of vehicles that would like to share their resources. The vehicles that belong to a VC should be able to communicate directly to each other. In general, a VC is formed only if there are no enough resources at the cloudlet.

The main goal of our work is to provide video steaming over the cloud-based VANET architecture. This is actually a challenging task given its high sensitivity to delay and bandwidth fluctuations. However, characteristics of a cloud-based VANET architecture facilitate providing video streaming service. The different components of our video streaming system and their interaction are going to be developed in a way that; (1) account for architectural characteristics of cloud-based VANET and (2) maximize the QoE of delivered video streams by optimizing jointly sender and receiver applications as well as midway involved entities.

## 3   The Engineering of Video Streaming System over a Cloud-Based VANET

In order to enable video streaming over a cloud-based VANET, we propose a complete video streaming system that aims to achieve a satisfactory Quality of

Experience (QoE) using (1) the flexibility and potential of cloud technology and (2) the adaptation capabilities of source and receiver video streaming sides. Basically, our video streaming solution integrates three main components (see Fig. 2):

1. A QoE-driven video streaming player that is installed on each vehicle.
2. A VM that is hosted at the roadside cloudlet and serves one or multiple video streaming clients. It is intended to play the role of a mobile video streaming server that is able to communicate with mobile streaming servers running on adjacent cloudlet.
3. A VM installed on the center cloud that manages and monitors all VMs instantiated at various cloudlets as well as their content. This is more related to remote management and monitoring of VMs in a distributed cloud environment. This issue is currently outside the scope of our work.

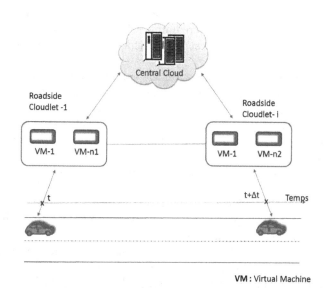

**Fig. 2.** QoE-driven video streaming architecture of cloud-based VANET

As we can see in Fig. 2, a vehicle is going to be served by a series of VMs running over crossed roadside cloudlets. The layout of all components installed at the cloudlet and the vehicle sides are presented in Fig. 3. As we can see, a cloudlet includes a manager of VM running in Dom0 that manages all VMs and is responsible for configuring running video streaming servers. Moreover, the cloudlet maintains a VDB (Video Data Base) and a PVDB (Popular Video Data Base). The latter is used in order to cache popular video contents. The VM (domU) used as a video streaming server includes the following main components:

1. The video streaming manager - cloudlet side: It receives clients requests and creates video streaming scheduling according to available resources, content distribution and vehicle information grid.
2. The video prefetching manager - cloudlet side: It fetches a requested content in its video source index. If the content is not found then the request in relayed to the central cloud.
3. The QoE-Controller – server side: It defines on-line streaming parameters as a function of available channel capacity and vehicle information grid.
4. The video streaming sender: It encodes, packetizes and sends video streaming chunks as a function of parameters set by the QoE-Controller – sender side.
5. The streaming buffering manager: It allocates and releases the internal VM buffer's space as a function of scheduled transfer tasks.

At the vehicle side, we propose a QoE-driven video streaming clients that is composed of the following key elements:

1. The video streaming manager - vehicle side: It receives clients requests and creates, if possible, a video streaming scheduling over a vehicular cloud. Otherwise, it relays the request to the video streaming manager - cloudlet side.
2. The video prefetching manager - vehicle side: It fetches a requested content in its video source index. If the content is not found then the request is relayed to the cloudlet.
3. The video streaming receiver: It receives video packet stream that are analyzed, filtered, decoded than forwarded to the streaming buffer manager.
4. The streaming buffering manager: It inserts correctly received video frames in the play-out buffer using configuration parameters calculated by the QoE-Controller.
5. The QoE-Controller – receiver side: It adapts the parameters of the play-out process as a function of received data rate and content. It mainly controls the play-out buffer delay and its content.
6. The QoE-Monitor: It probes played streams at different levels in order to measures QoE values of on-going video streaming sessions. This is realized using a set of technical metrics and installed QoE-models. The measured value are reported to QoE-Controller located at the vehicle and cloudlet sides.

Tables 1 and 2 give an exhaustive list of the main components of our proposed video streaming system installed at the cloudlet and vehicle sides. The QoE-Monitor aims to provide feedbacks about encountered QoE by the end-users. The measurement of QoE values is realized at the vehicle for a given configuration using a set of gathered local metrics. It is then sent to the QoE-controllers located at the vehicle and/or cloudlet side at specific time interval. The technical metrics considered by our QoE-monitor are the followings:

– The video prefetching delay: The time spent to prefetch a video from PVDB, VDB or in central cloud.

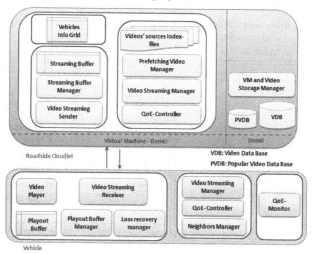

**Fig. 3.** The vehicle and cloudlet architectures

- The frame resolution and rate: It defines the spatial and temporal resolution of displayed frames that may be adapted during the service.
- The encoding scheme its encoding rates: It defines the used codec and its resulting bitstream rate.
- The packet size and interval: They are used by the packet stream packetizer in order to create data packets. The packet interval refers to the video delay included into a packet.
- The playout delay: The buffering delay at a vehicle before starting playback processes. This is a well-known techniques used to filter-out packet delay variation of received video chunks.
- The ratio of lost packets and the mean loss and inter-loss duration: This metrics capture characteristics of of encountered packet loss process.
- The one-way delay and its variation: The average transit delay from the source to the receiver.
- The number of rebuffering: The number of rebuffering events is the number of times the Video Player stopped to rebuffer frames after it started playing.

A QoE-Controller is deployed at the vehicle and cloudlet sides. They are responsible for tunning and selecting optimal video streaming key parameters in order to enhance QoE. The QoE-Controller residing at the vehicle side controls mainly play-out delay, startup delay, number of re-buffering, the space of the playout buffer and the loss concealment techniques. On the other hand, QoE-Controller residing at the cloudlet controls sending rate, delivery paths, packet time interval, redundancy scheme, handover strategy, etc. The operational mode of QoE-Controllers is going to be detailed in a future work.

**Table 1.** The video streaming components at the roadside cloudlet

| | Module | Role |
|---|---|---|
| The cloudlet server (Dom0) | VMs and video storage Manager | It manages VM and related storage spaces |
| | Video Data Base (VDB) | A storage space of vehicles' videos |
| | Popular Video Data Base (PVDB) | A storage space of most popular videos with respect to social networks |
| The Virtual Machine (DomU) | Prefetching Video Manager | It fetches video content in PVDB, VDB or in nearby roadside cloudlet or in central cloud. |
| | QoE-Controller | It adapts the transmission bitrate as well as the spatial and temporal resolutions of the video content according to bandwidth occupancy and playback buffer state |
| | Video Streaming Manager | It manages video content requests and creates a video streaming scheduling according to the content chunk distribution and vehicle mobility. It also manages handover across cloudlets |
| | Streaming Buffer Manager | It manage the internal streaming buffer of a VM used by the server to accelerate transmission of video chunks |

**Table 2.** The video streaming components at the vehicle

| Module | Role |
|---|---|
| QoE-Monitor | It measures and reports video quality value to QoE-Controllers. |
| QoE-Controller | It defines the configuration parameters used by a video player, such as startup delay and frame rate. |
| Video Streaming Manager | It handles video content requests and creates a video streaming scheduling. It may decide to cache a received video chunk in its local buffer |
| Loss recovery manager | It can ask for a missing video chunk from either the serving VM or its neighbors vehicles. |
| Video Player | It reads the video image from a playback buffer |
| Playout Buffer manager | It places received video chunk in their suitable location inside the playback buffer |

## 4    The Video Streaming Scheduling for Service Continuity

To provide a stable and satisfactory QoE of video streaming to mobile vehicles, a session management protocol should be used. Its main goal is to prevent video freezing during a handover process between cloudlets. To date, there is no a dedicated management protocol of video streaming session that is specifically designed for a roadside cloud. In order to maintain video streaming continuity, we assume that each cloud member runs a VM hosting a video streaming server. They can exchange control information about vehicles' mobility and video session. A streaming scheduling specifying the entity which is going to provide a given video portion at a specific time.

The video streaming scheduling may be built by the client, the cloudlet or the central cloud. Precisely, if a client is a member of a functional vehicular cloud, then it searches for the requested content in its local video index file that includes reference to available video content. If the content is available over the vehicular cloud, then a streaming scheduling is locally built. Otherwise, a request is sent to the nearest cloudlet that performs a similar processes. If the content is unavailable at the cloudlet, then the streaming scheduling is built by the central cloud. The video streaming scheduling is built as a function of the current vehicle position, its velocity and direction. The information about vehicle mobility may be obtained from the vehicle traffic mining process. A dual-connection is opened during a handover interval in order to perform a seamless transition. This assures a quick transition of the serving cloudlet that helps in maintaining service continuity. Currently, we are evaluating our video streaming service continuity protocol over cloud-based VANET. More details and results will be given in our future publications.

## 5    The Workflow of Video Streaming Service Components

### 5.1    The Video Streaming Server Workflow at the Roadside Cloudlet

The video streaming server installed at a roadside cloudlet follows the workflow presented in Fig. 4 using the UML activity diagram. Upon the reception of a video content request, the video manager call the prefetching video manager that checks if an image exists in its local PVDB and if not found in VDB using video index file. If the local image is found then a video streaming scheduling is built by the video streaming manager as a function of vehicle speed and direction, and subsequently sends to its neighbor cloudlets. However, if the video content does not exist at the cloudlet then the received client request is relayed to the center cloud that builds a streaming scheduling and sends it to all involved cloudlets in the conjunction with the suitable video content. In both cases, the video streaming process starts as soon as a streaming scheduling is received by all involved elements. Once a session is activated, the QoE-monitor reports periodically to the QoE-controller estimates regarding QoE values in order to select the configurations that optimize video streaming service.

### 5.2    The Video Streaming Client Workflow at the Vehicle

The vehicle adapts dynamically the configuration parameters of the playback process in order to optimize the QoE of played video. The workflow of our proposed video streaming player dedicated to VANETs is given in Fig. 5. The playback policy is supervised by the QoE-controller that set configuration parameters of the playback process. Moreover, the QoE-controller decides to send a request for retransmitting a missing video segment if its expected arrival time is less than its calculated play-out time. Furthermore, the QoE controller may force the QoE-monitor to send urgent QoE report to the serving cloudlet if an exceptional event is observed.

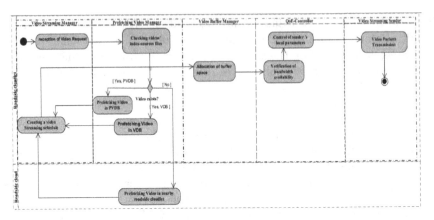

**Fig. 4.** The activity diagram of workflow realized in the roadside cloudlet

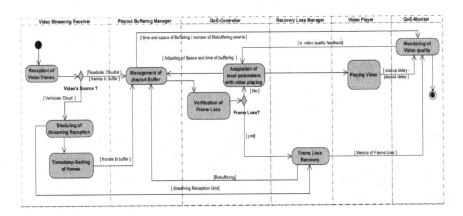

**Fig. 5.** The activity diagram of QoE-driven workflow realized in the vehicle

## 6   Conclusion

This work proposes a scheme and a strategy that is going to improve QoE of video streaming over VANET. The main idea consists of using an emerging cloud-based VANET architecture that helps in reducing quality impairment factors observed by ordinary VANETs. Each cloud member includes a VM in order to run video streaming component at server and client sides. Each roadside cloudlet configures installed VM that are responsible for prefetching, caching and streaming videos to vehicles. A video streaming scheduling is built at a session start-up in order to prevent video streaming interruptions. This framework is currently under investigation using simulation and experimentation. The results are going to be published in our future publications.

# References

1. Park, J.-S., Lee, U., Gerla, M.: Vehicular communications: Emergency video streams and network Coding. Journal of Internet Services and Applications 1, 57–68 (2010)
2. Naeimipoor, F.: Video streaming and multimedia broadcasting over vehicular Ad Hoc networks. PhD thesis, University of Ottawa (2013)
3. Bradai, A., Ahmed, T.: ReViV: Selective rebroadcast mechanism for video streaming over VANET. In: Proc. of the IEEE 79th Vehicular Technology Conference (IEEE VTC 2014), Seoul, Korea (2014)
4. Rezende, C., Mammeri, A., Boukerche, A., Loureiro, A.: A Receiver-based Video Dissemination Solution for Vehicular Networks with Content Transmissions Decoupled from Relay Node Selection. Ad-Hoc Network 17, 1–17 (2014)
5. Whaiduzzaman, M., Sookhak, M., Gani, A., Buyya, R.: A survey on vehicular cloud computing. Journal of Network and Computer Applications 40, 325–344 (2014)
6. Abuelela, M., Olariu, S.: Taking vanet to the clouds. In: Proceedings of the 8th International Conference on Advances in Mobile Computing and Multimedia
7. Olariu, S., Eltoweissy, M., Younis, M.: Towards Autonomous Vehicular Clouds. ICST Transactions on Mobile Communications and Applications 11, 1–11 (2011)
8. Hussain, R., Son, J., Eun, H., Kim, S., Oh, H.: Rethinking Vehicular Communications: Merging VANET with cloud computing. In: Proc. of IEEE 4th International Conference on Cloud Computing Technology and Science, Taipei, Taiwan (2012)
9. Yu, R., Zhang, Y., Gjessing, S., Xia, W., Yang, K.: Toward Cloud-based Vehicular Networks with Efficient Resource Management. IEEE Network 27, 48–55 (2013)

# Augmented Reality Based Traffic Sign Recognition for Improved Driving Safety

Lotfi Abdi[1], Aref Meddeb[2], and Faten Ben Abdallah[2]

[1] National Engineering School of Tunis
University of Tunis-El Manar, Tunis, Tunisia
lotfiabdi@hotmail.com
[2] National Engineering School Of Sousse
University of Sousse, Tunis, Tunisia
Aref.Meddeb@infcom.rnu.tn,
faten.benabdallah@enit.rnu.tn

**Abstract.** In recent years, automotive active safety systems have become increasingly common in road vehicles since they provide an opportunity to significantly reduce traffic fatalities by active vehicle control. Augmented Reality (AR) applications can enhance intelligent transportation systems by superimposing surrounding traffic information on the users view and keep drivers and pedestrians view on roads. However, due to the existence of a complex environment such as weather conditions, illuminations and geometric distortions, Traffic Sign Recognition(TSR) systems has always been considered as a challenging task. The aim of this paper is to evaluate the effectiveness of AR cues in improving driving safety by deploying an on-board camera-based driver alert system against approaching traffic signs such as stop, speed limit, unique, danger signs, etc. A new approach is presented for marker-less AR-TSR system that superimposes augmented virtual objects onto a real scene under all types of driving situations including unfavorable weather conditions. Our method is composed of both online and offline stages. An intrinsic camera parameter change depending on the zoom values is calibrated. A Haar-like feature with Adaboost has been used to train a Haar detector in the offline stage. Extrinsic camera parameters are then estimated based on homography method in the online stage. With the complete set of camera parameters, virtual objects can be coherently inserted into the video sequence captured by the camera so that synthetic traffic signs may be added to increase safety.

**Keywords:** Augmented Reality, 3D, SURF, Camera Calibration, Traffic Signs, OpenCV.

## 1 Introduction

Improving traffic safety is one of the most important goals of Intelligent Transportation Systems (ITS). In such systems, a video camera is installed in the interior of the vehicle and the environment is scanned to provide useful information for the driver (such as obstacles, traffic lights, speed limit, etc.). In fact,

© Springer International Publishing Switzerland 2015
M. Kassab et al. (Eds.): Nets4Cars/Nets4Trains/Nets4Aircraft 2015, LNCS 9066, pp. 94–102, 2015.
DOI: 10.1007/978-3-319-17765-6_9

an increasing effort has been dedicated to developing driver assistance systems based on computer vision in the past years, aiming to reduce the number and fatality of traffic accidents and focusing on several aspects such as pedestrian detection [4],[6], lane detection/lane departure warning systems [11],[19], or traffic sign detection/recognition [13],[12]. Augmented Reality (AR) is a technique that combines live views in real-time with virtual computer generated images, creating an augmented experience of reality.

In cars, AR is becoming an interesting means to enhance active safety in the driving task. Guiding a drivers attention to an imminent danger somewhere around the car is a potential application. In current status of driving technology, it is an important issue that let drivers obtain driving information easily. There are many advanced electronic devices used for driving safety assistance such as automatic navigation system and lane departure warning system. In-vehicle driver assistance technologies, such as AR cuing, may help direct driver attention to roadway hazards [7],[8],[14], improve target detection [20], and reduce collision risk [10].

AR combines natural and artificial stimuli by projecting computer graphics on a transparent plane [1]. The graphical augmentation can highlight important roadway objects or regions or provide informative annotations. From this point of view, object detection and recognition from in-vehicle camera images have been widely studied, in particular for pedestrians [5], traffic signs [9], and other targets. There are two main problems to solve before the widespread usage of AR. First, we have the problem of rendering and merging virtual objects along with the high quality video stream. The second problem can be stated as finding a transformation of virtual scene into the one perceived by the human scene [17]. It requires that virtual objects are placed in the correct 3D position and orientation; and comply with the human eyes scale factor. For every frame of video stream, virtual objects have to be placed in a correct position and orientation and rendered again. This is a complex and time consuming process[15].

The use of AR in a vehicular context is becoming widely used and various projects are exploring this technology as a way to increase road safety and the overall driving experience. Traffic signs or road signs are an important part of road environment as they provide visual messages, not only for drivers, but also for all road users. Detection algorithms based on edge detection are more resilient to changes in illumination. The interaction of backgrounds and natural lighting can affect the usability of AR graphics (e.g., text legibility), a phenomenon that has been measured in studies such as [2] and [3].

Limited research has been conducted on the effectiveness of AR cuing for traffic signs detection. A handful of manufacturers offer a video-based AR auxiliary display to aid drivers in maneuvering the vehicle and identifying potential hazards while backing up. As the automotive industry moves toward the smart car, it makes driving safer, more pleasant, and more convenient. While we are already seeing some successful video-based AR auxiliary displays (e.g., center-mounted backup aid systems), the application opportunities of optical see-through AR as presented on a drivers windshield are yet to be fully tapped; nor are the related visual, perceptual, and attention challenges fully understood.

In this paper we present a marker-less tracking method which relies upon the use of features already available in the scene, without adding specific patches or markers. The system is responsible for detection and identification of traffic signs, speed limits, and any additional information that might be useful for drivers. Significant amount of work have addressed traffic sign recognition and four main factors have been identified in TSR: 1)segment The image and extract a Region Of Interest (ROI); 2)verify the traffic signs in the ROI based on a binary classification; 3)recognize multi-class traffic signs obtained from detection; and 4)track the traffic signs in the video sequences and add augmented information to the objects properly.

The reminder of this paper is organized as follows: in Section 2 we describe our approach referred to as Augmented Reality Traffic Signs Recongition (AR-TSR). In section 3 we provide experimental results and we finally conclude by providing some future work direction.

## 2    AR-TSR Approach

Due to the limitations of traditional marker AR system, we make full use of Marker-less information of video frames to make our system more natural and effective. We also need to take into account the visual system of the driver.

The approach proposed in this paper aims to contribute to AR applications on which virtual images can be merged with real images in real-time, without using ÃŕÂñducial markers, and considering the angle of view of the observer and the position of the object of interest. The first phase of the system deals with the detection of traffic Signs using a scanning window with Haar cascade detector for each image of the input stream (target images), which eliminates most of the "not-objects". The second phase makes the system more robust by verifying the detected traffic signs based on Speeded Up Robust Features (SURF) detector and by adding augmented information to the objects properly. Our method is composed of two stages: online and offline. In in both stages we assume that the intrinsic and distortion parameters of the camera are known and do not change. These two stages are detailed in the following Sections.

### 2.1   Offline Stage

The offline phase may be summarized in the following two steps:

**Camera Calibration.** Camera calibration is the first and the most important step in any computer vision application. Camera calibration is a necessary step in 3D computer vision in order to extract metric information from 2D images. An offline camera calibration is performed by use OpenCV camera calibration routines and a planar chessboard pattern to estimate the internal parameters of the camera and its distortion coefficients. Intrinsic parameters define the optical characteristics and the internal geometry of the camera.

**Training of Haar-like Features.** Haar-like features were originally proposed in the framework of object detection in face recognition. We train an AdaBoost cascade using Haar-like features offline. A boosting algorithm is used here to train a classifier with Haar-like features of positive and negative samples. The Adaboost Algorithm trains iteratively a strong classifier which is the sum of several weak classifiers. Each stage is trained so that the false positives of the previous stage are labeled as negatives and added to the training set. The positive images are those containing the object (e.g. traffic signs), and negatives are those which do not contain the object.

## 2.2   On-line Stage

**Traffic Sign Detection.** In the detection step, the distinctive features of traffic signs shall be considered. Since traffic signs are normalized in specific colors and shapes, it is convenient to use those features to decide the candidate signs. The goal of our detection stage is to identify image regions that may contain a traffic sign. To ensure a high system performance, we focus on fast detection methods. We have based our research on one of the most outstanding approaches in object detection for real-time applications of the last decade i.e., the Viola-Jones face detector framework [18].

The initial candidate detection phase of a traffic sign recognition system has much computational costs because candidates in a large range of scales have to be searched in the complete image. The Viola-Jones detector works by sliding a detection window across an image. At each position, the classifier decides if there is a desired object inside the window. During the detection phase, the system scans each window of the input image and extracts Haar features of that particular window, which is then used to compare with the cascade classifier. Finally, only a few of these sub-windows accepted by all stages of the detector are regarded as objects. The detection process takes an image as input and provides the regions that contain the ROI at the output, as illustrated in fig 1. Firstly, we roughly find out all candidate ROIs in a 24x24 sliding window. Secondly, the candidate ROIs are resized to 50x50 windows and further verified. In order to reduce the search space and improve detection performance, we apply the SURF to extract key-points from output of the first detector stage ROIs.

During the online tracking stage, after extracting and describing the SURF key-points, the system matches the current image key-points with the set of key-points from the reconstructed model acquired in the offline phase. Then a candidate image is matched by individually comparing each feature of the candidate with the special database and then the ROI is determined to be a true positive. The false positive rate is reduced significantly when the system is verified with part based SURF detector. The recognition module performs finer validations over the ROIs and generates the final detection results.

**Pose Estimation and Augmentation.** In marker-less AR, the problem of finding the camera pose requires significantly complex and sophisticated algorithms, e.g. disparity mapping, feature detection, and object classification. The

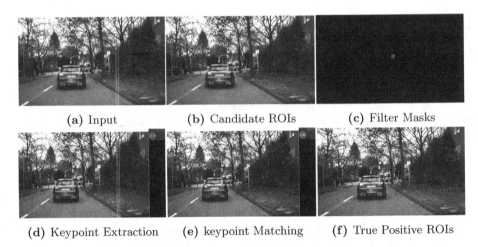

**(a)** Input        **(b)** Candidate ROIs        **(c)** Filter Masks

**(d)** Keypoint Extraction    **(e)** keypoint Matching    **(f)** True Positive ROIs

**Fig. 1.** A method for feature extraction of traffic sign detection

camera calibration allows the combination of virtual world and real world objects in a single display. In case of images or video, the relative position of an element on a screen can be calculated from camera parameters and relative position information of the camera with respect to the element.

After optimizing the matching process by RANSAC algorithm, a homography is applied to an ROI on an image and we apply the transformation of a planar object moving in the scene relative to a virtual camera. Firstly, the system takes four known points from the image of a scene and sets four separate tracking windows around the points. Based on these points, we calculate a camera calibration matrix. The mathematical model used is the projection transformation is expressed by (2), where $\lambda$ is the homogeneous scale factors unknown a-priori, $P$ is $3 \times 4$ projection matrix, $x = (x, y)$ represents the homogeneous coordinates of image features, $X = (X, Y, Z)$ represents the homogeneous coordinates of feature points in world coordinates, and $K \in R^{3 \times 3}$ is the matrix with the camera intrinsic parameters, also known as camera matrix. The joint rotation-translation matrix $[R|t]$ is the matrix of extrinsic parameters, $R = [r_x r_y r_z]$ is the $3 \times 3$ rotation matrix, and $T = [t]$ is the translation of the camera.

$$x = PX = K[R|t]X \tag{1}$$

$$
P = \overbrace{K}^{\text{Intrinsic Matrix}} * \overbrace{[R|t]}^{\text{Extrinsic Matrix}}
$$

$$
= \underbrace{\begin{pmatrix} 1 & 0 & x_0 \\ 0 & 1 & y_0 \\ 0 & 0 & 1 \end{pmatrix}}_{\text{2D Translation}} * \underbrace{\begin{pmatrix} f_x & 0 & 0 \\ 0 & f_y & 0 \\ 0 & 0 & 1 \end{pmatrix}}_{\text{2D Scaling}} * \underbrace{\begin{pmatrix} 1 & s/f & 0 \\ 0 & 1 & 0 \\ 0 & 0 & 1 \end{pmatrix}}_{\text{2D Shear}} * \overbrace{\underbrace{(I|t)}_{\text{3D Translation}} * \underbrace{\left( \frac{R|0}{0|1} \right)}_{\text{3D Rotation}}}^{\text{Extrinsic Matrix}} \tag{2}
$$

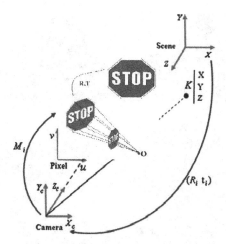

**Fig. 2.** Projection of Virtual Objects

In the final stage, the projection of virtual objects is accomplished once the pose is known. Having calculated the camera interior orientation and the camera exterior orientation for a video frame, the 3D can be drawn at the right position with the proper scale orientation and perspective in the scene of the real world, as shown in fig 2. With the complete set of camera parameters, virtual objects can be coherently inserted into the video sequence captured by the camera, so that synthetic traffic signs may be added to increase safety.

## 3   Experiment Results

To evaluate the performance of our AR-TSR method, we implement it using the hardware environment of Intel (R) Core (TM) i5 (2.5 Hz) and the software environment of Windows 7, Visual Studio 2010 using OpenGL and OpenCV Library. In this paper, we focus on the detection and recognition of speed limit, unique signs, and danger signs. The German Traffic Sign Recognition Benchmark (GTSDB) dataset [16] is used for verifying the effectiveness of our method.

### 3.1   Detection Performance

The first experiment, we separately evaluate the detection and classification modules. To evaluate the detector performance, we train a cascade of detectors using the evolutionary method with ordinal dissociated dipoles. The database used to train the detectors was collected from GTSRB dataset, the Belgian Traffic Signs Dataset (BelgiumTS), and our own images. In order to evaluate the systems robustness, we tested the accuracy of our algorithm when tracking the ROIs in the captured frames in various lighting and weather conditions, as shown in fig 3.

**Fig. 3.** Detection of traffic signs in adverse conditions

**Fig. 4.** Frames illustrating the insertion of virtual 3D object sign

We notice that the chances of missing true positives is comparatively less when compared with other systems. On the other hand, the false positive rate is reduced significantly when the system is tested with a SURF detector.

## 3.2   Recognition Performance

We evaluate the AR tracking by superimposing 3D graphics on target images. To provide driving-safety information using the proposed AR-TSR, various sensors and devices were attached to the experimental test vehicle, as shown in fig 4.

Our experiments demonstrate that the system can accurately superimpose virtual textures or 3D object to a user-selected planar part of a natural scene in real-time, under general motion conditions, without the need of markers or other artificial beacons.

# 4   Conclusions

In-vehicle contextual AR has the potential to provide novel visual feedback to drivers for an enhanced and more exciting driving experience. We have employed this approach to improve the accuracy of a traffic sign detector to assist the driver in various driving situations, increase the driving comfort, and reduce traffic accidents. We have demonstrated that AR can be very effective to enhance TSR. AR can be used to improve driving safety and minimize driving workload. The information provided is represented in such a way that it is easily understood, requiring little cognitive load on the driver. Further research needs to be conducted into the amount of information and the types of representations that can further minimize both driver's cognitive and visual loads, respectively.

**Acknowledgments.** This work was performed under the MOBIDOC device, part of the Support to Research and Innovation System project (PASRI), funded by the European Union (EU) and administered by the National Agency for Promotion of Scientific Research (ANPR).

# References

1. Azuma, R., Baillot, Y., Behringer, R., Feiner, S., Julier, S., MacIntyre, B.: Recent advances in augmented reality. IEEE Computer Graphics and Applications 21(6), 34–47 (2001)
2. Gabbard, J.L., Edward Swan III, J., Hix, D.: The effects of text drawing styles, background textures, and natural lighting on text legibility in outdoor augmented reality. Presence: Teleoperators and Virtual Environments 15(1), 16–32 (2006)
3. Gabbard, J.L., Swan, J.E., Hix, D., Schulman, R.S., Lucas, J., Gupta, D.: An empirical user-based study of text drawing styles and outdoor background textures for augmented reality. In: Proceedings of IEEE Virtual Reality 2005, pp. 11–18. IEEE (2005)
4. Geronimo, D., Lopez, A.M., Sappa, A.D., Graf, T.: Survey of pedestrian detection for advanced driver assistance systems. IEEE Transactions on Pattern Analysis and Machine Intelligence 32(7), 1239–1258 (2010)
5. Guo, H., Zhao, F., Wang, W., Jiang, X.: Analyzing drivers attitude towards hud system using a stated preference survey. Advances in Mechanical Engineering 2014 (2014)

6. Guo, L., Ge, P.S., Zhang, M.H., Li, L.H., Zhao, Y.B.: Pedestrian detection for intelligent transportation systems combining adaboost algorithm and support vector machine. Expert Systems with Applications 39(4), 4274–4286 (2012)
7. Ho, C., Reed, N., Spence, C.: Multisensory in-car warning signals for collision avoidance. Human Factors: The Journal of the Human Factors and Ergonomics Society 49(6), 1107–1114 (2007)
8. Ho, C., Spence, C.: Assessing the effectiveness of various auditory cues in capturing a driver's visual attention. Journal of Experimental Psychology: Applied 11(3), 157 (2005)
9. Hussain, K., Kaptan, V.: Modeling and simulation with augmented reality. RAIRO-Operations Research 38(02), 89–103 (2004)
10. Kramer, A.F., Cassavaugh, N., Horrey, W.J., Becic, E., Mayhugh, J.L.: Influence of age and proximity warning devices on collision avoidance in simulated driving. Human Factors: The Journal of the Human Factors and Ergonomics Society 49(5), 935–949 (2007)
11. McCall, J.C., Trivedi, M.M.: Video-based lane estimation and tracking for driver assistance: survey, system, and evaluation. IEEE Transactions on Intelligent Transportation Systems 7(1), 20–37 (2006)
12. Mogelmose, A., Trivedi, M.M., Moeslund, T.B.: Vision-based traffic sign detection and analysis for intelligent driver assistance systems: Perspectives and survey. IEEE Transactions on Intelligent Transportation Systems 13(4), 1484–1497 (2012)
13. Park, J.-G., Kim, K.-J.: Design of a visual perception model with edge-adaptive gabor filter and support vector machine for traffic sign detection. Expert Systems with Applications 40(9), 3679–3687 (2013)
14. Scott, J.J., Gray, R.: A comparison of tactile, visual, and auditory warnings for rear-end collision prevention in simulated driving. Human Factors: The Journal of the Human Factors and Ergonomics Society 50(2), 264–275 (2008)
15. Sobel, D., Jędrasiak, K., Daniec, K., Wrona, J., Jurgaś, P., Nawrat, A.M.: Camera calibration for tracked vehicles augmented reality applications. In: Innovative Control Systems for Tracked Vehicle Platforms, pp. 147–162. Springer (2014)
16. Stallkamp, J., Schlipsing, M., Salmen, J., Igel, C.: The german traffic sign recognition benchmark: A multi-class classification competition. In: The 2011 International Joint Conference on Neural Networks (IJCNN), pp. 1453–1460. IEEE (2011)
17. Topór-Kamiński, T., Krupanek, B., Homa, J.: Delays models of measurement and control data transmission network. In: Nawrat, A., Simek, K., Świerniak, A. (eds.) Advanced Technologies for Intelligent Systems. SCI, vol. 440, pp. 257–278. Springer, Heidelberg (2013)
18. Viola, P., Jones, M.J.: Robust real-time face detection. International Journal of Computer Vision 57(2), 137–154 (2004)
19. Wang, J.G., Lin, C.J., Chen, S.M.: Applying fuzzy method to vision-based lane detection and departure warning system. Expert Systems with Applications 37(1), 113–126 (2010)
20. Yeh, M., Wickens, C.D.: Display signaling in augmented reality: Effects of cue reliability and image realism on attention allocation and trust calibration. Human Factors: The Journal of the Human Factors and Ergonomics Society 43(3), 355–365 (2001)

# Evolving Traffic Scenarios to Test Driver Assistance Systems in Simulations

Torsten Steiner

Fraunhofer ESK,
Hansastrasse 32, 80686 Munich, Germany

**Abstract.** Nowadays, driver assistance systems involve an ever increasing degree of automatization. Costly effort is put into testing the individual components to ensure proper functioning by the vehicle manufacturers.

However, problems can also arise on a macroscopic scale, as vehicles and infrastructure are recently equipped with short range radio communication ("Car2X"). These problems caused by interaction are of even greater concern than "normal" bugs, as the final product might already have been deployed when the issues first become apparent.

Multi-Agent System (MAS) research refers to such issues as "emergent misbehavior". The said field also brought up an approach to automatically discover the worst consequences of the malfunctions. Hence, a given system under test can already be revised during development, saving a tremendous amount of resources.

The approach from MAS is adapted to the domain of testing driver assistance systems in traffic simulations. A green-light optimal-speed advisory (GLOSA) algorithm is used as an example in which conceptual problems are discovered by the testing system after simpler issues are eliminated.

## 1 Introduction

Traffic simulations have become a common tool for traffic engineers and advanced driver assistance system (ADAS) developers for testing and validating the performance of their new inventions or infrastructure modifications before deployment. The complexity of ADASs is on the rise due to an ever increasing amount of new sensors and algorithms for automotive applications. This fact already makes it hard for human testers to find all possible causes of errors in common driver assistance systems. However, if several of these systems start to interact (e.g. via Car-to-Car Communication) new use cases can be provided to drivers. As a consequence, several vehicles from different manufacturers will need to communicate and coordinate on future roads - which makes the problem of testing the systems even more difficult.

When performing simulative studies to evaluate the effects of a new ADAS on traffic there are several approaches. A common variant is to build large scenarios, trying to get them as close to reality as possible [14]. Be it by automatic or even manual optimization as in [9]. However, it is often quite hard to aquire

M. Kassab et al. (Eds.): Nets4Cars/Nets4Trains/Nets4Aircraft 2015, LNCS 9066, pp. 103–114, 2015.
DOI: 10.1007/978-3-319-17765-6_10

sufficiently accurate detector and traffic signal data to accurately simulate such large scenarios. Hence, [4] built a larger scenario using averaged parameters on a synthetic grid street setup. Another variant is to simulate minimal synthetic scenarios with the sole purpose being the testing of an ADAS with different parameters as in [7], [15].

This paper's contribution is the application of an approach from the area of MAS research [6] to the prototyping of ADAS in traffic simulations. Negative impacts of new systems can automatically be discovered and presented to developers in synthetic small scale scenarios. The said scenarios are automatically generated by a genetic algorithm. This algorithm uses a fitness function that compares the performance of the tested system to the performance of an unmodified system on the same scenario. Consequently, the testing system is able to learn how situations look like in which new ADAS developments lead to bad advice for the drivers. The small scale of the scenarios minimizes the effort to find programming errors or even conceptual problems during development.

To demonstrate the capabilities of this paper's contribution in practice, an instance of the widespread GLOSA application was taken from [7]. Since the testing system found issues in the GLOSA algorithm itself, improvements were implemented in the ADAS logic so that further test runs could be conducted. Finally, the procedure was aborted when a conceptual problem was brought up in a generated scenario. The refactoring required to circumvent that problem would require large changes to the algorithm and new concepts to be introduced, which is beyond the scope of a simple example.

The remainder of this paper is organized as follows: In Section 2 a description of GLOSA and its different implementations is given. The variant from [7] is listed for reference. Section 3 details the concepts of employing a genetic algorithm to find ADAS problems in traffic simulations while Section 4 lists the paramters for the specific tests conducted. Section 5 shows what was achived for the application on the GLOSA demo code. Finally, Section 6 compares the approach from this paper with other similar versions from other fields. Section 7 gives a conclusion and points out interesting new research options.

## 2    GLOSA in Traffic Simulations

A GLOSA driver assistance system is able to provide the driver with optimal speed recommendations on how to approach a traffic light, so that unnecessary stop-and-go movement is avoided. Consequently, GLOSA systems need to know the traffic signal schedules to provide their recommendations, i.e. the schedule data needs to be transferred to the vehicle in some way. Recent projects and simulations have used dedicated short range communication (DSRC) modules integrated in vehicles and infrastructure [7], [11], [9] as well as crowd sourced data from the drivers smartphones [8].

According to [8], the main benefits of a GLOSA assistance system are threefold: First, the fuel consumption is decreased. Second, traffic flow is smoothed and increased. Third, the environmental impact is decreased. It is also noted, that given speed recommendations which lie below the current speed of a vehicle do not necessarily increase the total travelling time. The latter is because GLOSA-enabled vehicles cross in the same signal phase as "normal" drivers but are already in motion, as they did not need to halt their vehicles completely.

There are different strategies to achieve the benefits listed above. Some of them can be found in [7], [15], [12], [4] and [3]. To demonstrate the approach used in this paper, the algorithm from [7] was chosen, because of its purely reactive simplicity. It is listed in Figure 1 for convenience.

1: Find the closest traffic light $TL$
2: Calculate the distance $d$ and time $T_{TL}$ to $TL$
3: Check phase as $T_{TL}$
4: **if** GREEN **then**
5:      Continue trip
6:      Target Speed $U_t = U_{max}$
7: **else if** RED **then**
8:      Calculate remaining Red Time $T_{red}$
9:      Calculate target speed for $T_{red} + T_{TL} : U_t$
10: **else if** YELLOW **then**
11:      Calculate remaining Yellow Time $T_{yellow}$
12:      Check for possible acceleration
13:      Calculate target speed for $T_{yellow} + T_{red} + T_{TL} : U_t$
14: **end if**
15: Advisory speed $= MAX(U_t, U_{min})$ & $MIN(U_t, U_{max})$

**Fig. 1.** The GLOSA algorithm which was used as an example for problems, that can be found in a given ADAS. Vehicles receive signal phase and timing (SPAT) [5] messages from a traffic signal. From this data, $d$ and $T_{TL}$ can be computed. Based on this computation, recommendations about acceleration or deceleration can be given to the driver. For more details see [7].

## 3   Evolutionary Testing of ADAS in Traffic Simulations

The main idea of evolutionary testing in ADAS is based on a learning component [6] ("Learner" in Figure 2), that automatically creates different traffic scenarios in which the ADAS under test causes problems. Due to the potentially huge search space (please find an outline of some possibilities in Section 4) a genetic algorithm was chosen for this module.

As a consequence, the general scheme of the testing system is to start on a randomly initialized set of parameters to create a set of traffic scenarios (*generation*) to be evaluated. An evaluation of a single scenario (*individual*) consists of two steps. The first step is to simulate each scenario using an unmodified driver's behavior, while the second step uses the ADAS to influence the behavior. Both steps can of course be parallelized. The output of each step are one or more real valued numbers on a scale defined by the user (e.g. total $CO_2$ output or total waiting time). A *fitness function* is then used to incorporate all values from the

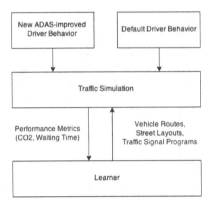

**Fig. 2.** Overview of the testing approach. This work used a genetic algorithm for the learner and SUMO for the traffic simulation component.

previous stage and guide the search in the desired direction. *Genetic operators* are then applied to the created scenarios to build a new generation of individuals to be used for the next iteration. After a given number of generations the process is halted.

There are several traffic simulators that could perform the simulations during the evaluation of an individual. For this work, the "Simulation of Urban Mobility" (SUMO) traffic simulator was chosen as it provides enough features to find problems in high level interactions of vehicles on the road. It should be noted that different simulators yield different benefits and that the choice of a simulator greatly depends on the area one wants to find problems in.

### 3.1 Individual Encoding

SUMO offers a plethora of different configuration parameters to build complex traffic scenarios. As the work presented here only serves as a proof of concept, a choice is needed about which of the parameters to include in the individuals for the genetic algorithm. The employed individual encoding features the following traffic simulation components:

**Road Topology.** A modification of the environment during the evolution is possible, i.e. the layout of streets can be changed in an individual. A design decision was made to use a triangular grid as a base layout, so that more complex intersection layouts and possibilities for vehicles to interact in the simulation can be provided, compared to a grid layout. Consequently, the number of (undirected) streets that meet in an intersection is limited to six, while the presence of each connection on the base graph is controlled by a single bit.

More options open up as each edge in the underlying graph can contain several lanes, each of which can have different turning restrictions. The approach of using a triangle grid compared to e.g. randomly generated junction node locations also avoids the problem of scenarios being regarded as broken by SUMO's parser, as scenarios in which streets cross without an intersection are regarded as invalid.

**Traffic Signal Locations and Schedules.** What is more, it can be determined whether or not a junction should be governed by a traffic signal at all. If the outcome is that there is a signal, the schedules of this signal can also be modified. A constraint was made that limits the search space at this point. Namely, when choosing the signal schedules in a random fashion conflicting streams are a frequent outcome. Since such scenarios do not occur in reality, the interpretation of an individual also does not output them for the simulation.

**Traffic Flows.** Finally, individuals can contain different routes for different vehicle streams, while streams can contain variable numbers of vehicles themselves. The behavior of the vehicles is left to be controlled by user provided applications (i.e. the ADAS under test). Hence, no further information about it is encoded in the individual.

Considering all the possible parameters that make up a traffic simulation there are of course plenty of things which can not be touched in the current version of the presented software system, since this paper only outlines the concept and a simple application. Generally, everything that has not been specifially mentioned before is left to be the default SUMO 0.22 parameter for the given value. Values that are set but left unchanged include the speed limit (set to a static value of 50 km/h for an average urban traffic situation). There are also no accidents and no further obstacles (except for slow vehicles themselves) in the simulations conducted. Nevertheless, it should be noted, that the effort to make parameters or events like the aforementioned ones "reachable" to the genetic algorithm is rather small. When integrating further events, one is basically only limited by the features of the chosen traffic simulator.

## 3.2    Genetic Operators

The genetic operators employed are twofold. First, a single point mutation can be used to make simple modifications to the topology, i.e. single bit switches determine which of the underlying graph's edges are being used to create the street network later on. Another single point mutation is available to change the timings in traffic signal programs. Second, a crossover operation is available to combine different parts from two parental individuals to create new individuals. This operation takes special care to not "cut" the individuals encoded parameters at the wrong place. This is because swapping parts of traffic signal logic into topology parts would result in invalid scenarios at a later point in the generation process.

Furthermore, special care had to be taken in regard to problems caused by changes to the topology of an individual. For example, scenarios might be changed in a way that takes single segments out of the street grid so that previously generated routes become invalid. This case triggers a repair mechanism in the implementation that fixes the errors: Whenever an existing vehicle's route is broken during a topology mutation it is repaired optimizing for the longest possible route so that interactions between vehicles are maximized.

### 3.3 Fitness Function

In the same manner as in [6] it was found that an obvious choice for a fitness function $fit$ would be to use the raw difference between one or more metrics of simulation output values for a given individual $i = (topo, sl, ss, flows)$ - where $topo$ is the topology, $sl$ traffic signal locations, $ss$ traffic signal schedules and $flows$ the generated vehicles routes.

For example, a simple fitness function could be $fit_{CO_2}(i) = eval_{ADAS_{CO_2}}(i) - eval_{base_{CO_2}}(i)$, which denotes the total difference between all $CO_2$ output by all vehicles of a given $i$, evaluated for the ADAS by the evaluation function $eval_{ADAS_{CO_2}}$ on the one hand and for the basic driver's behavior $eval_{base_{CO_2}}$ on the other hand. In the same manner as for $CO_2$ one can also use the total waiting time $twt$ as a metric, obtaining a fitness function such as $fit_{twt}(i) = eval_{ADAS_{twt}}(i) - eval_{base_{twt}}(i)$ - where $twt$ represents the time spent by drivers waiting in front of traffic lights or in traffic jams.

As the GLOSA algorithm contains no adaptive elements these simple fitness measures already sufficed to create scenarios in which issues showed up.

## 4  Applying the Testing Approach to GLOSA Traffic Simulations

To apply the testing system to drivers behaving according to the algorithm from Figure 1 some more assumptions and settings were made, which the following paragraphs are going to describe.

Basically, the initial implementation of the GLOSA logic was kept as close as possible to [7]. That means, that the SUMO traffic simulator was used as a base for the simulations conducted. Consequently, its traffic flow model [10] is used as a fallback, as soon as the GLOSA algorithm does not compute any recommendation. This might be the case when there is no traffic light on the upcoming route, or the next traffic light is too far away to be in radio range. Also, the prototypical ADAS is connected to SUMO via the TRACI interface, so vehicles in the simulation can be given GLOSA speed recommendations.

To keep things simple, random influences that do not lead to the test goal were kept out of the simulations. Concretely, the evaluation runs were done without further simulator-coupling (e.g. a network simulator was not used), as the point of applying the testing approach is to find negative highlevel interactions which are caused by following the final ADAS advice. Hence, it is assumed that the vehicles "know" the traffic signal schedules and can compute their recommended speed accordingly (i.e. the communication links always work). What is more, the drivers always accept the GLOSA recommendations as long as there are no collisions involved. This means that slower vehicles in front are not over-taken. However, it is perfectly possible to build more complex simulation setups in the future to provide for even larger possibilies of failure from different sources.

Regarding the configuration of the genetic algorithm the following settings were made: The street layout used in the experimental runs was built based on a quite small number (2) of triangles to construct the concrete SUMO scenario on. The number of triangles was chosen, so that a small street net is produced which guarantees a quick overview of what is happening to the developer.

The number of lanes of a street coming into an intersection was configured to be between zero (no connection to a junction at all) and four. Note that this refers to the number of lanes in one direction on a single street - consequently, there can be a total of eight lanes on a single street on a given intersection.

Traffic signal schedules were created to contain values between three and 64 seconds for a phase.

The vehicles routes were made modifiable in different ranges for the appli-cation of the testing system to the given GLOSA algorithm. First, a series of runs was conducted with only a single vehicle in the simulation, so that simple implementation issues (such as parsing or interpreting SUMO's TRACI output incorrectly) could be resolved quickly. Afterwards, the genetic algorithm was al-lowed to insert between two and four vehicle streams into the traffic scenario. Each of these streams could contain between three and 15 vehicles.

Traffic scenarios were not aborted but simulated until every inserted vehicle had reached its final destination, i.e. it left the simulation. Hence, the number of simulated timesteps variied from scenario to scenario and was only indirectly influenced by the learning system via the aforementioned parameters.

Finally, $fit_{twt}$ was used as a fitness function, so that speed modulation had no impact on an individual's fitness as it would have been the case when using $fit_{CO_2}$. This choice was made because the learning system would run into sce-narios in which vehicles crossed the stop line just as a phase switch occurred. Consequently, the GLOSA algorithm would always oscillate between break and acceleration state, raising the total $CO_2$ output of an individual. This was re-garded as a minor detail to be fixed, compared to the conceptual issues described later.

## 5   Results

To conduct the experimental runs, the genetic algorithm was configured as de-scribed in the previous section. The ADAS logic used to compute the GLOSA recommendations was taken from [7] and is given in Figure 1 for reference.

### 5.1   Quantitative Results

Quantitative results are listed in Table 1. To obtain the data for each row a series of ten runs was conducted to account for random effects of the genetic algorithm. What is more, the number of generations used was always 20, while the number

**Table 1.** Results for the testing system's efficiency. "Average" denotes the average of all values of $\frac{ADAS_{twt}}{base_{twt}}$ over a series of runs, while "Maximum" stands for the result of the best run in a series. See Section 3.3 for the according definitions.

| # flows | Average | Maximum |
|---------|---------|---------|
| 2 | 27.95 | 105.86 |
| 3 | 7.06 | 40.29 |
| 4 | 2.07 | 3.83 |

of individuals per generation was kept at 24. There were always two vehicles in a flow. Since the combined total waiting time of all vehicles in a traffic scenario can be zero, those scenarios were filtered from the testing system's output, so that relative increases could be computed. It is striking that the testing system could generate scenarios with large losses in traffic efficiency. The main cause for inefficiencies is described in the next section. It should be noted that the runs conducted were done using the improved version of the GLOSA algorithm from [7] (i.e. a version including all the changes described in the next section).

### 5.2    Qualitative Results - Improving on a Reactive Algorithm

When the approach was applied to practical simulations, the first problems found were simple programming errors as they were mentioned before. The general process here was to evolve simulation scenarios in which such errors occurred, fix the corresponding problem and introduce the scenario as a testcase for the ADAS logic itself. The addition of an evolved scenario as a testcase was also kept as the errors got more complex in later runs, since it prevented to reintroduce problems into the system which were already fixed before. For the early stage of development only a single vehicle was used for the simulations. Only after the search did not yield any scenario in which the GLOSA logic performed worse than SUMO's basic driver behavior the genetic algorithm was allowed to use more than one vehicle.

After these first trivial mistakes were fixed, two problems in the algorithm from Figure 1 were found by the genetic algorithm. When looking at those scenarios manually, both of them displayed situations in which vehicles would drive remarkably slow. Looking at the code paths used by these slow vehicles in the GLOSA algorithm exposed the root of the problem to be in line three of the algorithm. More concretely, the time for a given vehicle to reach the next traffic light $T_{TL}$ was computed by Equation (1). In the equation, $d$ is the distance to the traffic signal, $v$ the vehicle's current velocity and $a$ the vehicle's current acceleration.

$$T_{TL} = \begin{cases} \frac{d}{v}, & \text{when } a = 0 \\ -\frac{v}{a} + \sqrt{\frac{v^2}{a^2} + \frac{2d}{a}}, & \text{when } a \neq 0 \end{cases} \tag{1}$$

With a scenario pointing at the problem is was obvious to see, that the given GLOSA algorithm did not cover the case of $a = 0$, while $v \neq 0$ (and the speed limit allowed a higher velocity $v_{max}$). More concretely, if the aforementioned case was hit, $T_{TL}$ was set to an incorrect value as a consequence and the remainder of the algorithm would only output incorrect values. To correct the error, the computation of $T_{TL}$ was extended for that case to be as given in (2) with $t_{v_{max}} = \frac{v_{max} - v_0}{a}$

$$T_{TL} = t_{v_{max}} + \frac{d - (v_0 * t_{v_{max}} + 1/2 * a_{max} * t_{v_{max}}^2)}{v_{max}}, \qquad (2)$$

After the above computation was integrated the next iteration of the test system brought up a similar issue. Again, the error location was in the $T_{TL}$ computation and hence provided incorrect input for the remaining algorithm. Since [7] used the current acceleration to compute $T_{TL}$ the case of a possible stronger acceleration is disregarded. To improve the algorithm the maximal acceleration of the given vehicle was used instead changing $t_{v_{max}}$ in Equation 2 to be $\frac{v_{max} - v_0}{a_{max}}$, with $a_{max}$ being the vehicle's maximum acceleration.

### 5.3   Conceptual Problems Detected

Finally, after all problems from the previous section were fixed as described, the genetic algorithm ended up creating a scenario in which a conceptual problem of the employed GLOSA approach became apparent. The scenario is depicted in Figure 3. One can see a number of vehicles closing in on an intersection. Vehicle number (1) moves very slowly because its assistance system hands out advice to do so, knowing that the upper signal will turn green in some seconds. However, the following vehicles (2-4) are blocked by vehicle (1). As a consequence, (2-4) can not pass the junction as it would have been possible had the GLOSA system not been in place in (1).

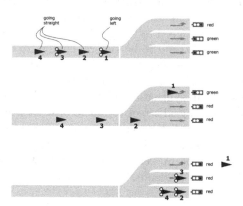

**Fig. 3.** The conceptual problem discovered in the GLOSA algorithm from [7]. The snapshots depict a situation at a traffic signal. Time flows from top to bottom. Vehicle (1) is slow due to GLOSA advice and blocks (2), (3) and (4). Consequently, three vehicles are forced into stop-and-go movement while only a single one can drive efficiently.

This is the point at which the decision was made to interrupt the test runs on the GLOSA algorithm. It became apparent that there are more elaborate concepts needed to resolve the situation, so that the overall waiting time and $CO_2$ output are still kept to a minimum. It should be noted that the problem is already known in the literature, e.g. [11] found the situation and recommends the usage of GLOSA only for "simple" intersections without overlapping lanes. However, future coordination mechanisms could certainly also be used to resolve such situations, so that GLOSA can also be provided for more complex intersections. For example, vehicles could dynamically negotiate a solution while approaching a traffic light.

## 6    Related Work

As mentioned before the initial idea for the creation of the presented testing system was taken from [6] which applied the general testing approach to the domain of the Pickup and Delivery Problem. Later, the approach was applied to attack vehicular ad hoc networks [2] which comes closest to the work presented in this paper. However, the focus of [2] is on mobile networks, which are being attacked by malicious agents while this work concentrates on effects caused by bad advice given to drivers via assistance systems. What is more, the environment is never modified as a part of the simulation.

Another approach that comes close to the work presented here was shown in [1], however the domain of application were air traffic scenarios. Consequently, the environment was spatially unconstrained (airspace) except for other planes. On top of that, the goal was to find scenarios with a high complexity as the algorithms were expected to perform poorly under these conditions. Also, (and in the same manner as [13]) the employed optimization function was not crafted to find misbehaviors by using another given system.

When it comes to ADAS evaluations there is a general issue of how to pick a good simulation scenario layout for the evaluation of new systems/algorithms. The problem is that scenarios need to be specific enough to show the benefit of a given system, while they also need to be general enough to demo that the given system also works under other conditions. Generally, there are three kinds of simulation studies for new assistance systems used in the literature. First, using a small number of very small synthetic scenarios [7], [13]. Second, a few realistic scenarios [11], [14] or third, a grid street layout to base their evaluations on as in [4]. Studies that decide for realistic scenarios mostly have to deal with the bad availability of traffic flow or traffic signal schedule data.

However, there seems to be no general approach that maps the search technique to traffic simulations as presented in this paper. Scenarios are always static and no search is performed.

## 7    Conclusion

This paper has presented the application of a semiautomatic testing process for driver assistance systems. A simple GLOSA algorithm was taken as an example to show what kind of issues the testing system can reveal in practice. It was shown that there is a conceptual problem in the purely reactive GLOSA algorithm from [7]. A driver who follows correct GLOSA advice can block other drivers from crossing a traffic signal at green in a situation as shown in Figure 3.

It was proposed to develop a Car2Car approach to fix the problem, as it was shown that a simple broadcast of traffic light phase and timing (SPAT) [5] is not enough for every situation. This would make more complex coordination mechanisms a necessity. Work on the introduction of such mechanisms has only started recently and can hopefully profit from the system presented here, as the approach also works for more adaptive systems when the fitness function is changed accordingly.

Future extensions and possible applications of the presented test system are manifold. The testing system was not employed to its maximum capabilities, since the GLOSA algorithm was purely reactive. Hence, the application to systems like [13] or the aforementioned Car2Car coordination mechanism would be especially interesting, since [6] already showed how self-adaption in systems can be automatically exploited by the search algorithm.

Also, the application of the principle is not limited to the comparision to a simulators basic driver model. The basic model can easily be swapped for another ADAS. This variant could be used to improve on a working assistance system when adding new features, while making sure not to break performance in the process.

What is more, one could deploy several vehicles with different ADASs in a single scenario. The test system in its presented form is applicable to all ADASs that change a driver's behavior. Hence, it would be simple to also use it on simulations in which several different ADASs interact. Unforeseen interactions could be brought up and fixed before they might happen in reality. This point is expected to gain further importance in the near future as a lot of manufacturers are focussing on the development of autonomous vehicles.

# References

1. Alam, S., Shafi, K., Abbass, H., Barlow, M.: Evolving Air Traffic Scenarios for the Evaluation of Conflict Detection Models. In: 6th Eurocontrol Innovation Research Workshop and Conference, Eurocontrol Experiment Research Centre, pp. 1–8 (2007)
2. Bergmann, K.: Vulnerability Testing In Wireless Ad-hoc Networks Using Incremental Adaptive Corrective Learning. Dissertation, University of Calgary (2014), http://theses.ucalgary.ca/handle/11023/1504
3. Chao-Qun, M., Hai-Jun, H., Tie-Qiao, T.: Improving Urban Traffic by Velocity Guidance. In: 2008 International Conference on Intelligent Computation Technology and Automation (ICICTA), vol. 2, pp. 383–387. IEEE (October 2008), http://ieeexplore.ieee.org/lpdocs/epic03/wrapper.htm?arnumber=4659788
4. Eckhoff, D., Halmos, B., German, R.: Potentials and limitations of Green Light Optimal Speed Advisory systems. VNC (Section IV) (2013), http://www7old.informatik.uni-erlangen.de/ eckhoff/publications/pdf/ eckhoff2013potentials.pdf

5. ETSI: TS 102 894-1 - V1.1.1 - Intelligent Transport Systems (ITS); Users and applications requirements; Part 1: Facility layer structure, functional requirements and specifications 1, 1–56 (2013)
6. Hudson, J., Denzinger, J., Kasinger, H., Bauer, B.: Efficiency Testing of Self-Adapting Systems by Learning of Event Sequences. In: ADAPTIVE 2010. pp. 200–205 (2010)
7. Katsaros, K., Kernchen, R., Dianati, M., Rieck, D.: Performance study of a Green Light Optimized Speed Advisory (GLOSA) application using an integrated cooperative ITS simulation platform. In: 2011 7th International Wireless Communications and Mobile Computing Conference, pp. 918–923. IEEE (July 2011)
8. Koukoumidis, E., Peh, L., Martonosi, M.: SignalGuru: leveraging mobile phones for collaborative traffic signal schedule advisory. In: Proceedings of the 9th International Conference on Mobile Systems, Applications, and Services, June 28-July 01, pp. 127–140. ACM (2011)
9. Krajzewicz, D., Bieker, L., Erdmann, J.: Preparing Simulative Evaluation of the GLOSA Application. elib.dlr.de, pp.1–11 (October 2012), http://elib.dlr.de/78905/1/ITSW2012_GLOSA.pdf
10. Krauß, S.: Microscopic modeling of traffic flow: Investigation of collision free vehicle dynamics. D L R - Forschungsberichte (1998)
11. Niebel, W.: Cost-Benefit-Based Implementation Strategy for Green Light Optimised Speed Advisory (GLOSA). Activities of Transport Telematics 2013(C), 312–320 (2013), http://link.springer.com/chapter/10.1007/978-3-642-41647-7_38
12. Sanchez, M., Cano, J.C., Kim, D.: Predicting Traffic lights to Improve Urban Traffic Fuel Consumption. In: 2006 6th International Conference on ITS Telecommunications, pp. 331–336. IEEE (June 2006)
13. Seredynski, M., Mazurczyk, W., Khadraoui, D.: Multi-segment Green Light Optimal Speed Advisory. In: 2013 IEEE International Symposium on Parallel & Distributed Processing, Workshops and Phd Forum, pp. 459–465 (May 2013)
14. Sommer, C., Eckhoff, D., Dressler, F.: Improving the Accuracy of IVC Simulation Using Crowd-sourced Geodata. PIK - Praxis der Informationsverarbeitung und Kommunikation 33(4), 278–283 (2010), http://www.degruyter.com/view/j/piko.2010.33.issue-4/piko.2010.047/piko.2010.047.xml
15. Wegener, A., Hellbruck, H., Wewetzer, C., Lubke, A.: VANET Simulation Environment with Feedback Loop and its Application to Traffic Light Assistance. In: 2008 IEEE Globecom Workshops, pp. 1–7. IEEE (November 2008)

# Rail

# QoS-Aware Radio Access Technology (RAT) Selection in Hybrid Vehicular Networks

Zeeshan Hameed Mir[1], Jamal Toutouh[2], Fethi Filali[1], and Enrique Alba[2]

[1] Qatar Mobility Innovations Center (QMIC), Qatar Science and
Technology Park (QSTP), PO Box 210531, Doha, Qatar
{zeeshanh,filali}@qmic.com
[2] Dept. de Lenguajes y Ciencias de la Computación,
University of Malaga, Malaga, Spain
{jamal,eat}@lcc.uma.es

**Abstract.** The increasing number of wireless communication technologies and standards bring immense opportunities and challenges to provide seamless connectivity in Hybrid Vehicular Networks (HVNs). HVNs could not only enhance existing applications but could also spur an array of new services. However, due to sheer number of use cases and applications with diverse and stringent QoS performance requirements it is very critical to efficiently decide on which radio access technology (RAT) to select. In this paper a QoS-aware RAT selection algorithm is proposed for HVN. The proposed algorithm switches between IEEE 802.11p based ad hoc network and LTE cellular network by considering network load and application's QoS requirements. The simulation-based studies show that the proposed RAT selection mechanism results in lower number of Vertical Handovers (VHOs) and significant performance improvements in terms of packet delivery ratio, latency and application-level throughput.

**Keywords:** IEEE 802.11p, LTE, RAT Selection, Hybrid Vehicular Networks.

## 1 Introduction

Recently, several studies [1–4] urged to combine different radio access technologies into a unified Hybrid Vehicular Networking (HVN) architecture. Multiple radio access technologies for vehicular communications could not only enhance several existing applications in the road safety, traffic efficiency, and infotainment domains, but could also spur an array of new services. However, successful implementation of such hybrid architecture is often attributed to efficient management of combined radio resources. Central to this are the Radio Access Technology (RAT) selection algorithms which carefully choose the most suitable access technology while preserving the connectivity through Vertical Handover (VHO). For this purpose, standards like Communications Architecture for Land Mobile environment (CALM) [5] and Media Independent Handover (MIH) or IEEE 802.21 [6] can be utilized in the vehicular networking environment. It is highly desirable

© Springer International Publishing Switzerland 2015
M. Kassab et al. (Eds.): Nets4Cars/Nets4Trains/Nets4Aircraft 2015, LNCS 9066, pp. 117–128, 2015.
DOI: 10.1007/978-3-319-17765-6_11

to limit the number of unnecessary VHOs because of the higher VHO signaling cost and the delay incurred which often translate into data throughput lost.

To fully exploit the potential of HVN architecture we consider to combine IEEE 802.11p [7] based ad hoc network and infrastructure-based LTE [8] cellular network. It is envisioned that the proposed HVN architecture would support different types of uses cases and applications such as road safety, traffic efficiency and infotainment. The applications exchange messages called *beacons* at regular intervals and the frequency with which beacons are transmitted is termed as *beaconing frequency*. Since each application has its own set of functional and performance requirements, typically the beaconing frequency varies between 1Hz to 10Hz. The IEEE 802.11p standard provides ad hoc networking capabilities to exchange messages directly and is particularly suitable for low to medium range and delay sensitive vehicular networking applications. On the other hand LTE by 3GPP promises to offer medium to large communication range, higher data rates with moderate delays. Each beacon is sent to the base station (eNodeB), which traverse through the core network before reaching an Intelligent Transportation Systems (ITS) Server. The ITS Server acts as a rendezvous between the senders and receivers and transfers the beacon messages back to sender's neighboring vehicles through broadcasting by the eNodeB.

RAT selection algorithms have been extensively studied in heterogeneous mobile networks [9]. In context of vehicular communications most of studies focused on protocol switching algorithms between co-located WLAN and WWAN access technologies. To provide seamless connectivity, the VHO decisions are made either by predicting location information or by measuring multiple performance criteria. The former approach relies excessively on the accuracy of prior knowledge such as call duration and hot-spot dwell time. Whereas the later approach results in higher VHO frequency [10].

In this paper we proposed an efficient QoS-aware RAT selection algorithm which switches between IEEE 802.11p and LTE access technologies by performing VHO. Coordinated by a Distributed Radio Resource Management (DRRM) [9] entity, the IEEE 802.11p interface exchanges periodic beacon messages directly in an ad hoc manner. Alternatively, based on the network load and QoS requirements imposed by vehicular networking applications, the DRRM can choose to perform vertical handover to the LTE interface. However, in order to lower the frequency of VHO and associated cost the proposed mechanism first tries to locally solve the network load issue through beaconing frequency reduction [11] as permissible by application's QoS requirements. The study shows that the *QoS-aware RAT selection* and *Beaconing Frequency Adaptation* mechanism result in fewer number of VHOs while satisfying QoS requirements by different types of applications. The proposed mechanism preformed significantly well in terms of packet delivery ratio, latency and application-level throughput.

The rest of this paper is organized as follows. The related work is described in Section II and the proposed QoS-aware RAT selection algorithm is explained in Section III. The performance evaluation is provided in Section IV. Finally, the paper is concluded in Section V.

## 2   Related Work

Much work has been done in heterogeneous mobile networks, and efficient selection of radio access technology (RAT) is one of most addressed research issues. This section summarizes the work on RAT selection in mobile networks and reviews studies on heterogeneous wireless network in vehicular environment.

Studies on RAT selection in mobile networks can be largely classified into three categories: i.e., random, single-criterion, and multiple-criteria based algorithms [9]. In random RAT selection, all new or VHO (vertical handover) calls are handled by one of the available access technology. The simplicity of implementation comes at the cost of higher call blocking and dropping probability. The single and multiple criteria approaches differ in using either only one or several requirements while evaluating the suitability of a network. Work falling into the former category takes into account a single criterion such as load balancing, coverage, user satisfaction and service types. The later approaches consider diverse performance metrics and parameters to decide on the candidate access technology. It includes Analysis Hierarchy Process (AHP), Simple Additive Weighting (SAW), Multiplicative Exponent Weighting (MEW) and fuzzy logic-based methods. The single criterion approaches improve system performance in certain specific aspects while multiple criteria approaches provide optimized solutions, however they are complicated to implement.

Heterogeneous network architectures for vehicular communications have been realized by mean of accessing Wireless Local Area Network (WLAN) and Wireless Wide Area Network (WWAN) technologies in parallel. Earlier work in this domain exploit co-located Access Points (APs) and cellular technologies such as CDMA2000 [12] and UMTS [13] to implement hybrid communication paradigm for vehicular networking. These studies were focused on providing hybrid V2X communication protocol with the help of VHO between Vehicle-to-Vehicle (V2V) and Vehicle-to-Infrastructure (V2I) communications. However the main difference is the VHO strategy which they employed. Anna et. al. in [10] proposed a switching protocol decision metric based on the cost function which is measured by taking into account delay and radio resource utilization time associated with the alternative paths. The VHO decision based on multiple performance criteria results in higher number of VHOs (i.e., ping-pong effect) which often leads to protocol instability [13].

Similarly, the VHO decision in [12] is based on metrics like service type, congestion and location prediction. Based on the predicted dwell time at a hot-spot, if the user is expected to stay, WLAN become the preferred choice; otherwise WWAN is the preferred choice. For real-time type services, WWAN is selected and for non-real-time service WLAN, only if WWAN is not congested. In Hasib's work it is assumed that the call duration and the hot-spot dwell time are known in advance, which is quite hard to achieve because vehicular network topology changes rapidly and in an unpredictable manner.

# 3    Proposed RAT Selection Algorithm

It is assumed that each end user implements a distributed strategy for managing multiple radio resources, called *Distributed Radio Resource Management (DRRM)* entity [9]. Unlike the *centralized* or *hierarchical* approaches, the DRRM entity independently makes the RAT selection decisions. DRRM is not only responsible for providing coordination among participating access technologies which are managed locally by their respective *Radio Resource Management* (RRM) entities but also among different DRRM entities.

## 3.1    QoS-Aware RAT Selection

The IEEE 802.11p RRM entity is in charge of analyzing the IEEE 802.11p network load by using the *Network Load Monitor* (NLM) mechanism, which monitors the length of the queues in order to determine the current network load. If the queue lengths are below a given threshold limit, the DRRM entity broadcasts beacons via its IEEE 802.11p interface. However, if the queue lengths exceed certain threshold limit, it considers that the current network load could lead to a congestion situation which in turns causes severe performance degradation. The threshold limit is defined by the parameter *NLM-Threshold* which often varies between 80% to 90% of the total queue capacity.

To locally resolve the network load problem, the DRRM entity initiates the Beaconing Frequency Adaptation (BFA) mechanism which allows the applications to adapt and operate the IEEE 802.11p interface with new set of communication requirements. Therefore, the use of LTE radio access technology and the associated cost of performing VHOs can be minimized. The proposed QoS-aware RAT selection algorithm can be summarized as follow:

**Step 1:** On finding that the network load exceeds the predefined threshold limit i.e., NLM-Threshold, the DRRM entity triggers the BFA mechanism which reduces the number of beacons transmitted in the ad hoc network. The BFA mechanism adjusts the beaconing frequency of an application by adapting its QoS requirements.

**Step 2:** If the local adjustment of an application's beaconing frequency fails to lower the network load enough, in the next step the DRRM entity initiates a request to the neighboring vehicles to apply the BFA mechanism. On receiving such requests the DRRM entity at each neighboring vehicle tries to adapt its application's beaconing frequency.

**Step 3:** If applying above two steps brings down the network load below the NLM-Threshold, the DRRM entity suggests to broadcast the beacons through its IEEE 802.11p interface with the reduced beaconing frequency. However, if the network load is still high and the beaconing frequency cannot be further reduced without significantly sacrificing the QoS requirements, a VHO is performed. All the subsequent beacons are sent through the LTE interface for certain duration. This duration is usually short mainly due to vehicular mobility where topology and the network load changes rapidly. Fig. 1, illustrates the QoS-aware RAT selection algorithm.

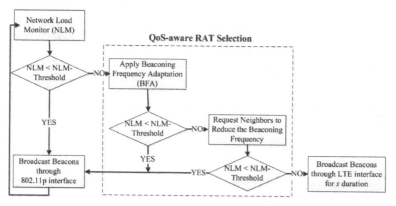

**Fig. 1.** Flowchart: QoS-aware RAT selection algorithm

## 3.2 Beaconing Frequency Adaptation (BFA)

By adjusting the QoS requirements of an application according to the network load conditions the Beaconing Frequency Adaptation (BFA) mechanism improves the network efficiency and reduces the number of VHOs and the associated cost. Fig. 2 summarizes the BFA procedure which is either triggered locally or as a result of a request received by one or more of the neighboring vehicles. It starts with the applications reporting their current QoS requirements to the DRRM entity. It is assumed that these requirements can be characterized using three parameters namely initial beaconing frequency *bFreqInitial*, beaconing frequency reduction factor *rFactor* and maximum beaconing frequency reduction tolerance *rTolerance*. Based on these parameters, the BFA mechanism calculates the reduced beaconing frequency *bFreqReduced* given as,

$$bFreqReduced = \lceil bFreqReduced - (rFactor\% \times bFreqInitial) \rceil$$

After initially setting bFreqReduced to bFreqInitial, an iterative procedure is carried out by the DRRM entity which checks whether the reduction in initial frequency is permissible as per application's QoS requirements defined by the parameter rTolerance. If the beaconing frequency can be reduced, the DRRM entity requests the application layer to decrease its initial beaconing frequency by the given rFactor. The BFA mechanism finishes either when an application can't tolerate further decrease in its beaconing frequency or the network load is reduced to the level where beacons can be efficiently transmitted over the IEEE 802.11p interface.

An application's QoS requirements are preserved by using rTolerance and rFactor parameters. The parameter rTolerance is the maximum tolerable reduction in beaconing frequency by an application, given as the percentage of the initial beaconing frequency (bFreqInitial). This parameter ensures that the application functions properly along with its QoS requirements without losing the useful information to the neighboring vehicles. Whereas the parameter rFactor

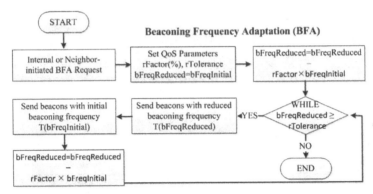

**Fig. 2.** Flowchart: Beaconing Frequency Adaptation (BFA)

is used to gradually decrease the beaconing frequency in relatively smaller steps instead of reducing it directly by the rTolerance. For example, in a scenario where an application sets bFreqInitial at 10Hz, with rTolerance and rFactor equal to 50% and 25% of the bFreqInitial, respectively. For the first, second and third iteration of the BFA mechanism the parameter bFreqReduced is calculated as 8Hz, 6Hz, and 4 Hz, respectively. From the implementation perspective two timers were defined as well.

1. The timer T(bFreqReduced) defines the maximum time period an application can operate at reduced beaconing frequency without compromising the QoS requirements. During this duration the vehicles would broadcast beacons with a frequency lower than the value initially set, as illustrated in Fig. 3(a).
2. The timer T(bFreqInitial) defines the minimum time period that an application must operate at initial beaconing frequency right after the T(bFreqReduced) epoch, as shown in Fig. 3(b).

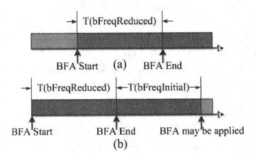

**Fig. 3.** The timers: (a) T(bFreqReduced) and (b) T(bFreqInitial)

## 4    Performance Evaluation

This section evaluates and compares the QoS-aware RAT selection algorithm using self-developed simulation tool and consists of two types of simulation studies.

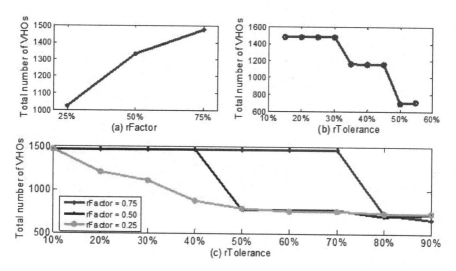

**Fig. 4.** Impact of QoS parameters: (a) rFactor, (b) rTolerance and (c) Combined rFactor and rTolerance vs. Number of VHOs

Firstly, the proposed algorithm is evaluated for different values of QoS parameters such as rFactor, rTolerance, T(bFreqReduced) and T(bFreqInitial) and their impact on the number of VHOs. Secondly, a comparative study is provided which evaluated several RAT selection mechanisms in terms of packet delivery ratio (PDR), latency and application-level throughput or goodput.

## 4.1    Simulation Environment

The road network represents a highway scenario of length 1km with three lanes each 5m wide. There are 150 vehicles participating, with varying speed between minimum 50km/h to maximum 130km/h. For modeling IEEE 802.11p simulation the Three-Log Distance propagation model is used with 5.8GHz radio operating at 6Mbps data rate. The communication range is set to 250m. As for the of LTE part a simplified Radio Access Network (RAN) is modeled with one eNodeB, thus a single cell environment operating at 900 MHz with a bandwidth of 10Mhz. The application running at each vehicle transmits 100 bytes beacons at varying beaconing frequencies. Each simulation runs for 100 seconds, and the obtained results are the averaged over 10 different simulation instances.

## 4.2    Simulation Study

**Impact of QoS Parameters.** Fig. 4(a) shows that with the increase in rFactor, the number of VHO increases. Even with a moderate reduction factor of 25% the number of VHOs are quite high. For more aggressive increments in rfactor the number of VHOs grows significantly. Since the maximum beaconing frequency

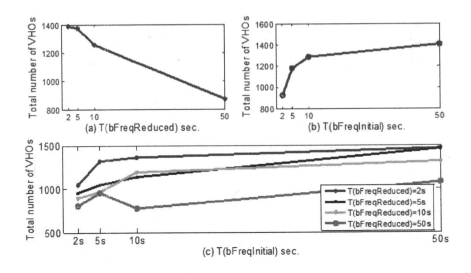

**Fig. 5.** Impact of timer values: (a) T(bFreqReduced), (b) T(bFreqInitial) and (c) Combined T(bFreqReduced) and T(bFreqInitial) vs. Number of VHOs

is set to 10Hz, the rTolerance is achieved at a very early iterations of the BFA mechanism. Therefore for the subsequent iterations, the parameter rTolerance wouldn't let BFA mechanism to apply. This causes network load to increase and thus high number of VHOs. Fig. 4(b) shows that overall with the increase in rTolerance, the number of VHOs decreases. The higher rTolerance values let applications to reduce the beaconing frequency at maximum which leads to lower network load and therefore less number of VHOs. Fig. 4(c) shows the combined effect of parameters rTolerance and rFactor on the number of VHOs. The constant number of VHOs is due to smaller changes between the consecutive values of rTolerance. Unless the rTolerance parameter value is considerably greater than that of rFactor (i.e., applications are more flexible) the effect of increasing reduction factor on the number of VHOs remains less significant.

Fig. 5(a) shows that the increase in T(bFreqReduced) (i.e., an application can operate at reduced beaconing frequency for longer duration without sacrificing the QoS requirements) results in lower number of VHOs. Since, an application can tolerate to operate at reduced beaconing frequency longer, there are fewer chances of network load to increase beyond the threshold limits, therefore requires fewer number of VHOs. Fig. 5(b) shows that the increase in T(bFreqInitial) (i.e., an application is required to stay longer at the initial beaconing frequency right after T(bFreqReduced) duration) causes higher number of VHOs. An application tends to operate at original beaconing frequency for longer duration, which cause significant increase in network load. The frequent violation of the threshold limit which is often can't be handled by the BFA procedure result in higher number of VHOs. Generally, as the T(bFreqInitial) increases, for all the

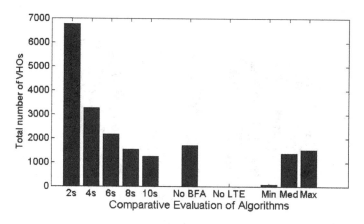

**Fig. 6.** Number of VHO for different RAT selection schemes

simulated values of T(bFreqReduced) the number of VHOs increases, as given in Fig. 5(c). No matter for what duration of time an application can tolerate the reduction of original beaconing frequency, if it requires attaining the initial beaconing frequency longer afterwards this would increase the network load to the level where VHO cannot be avoided. Similarly, as the timer T(bFreqReduced) value increases, for all the simulated values of timer T(bFreqInitial), the number of VHO decreases. Shorter an application can tolerate to stay at original beaconing frequency, fewer the chance are for the network load to increase beyond the specified threshold limit. Therefore fewer numbers of VHOs are required to satisfy the application QoS requirements.

**Comparative Study.** For a comparative study, the proposed QoS-aware RAT selection mechanism is compared with number of other schemes, including:

1. Periodic RAT selection: The decision of switching between two access technologies is carried out in discrete period in time (i.e., proactive handover [14]). Simulations were performed for several epochs from 2s to 10s.
2. No BFA: In this scheme, every time the network load exceeds the predefined NLM-Threshold value, the algorithm performs VHO. This is similar to load balancing among multiple RAT with a fixed threshold value [15].
3. No LTE: It is assumed that there is no LTE interface available i.e., only the performance of IEEE 802.11p based vehicular ad hoc network is evaluated.

Fig. 6 shows the number of VHOs performed by each scheme. As expected, for the periodic RAT selection this metric value decreases with the increase in periodicity interval. The number of VHOs in the No BFA scheme is quite comparable with periodic scheme for values between 6s and 8s. For the proposed QoS-aware RAT selection mechanism the values of minimum, median, and maximum number of VHOs are plotted. The minimum number of VHOs is significantly lower than any other algorithm, whereas the median and maximum values are equivalent to the periodic scheme with period in between 8s and 10s. The fewer number

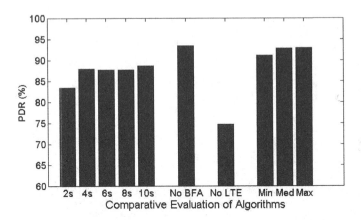

**Fig. 7.** Packet Delivery Ratio (%) for different RAT selection schemes

of VHO signifies less reliance on the LTE interface while reducing VHO cost in terms of latency and the corresponding lost in data throughput.

The number of VHOs, significantly impact other performance metrics. Fig. 7 illustrates the packet delivery ratio (PDR) statistics. The PDR for the periodic switching scheme varies between 80% to 90%. Higher number of VHOs results in higher delays which in turn result in lower delivery of beacons that could have been delivered during the VHO delays. The PDR for No BFA and our proposed mechanism are quite comparable whereas No LTE suffers from severe reliability issues which are mainly due to higher network load.

As shown in Fig. 8, in No BFA the performance in terms of lower number of VHOs and higher PDR is completely offset due to higher latency. No LTE, results in lower beacon exchange latency because of the direct communication among the vehicles. By switching access technologies only when it is necessary

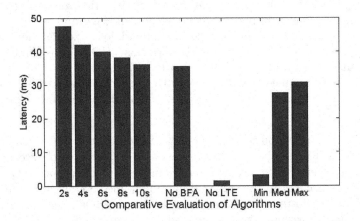

**Fig. 8.** Latency for different RAT selection schemes

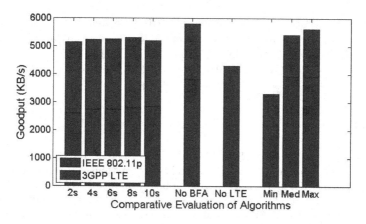

**Fig. 9.** Goodput for different RAT selection schemes

without sacrificing the QoS requirements for an application, overall the proposed RAT selection mechanism achieved considerably lower latency.

Fig. 9 compares different schemes in terms of goodput. The bar plots are stacked comparing the contribution of each access technology to the total achievable goodput. Schemes with dual-interfaces attain comparable goodput, however the contribution by each access technology differs. In periodic switching role of each interface is similar. No BFA performs well, however at the cost of significantly higher delays with higher involvement of the LTE interface. For the proposed RAT selection mechanism the IEEE 802.11p interface delivers most of beacons whereas the use of LTE interface is reasonably lower than all other schemes.

## 5   Conclusion

In hybrid vehicular networks, efficient RAT selection while simultaneously achieving QoS requirements is a challenging task. In this paper a RAT selection algorithm is proposed in context of IEEE 802.11p based infrastructure-less and LTE based infrastructure-based cellular networks. The key idea is to use parameters like network load and desired QoS application requirements to make switching decisions between the two radio access technologies. In order to reduce the number of vertical handovers (VHOs), the algorithm reduces the beaconing frequency as permissible by the application's QoS requirements. Simulations show that by locally resolving the network load issues result in lower VHO frequency. Moreover, a comparative study with several other competitor mechanisms show that the proposed work achieve considerable performance improvements in terms of packet delivery ratio, latency and application-level throughput or goodput.

**Acknowledgments.** This work was made possible by NPRP Grant No.: 5-1080-1-186 from the Qatar National Research Fund (a member of The Qatar Foundation). The statements made herein are solely the responsibility of the authors.

J. Toutouh was supported by Grant AP2010-3108 and Est13/00988 of the Spanish Ministry of Education. This research has been partially funded by project number 8.06/5.47.4142 in collaboration with the VSB-Technical University of Ostrava) and UMA/FEDER FC14-TIC36. University of Malaga, International Campus of Excellence Andalucia Tech.

# References

1. Park, Y., Kuk, S., Kim, H., Ha, J., Liang, C.J., JeongGil, K.: A feasibility study and development framework design for realizing smartphone-based vehicular networking systems. IEEE Transactions on Mobile Computing (TMC) 99 (2014)

2. Hameed Mir, Z., Filali, F.: Lte and ieee 802.11p for vehicular networking: A performance evaluation. EURASIP Journal on Wireless Communications and Networking 2014(1), 89 (2014)

3. Hameed Mir, Z., Filali, F.: On the Performance Comparison between IEEE 802.11 p and LTE-based Vehicular Networks. In: IEEE 79th Vehicular Technology Conference (VTC2014-Spring) (May 2014)

4. Vinel, A.: 3gpp lte versus ieee 802.11 p/wave: which technology is able to support cooperative vehicular safety applications? IEEE Wireless Communications Letters 1(2), 125–128 (2012)

5. ISO: Intelligent transport systems-communications access for land mobiles (calm)-architecture. ISO/DIS 21217 (2006)

6. IEEE: Local and metropolitan area networks: Media independent handover services. IEEE Draft Standard P802.21/D13 (2008)

7. IEEE: Ieee standard for information technology–local and metropolitan area networks–specific requirements–part 11: Wireless lan (mac) and (phy) specifications amendment 6:wave. IEEE Std 802.11p-2010 (2010)

8. LTE: Overview of 3gpp release 8, http://www.3gpp.org/Release-8 (2010)

9. Wu, L., Sandrasegaran, K. (eds.): A Study on Radio Access Technology Selection Algorithms. Springer (2012)

10. Maria Vegni, A., Inzerilli, T., Cusani, R.: Seamless Connectivity Techniques in Vehicular Ad-hoc Networks. In: Advances in Vehicular Networking Technologies. InTech (2011)

11. Bansal, G., Cheng, B., Rostami, A., Sjöberg, K., Kenney, J.B., Gruteser, M.: Comparing LIMERIC and DCC approaches for VANET channel congestion control. In: 6th IEEE International Symposium on Wireless Vehicular Communications, WiVeC 2014, Vancouver, BC, Canada, September 14-15, pp. 1–7 (2014)

12. Hasib, A., Fapojuwo, A.: Analysis of common radio resource management scheme for end-to-end qos support in multiservice heterogeneous wireless networks. IEEE Transactions on Vehicular Technology 57(4), 2426–2439 (2008)

13. Vegni, A., Little, T.: Hybrid vehicular communications based on v2v-v2i protocol switching. Intl. Journal of Vehicle Information and Communication Systems (IJVICS) 2(3/4) (2011), doi:10.1504/IJVICS.2011.044263

14. Liu, X., Li, V., Zhang, P.: Nxg04-4: Joint radio resource management through vertical handoffs in 4g networks. In: Global Telecommunications Conference, GLOBECOM 2006, pp. 1–5. IEEE (November 2006)

15. Tolli, A., Hakalin, P., Holma, H.: Performance evaluation of common radio resource management (crrm). In: IEEE International Conference on Communications, ICC 2002, vol. 5, pp. 3429–3433 (2002)

# Performance Analysis of ITS-G5 for Dynamic Train Coupling Application

Hong Quy Le, Andreas Lehner, and Stephan Sand

Germance Aerospace Center (DLR)
Institute of Communications and Navigation
Hong.Le@dlr.de

**Abstract.** Virtual coupling is a technique that shall allow trains driving on the same track with quasi-constant distance. This would also enable dynamical joining and splitting of trains while driving, thus providing the flexibility for railway operators to adapt to the changing traffic demands and to increase the throughput on todays overloaded lines. In order to realize dynamic train coupling, position and speed information must be reliably exchanged between trains with very low latency. Cooperative transportation systems (C-ITS), where road vehicles cooperate by exchanging messages, has received a lot of attention recently. In Europe, ITS-G5, which uses IEEE 802.11p technology for radio access, has been chosen for C-ITS. IEEE 802.11p offers the ability of direct communications between vehicles, i.e. ad hoc communications, for up to a few kilometers. The idea is to exploit IEEE 802.11p for dynamic train coupling. In this work, we discuss the use and the performance of IEEE 802.11p for Train-to-Train (T2T) communications along with Car-to-Car (C2C) communications. We address the influence of C2C communication on the performance of T2T communication and simple methods to reduce the interference from C2C users on T2T users.

## 1 Introduction

Portion working refers to the operational practice of coupling two or more trains together over common sections. Today coupling is a time consuming procedure which can only be performed during a stop in a station. To efficiently implement portion working and to increase the route throughput in general, trains should have the ability of forming together into a longer train and also separating again while driving. The trains should be no longer mechanically coupled as today's technology, but electronically via wireless communication - without physical connection to each other. This concept is referred as *Dynamic Train Coupling*. The aim here is to safely control the spacing between train sets such that they can be regarded as a single train by exchanging information about distance, relative velocity and acceleration. On the trip, the train sets are electronically coupled and drive together as a single train (platoon), supported by optical or radar measurements of the distance to the vehicle in front. They can dynamically join and leave when needed. For this to work, the train sets locate themselves using route

M. Kassab et al. (Eds.): Nets4Cars/Nets4Trains/Nets4Aircraft 2015, LNCS 9066, pp. 129–140, 2015.
DOI: 10.1007/978-3-319-17765-6_12

maps, GNSS and sensors like odometers, accelerometers and gyros. Then they transmit this data via direct mobile to mobile communications. No installation of additional signals or guards on the rail tracks will be needed. Each train shall use the the status information from other trains to control its own acceleration and speed with the help of a linear longitudinal distance controller.

The reliability and safety of dynamic coupling depends highly on the real-time status information update which depends on the reliability of the wireless transmission. The quality of the direct wireless transmission during dynamic coupling depends not only on the location and on the absolute velocity, i.e. the Doppler bandwidth of the multipath channel, but also on the relative speed, i.e. on the maneuver. The relative velocity causes the Doppler shift of the direct radio signal. This relative offset between the Doppler shift of LOS signal and the Doppler shift of multipath signals influence both the synchronization and the bit error rate (BER). Both of which ultimately affects the Message Error Rate (MER). The following table shows the ranges for absolute velocity, relative velocity, and required communication range for the different maneuver scenarios in different environments according to the concept of a Next Generation Train (NGT), which has been developed in an identically named research project at the German Aerospace Center DLR.

**Table 1.** Maneuver scenarios and requirements

| Maneuver | Near stations | Environment | Absolute velocity | Relative velocity | Communication range |
|---|---|---|---|---|---|
| coupling, de-coupling | near stations | urban, suburban | 0 - 100 km/h | 0 - 50 km/h | 0-3 km |
| coupling, de-coupling | en-route | rural | 100 - 300 km/h | 0 - 100 km/h | 0 - 10 km |
| platooning | near stations | urban, suburban | 0 - 100 km/h | 0 - 10 km/h | 0 - 500 m |
| platooning | en-route | rural | 100 - 400 km/h | 0 - 10 km/h | 0 - 1000 m |

## 1.1    Communications Systems for Train-to-Train Communications

Conventional mobile communication between trains is based on cellular mobile communication technologies, e.g. GSM-R, and the controlled distribution of the data by a centralized control center, e.g. signal tower. Though GSM-R specification already takes into account higher requirements than GSM, e.g. with respect to the availability, the call setup time through special "Fast Call Set-up" still takes two seconds [1]. With additional coverage of cells and sectors in the radio network, it is furthermore ensured with GSM-R, that the hand-over time remains under one second [2]. Likewise, radio resources are reserved for high-priority services, e.g. emergency calls. This, compared to GSM, is a trade-off between higher service quality for high priority services and a lower efficiency in the use of the spectrum resource. Despite this, requirements of time-critical safety applications are not met in general. The latency of existing connections is in the range of 200-500 ms [3][4]. Due to distributed stations, GSM-R has long communication range. However, the large latency in the data transmission makes GSM-R less suitable for time-critical application like dynamic train coupling.

In contrast to centralized mobile communication, decentralized direct mobile communication between trains does not need base stations and indirect communication via centrally organized networks. It allows instantaneous connection [5] and low latency ($\mu$s to some ms [6]) data transmission for real-time applications such as longitudinal distance control for train platooning. In general the reliability of this kind of transmission increases with reduced distance between mobile users. However, the performance depends on the following factors which are relevant to dynamic coupling communication scenarios: propagation conditions as shadowing and multipath, i.e. communication range and data rate in direct mode, different frequency usage scenarios, i.e. different intra system interference conditions, different movement scenarios, and different user density scenarios.

An existing decentralized mobile communication system that has been assessed in [6] for T2T communication is TETRA in Direct Mode Operation (DMO) [5]. With TETRA in 400 MHz UHF band, a relatively large communication range is achievable even for non-LOS. With maximum transmit power of 40 dBm in DMO, the range in the railway environment is typically 3 km (urban) and up to 20 km (rural). 25 kHz bandwidth is available in each channel. The standard supports data rate of 7.2/14.4/21.6/28.8 kbits/s [5]. For strong multipath environment, smaller data rates are used to increase the transmission reliability.

The relatively large communication range of TETRA fits the needs of safe virtual coupling of trains in dynamic train coupling scenarios during the approach phase. But the limited data rate does not support safe operation at close distances. Therefore in addition a link with a higher data rate and a range of approximately 1-2 km is required.

## 2   ITS-G5 for T2T Communications

ETSI TC ITS has standardized ETSI ITS-G5 [8], a Vehicular Ad-hoc NETwork (VANET) communication standard based on IEEE 802.11p [9]. ETSI ITS-G5 mainly describes the physical (PHY) and medium access control (MAC) sublayer of ITS stations operating in the 5.9 GHz frequency band. It covers the frequency ranges G5A, G5B and G5C, of which G5A is dedicated for safety and safety related applications. Other applications have to use the G5B or G5C frequency bands. Since our interests lie in the area of safety applications, this paper is focusing on ITS-G5A. The PHY layer of G5A defines three 10 MHz channels, one control channel (CCH) and two service channels (SCH1 and SCH2), which allow vehicles to send with transmit power of up to 33 dBm. The modulation scheme which is used for ITS-G5A is Orthogonal Frequency Division Muliplexing (OFDM). This technique provides data rates from 3 Mbits/s up to 27 Mbits/s per channel.

## 2.1    Challenges

One of the main challenge in the design of an ad hoc network is to effectively control the common medium access. While in cellular networks the media access is usually controlled by base stations, and the cell arrangement and frequency reuse is optimized to cause minimum interference from the nodes in neighboring cells, the character of vehicular ad hoc networks requires distributed solutions that strongly depend on the node density and on the communication range, respectively the interference range of nodes in the neighborhood [15].

When using the control channel CCH of ITS-G5A for T2T communications, the CCH channel must be shared not only between T2T users but also between T2T and C2C users. The MAC layer of ITS-G5A uses a Carrier Sense Multiple Access with Collision Avoidance (CSMA/CA) scheme to access the shared media. CSMA/CA is known to perform well in non-congested networks, but degrades dramatically with a strong increase of network load [10]. Therefore, for scenarios, where the density of C2C users is low, a good performance of ITS-G5A for T2T can be expected. However, for scenarios with a high density of C2C users, i.e. especially when the railway is adjacent to densely used roads, a high interference from C2C on T2T can be expected. Thus, the influence of C2C on T2T must be taken into account when using ITS-G5A for dynamic coupling, and methods to lower the interference form C2C users must be developed.

## 2.2    Performance Improvement Methods

Generally, in order to increase the reliability of T2T communication when sharing the ITS-G5A channel with C2C communication users, interference reduction methods can be exploited.

**Increase of T2T Transmit Power.** In road-traffic 20 dBm transmit power is recommended for C2C communication to reduce interference and allow more nodes to transmit simultaneously [14]. For road safety applications, the status information from the closest cars is most important. Thus the communication range can usually be reduced. However, in T2T communication the requirement on the communication range is more stringent, because the stability of a platoon can only be ensured when each vehicle receives not only the data from the vehicle in front but also from the platoon leading vehicle [16]. Thus, a higher communication range is needed for the longer railroad vehicles. A simple solution is using the maximum allowed ITS-G5A transmit power for T2T communication. Due to the very low maximum amount of train-sets within the communication range compared to cars, the interference of high power T2T packets on the road users is supposed to have low impact.

**Reduce Packet Length.** Packets with shorter duration have lower error probability of transmission error for a given Bit-Error-Rate (BER) than packets with longer duration. Compared to road traffic safety applications, dynamic coupling application requires less information. This allows the use of shorter packet length for T2T communications. According to [17], a packet size of 128 bytes is sufficient on todays Wired Train Bus (WTB), There are reserved bytes available in these packets [18], which can be used for additional data and authentication bits that are required for a wireless approach supporting dynamic coupling application.

**Use Directional Antennas.** There are some basic differences between traffic on road and rail. For example, in road traffic cars can freely change lanes to overtake other cars. In contrast to that, in rail traffic trains move on a fixed track and they can not overtake other trains on the same track. For railway dynamic coupling application exploiting T2T communications, the trains are only interested in the messages from the trains in front and the trains from behind it. In rural area, the rail track is mostly straight or with large radius curves. These characteristics allow the use of directional antennas. The advantage of using directional antennas is twofold. First, it reduces the interference from C2C users. Second, it increases the received signal power at the train receivers.

## 3   Analysis of ITS-G5A for T2T Communication

To investigate the performance of ITS-G5A for T2T communications, we consider a "worst case" scenario, where a very high level of interference from C2C communication is assumed. The scenario consists of a 10 km railway track parallel to a 10 km highway with 3 lanes in each direction as depicted in Fig. 1. For each direction, the maximum allowed speed on each lane is 32 m/s, 36 m/s, and 40 m/s respectively. The vehicles are generated in SUMO (traffic simulator) [11]. In each simulation step, the position of the cars and trains are fed to Veins (network simulator) [12]. Vehicles are generated for each lane with the vehicle arrival rate of 1000 vehicles/hour. The vehicles can change lane, and can over take other vehicles. The resulting vehicle density is then about 70 vehicles/km of highway. With a communication range of 1500m, there will be approximately 210 cars in the communication range of the trains. In total, approximately 700 vehicles on the 10 km section of the highway at the same time. All vehicles are moved every 100ms. The trains are also generated and controlled by SUMO. Each train is 120 m long according to the NGT specification. They are moving at a speed of 70m/s and with a distance of 100m between each other, which is regarded as a critical distance, because optical distance measurements might already fail. Thus the platoon stability and safety would only rely on the wireless communications. There are a total of 6 trains in this scenario. Due to the larger number of cars compared to trains, we expect from T2T communication a negligible interference on the average performance of C2C communication. To avoid edge effects, only the data from the middle part of the highway has been collected, i.e. only the transmission and reception carried out when the transmitter is situated between 1500m and 8500m have been analyzed.

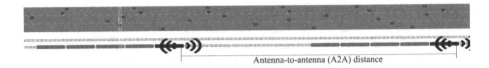

**Fig. 1.** Simulation traffic scenario

## 3.1    Performance Metrics

Two different performance metrics have been selected for evaluation, describing the overall performance of 802.11p for dynamic train coupling: Update delay and end-to-end delay.

**Update Delay.** is defined as the time elapsed between two consecutive successfully received messages from a specific TX at a specific RX. This performance metric measures the time between updated information from the transmitter that reaches the receiver.

**End-to-end Delay.** is the time elapsing from message generation at the application of the transmitter until it arrives at the application layer of the receiver. The end-to-end delay is a relevant metric for dynamic train coupling because it already accounts for other delay metrics, for example: Processing delay, queuing delay, contention delay, propagation delay, and packet transmission time.

## 3.2    Radio Propagation Model

Radio propagation models are an important part of the evaluation of vehicular networks. ITS-G5 operates on 5.9 GHz frequency band and in an ad-hoc network topology. Signals transmitted at such high carrier frequency are considered to be highly affected by the many metallic structures and objects in the railway environment.

Channel characterization through measurements in road traffic application was already conducted [12], but the specific T2T situation has not been investigated yet. As observed from measurement in VHF band [7], the T2T channel might be different to the C2C channel. Due to the lack of T2T channel characterization at 5.9 GHz we consider in this report, a simple pathloss model for radio propagation. However, a more accurate channel model shall be determined from measurements that are planned as future work.

## 3.3    Simulation Results

The parameter set that has been used for simulations is shown in Table 2. For each scenario, we run 30 Monte Carlo simulations.

**Table 2.** Simulation parameters

| Beacon length | 400 bytes, 128 bytes (depending on scenario) |
|---|---|
| Beacon rate | 10 Hz |
| Beacon priority | 3 (highest) |
| Channel model | simple pathloss model with exponent 2.35 |
| Carrier frequency | 5.89 GHz |
| Carrier sense threshold | -89 dBm |
| Noise power | -99 dBm |
| Transmit power | 33 dBm, 20 dBm (depending on scenario) |
| Transmission rate | 6 Mbps |
| Antenna pattern | omni-directional, bidirectional (depending on scenario) |
| BER, PER | measurement based model (default provided by Veins) |

**Scenario 1: 33 dBm Transmit Power and 400 Bytes Packet for Cars and Trains.** The result for the worst case scenario with respect to interference, when cars and trains use 33 dBm transmit power and 400 bytes packets, is shown in Fig. 2. The distance in the legend of the plot shows the antenna-to-antenna (A2A) distance between the trains, e.g. the antenna-to-antenna distance between the first train and the second train is 220 m which is the sum of the distance between two trains (set to 100 m for these simulations) and the length of the first train (cf. Fig. 1). Similary, the A2A distance of other train pairs can be calcualted. As shown in Fig. 2, the further the A2A distance between the trains, the worse the update delay. The reliability decreases with the distance. For example, the probability that the update delay exceeds 0.5 s is $3 \cdot 10^{-3}$ for A2A distance of 220 m and $7 \cdot 10^{-2}$ for A2A distance of 440 m.

**Scenario 2: 33 dBm Transmit Power for Cars and Trains, 400 Bytes Packet for Cars and 128 Bytes Packet for Trains.** Generally, because of the difference between road-traffic and railway-traffic, the data that needs to be included in the CAM messages for cars is much larger than that for trains. In the following simulation, we consider a packet length of 128 bytes sufficient for trains (including all protocol overhead). The results are shown in Fig. 2. Compared to Scenario 1, it is clear that by using a shorter packet length, the update delay is improved for the trains. This is as expected, as for the same SINR, a shorter packet length results in lower PER for the same BER. By using 128 bytes long packets, an improvement of a factor of 2 is achieved at 220 m A2A distance and a factor of 3 at 440m A2A distance for a delay of 0.5 s.

**Scenario 3: 20 dBm Transmit Power for Cars and 33 dBm for Trains and 400 Bytes Packet.** In this simulation, we used 20 dBm transmit power for cars and the full transmit power of 33 dBm for trains. Both cars and trains transmit packets with 400 bytes. The results are shown in Fig. 3. Compared with the first two scenarios, the benefit of lowering the transmit power of cars is vital. Because of lower interference and contention, the update delay performance is

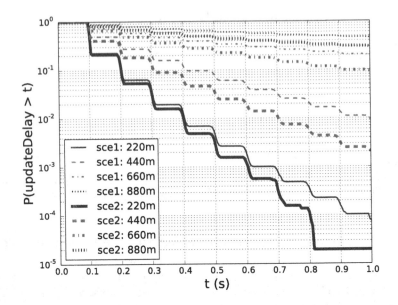

**Fig. 2.** Comparison of update delay for Scenarios 1 and 2

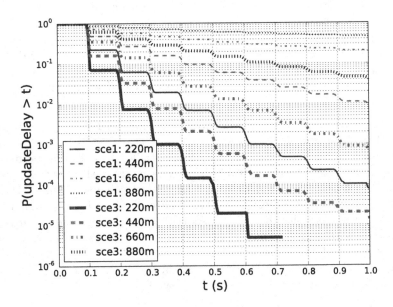

**Fig. 3.** Comparison of update delay for Scenarios 1 and 3

improved a lot at all A2A distances. At an A2A distance of 220 m, the probability that the update delay exceed 0.5 s is $4 \cdot 10^{-5}$, which is an improvement of a factor 50 compared to Scenario 1 and a factor 25 compared to Scenario 2.

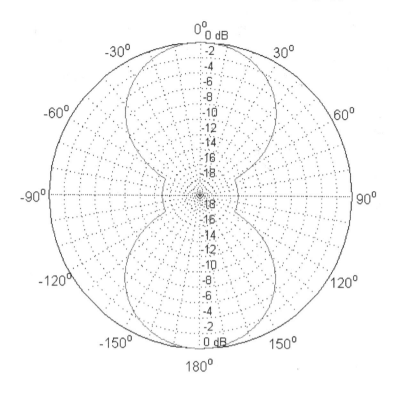

**Fig. 4.** Bi-directional antenna pattern

**Scenario 4: 33 dBm Transmit Power, Omni-directional Antenna for Cars and Bi-directional Antenna for Trains.** In this simulation, a simple bi-directional antenna with two main beams pointing to the front and behind of each train is used. The radiation pattern is shown in Fig. 4. The maximum antenna gain is 5 dB with 60° half-power-beam-width. The maximum suppression to the side is −10 dB. The transmit power of the trains is reduced to 28 dBm for a fair comparison with the other scenarios. The simulation results are shown in Fig. 5. With a directional antenna, the performance is increased at all A2A distances. The probability that the update delay exceeds 0.5 s is approximately $2 \cdot 10^{-5}$ at an A2A distance of 220m, which is an improvement of a factor 100 compared to Scenario 1 or a factor 2 compared to Scenario 3.

**End-to-end Delay.** The cumulative distribution function (CDF) of the end-to-end delay for the above four scenarios is presented in Fig. 6. The CDF is calculated as the average end-to-end delay of all messages at all the trains. The end-to-end delay of unsuccessful messages is assumed to be infinity. Clearly, Scenario 1 has the worst performance and Scenario 4 the best one. The probability of successful messages is only 69% in Scenario 1, 78% in Scenario 2, 92% in Scenario 3, and 93% in Scenario 4. In Scenario 3, in which the cars use 20 dBm transmit

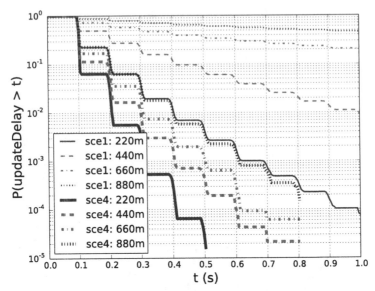

**Fig. 5.** Comparison of update delay for Scenarios 1 and 4

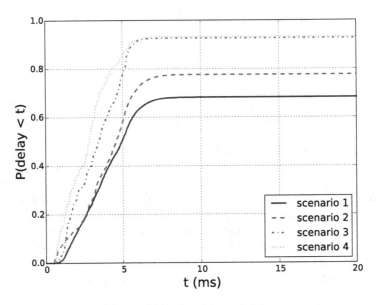

**Fig. 6.** CDF of end-to-end delay

power, the end-to-end delay of the trains is reduced due to less interference from the cars. In Scenario 4, in which the trains use directional antennas, the longer sensing range is compensated by the narrower interference region and higher packet reception probability. Hence, the lowest end-to-end delay is achieved in this scenario.

# 4    Conclusion and Future Work

In this paper, we have investigated the exploitation of ITS-G5 for dynamic coupling in rail transportation. As a result we have presented delay and latency statistics that are necessary for safety analysis of maneuvers. Within the NGT project the longitudinal distance controller is currently designed and will be simulated to determine the distance range between vehicles and the maximum number of train sets within a platoon that ensure safe operation when taking disturbances like wind forces or the loss of transmitted data packets into account.

We have addressed the challenges for the coexistence of T2T communication and C2C communication. Numerical simulations have been conducted to evaluate the performance of ITS-G5 for T2T communication with performance improvement methods under the interference from C2C communication. According to the results, the performance of ITS-G5 for T2T communication can be improved by increased transmit power, reduced packet length, or the use of directional antennas. Note that many more C2C messages than T2T messages have been transmitted as the number of cars has been 100 times more than the number of trains. Thus, we expect negligible interference from the T2T communication on the average performance of C2C communication, which needs to be further studied.

In the simulations, we have used a simple radio channel model. Thus, a more detailed investigation of the radio channel through measurements is necessary. Therefore, a next step is to use ITS-G5 in the T2T communication environment. Moreover, we plan to consider rail track curvatures in our simulations, where the mismatched between the moving direction of the trains, e.g. during a curved track, must be accounted for. It is furthermore planned to investigate what happens if there is no line-of-sight connection between the trains.

# References

1. Hillenbrand, W., Hofestaedt, H.: GSM-R Traffic Model for Radio-based Train Operation. World Congress Railway Research WCRR 2001, Cologne, Germany (2001)
2. Kastell, K., et al.: Improvements in Railway Communication via GSM-R. In: Proceedings VTC Spring 2006, pp. 3026–3030 (2006)
3. ERTM/ETCS-Class 1.GSM-R Interfaces Class 1 Requirements Subset-093-V230, 2005.10.10 (2005)
4. UIC Project EIRENE System Requirements Specification V.15
5. ETSI EN 300 396-3 V1.3.1(2006-2008). Terrestrial Trunked Radio (TETRA); Technical requirements for Direct Mode Operation (DMO); Part 3: Mobile station to mobile station (MS-MS) Air Interface (AI) protocol
6. Lehner, A., Rico Garcia, C., Strang, T.: On the Performance of TETRA DMO Short Data Service in Railway VANETs. In: Wireless Personal Communications, Springer Netherlands (2012), doi:10.1007/s11277-012-0656-9 ISSN 0929-6212
7. Lehner, A., Rico García, C., Strang, T., Heirich, O.: Measurement and Analysis of the Direct Train to Train Propagation Channel in the 70 cm UHF-Band. In: Strang, T., Festag, A., Vinel, A., Mehmood, R., Rico Garcia, C., Röckl, M. (eds.) Nets4Trains/Nets4Cars 2011. LNCS, vol. 6596, pp. 45–57. Springer, Heidelberg (2011)

8. ETSI ES 202 663, Intelligent Transport Systems: European profile standard on the physical and medium access layer of 5 GHz ITS, Draft Version 0.0.6 (2009)
9. IEEE 802.11 WG, IEEE P802.11p/D8.0, Draft Standard for Information Technology - Telecommunications and information exchange between systems - Local and metropolitan area networks - Specific requirements, Part 11: Wireless LAN Medium Access Control (MAC) and Physical Layer (PHY) specifications, Amendment 7: Wireless Access in Vehicular Environments, Draft Version 8.0 (2009)
10. Brakemeier, A.: White Paper on Network Design Limits and VANET Performance, Version 0.5, Car2Car Communication Consortium (2008)
11. Krajzewicz, D., et al.: SUMO (Simulation of urban mobility). In: Proceedings of the 4th Middle East Symposium on Simulation and Modelling (2002)
12. Sommer, C., German, R., Dressler, F.: Bidirectional coupled network and road traffic simulation for improved IVC analysis. IEEE Transactions on Mobile Computing 10(1), 3–15 (2011)
13. Sjoeberg, K., et al.: Measuring and using RSSI of IEEE802.11p. In: 17th World Congress on Intelligent Transportation Systems, ITS (2010)
14. Sjoeberg, K.: Medimum access control for vehicular ad hoc networks. Ph.D. dissertation, Chalmers University of Technology (2013)
15. Rico Garcia, C., Lehner, A., Robertson, P., Strang, T.: Performance of MAC protocols in beaconing Mobile Ad hoc Multibroadcast Networks. In: Vinel, A., Bellalta, B., Sacchi, C., Lyakhov, A., Telek, M., Oliver, M. (eds.) MACOM 2010. LNCS, vol. 6235, pp. 263–274. Springer, Heidelberg (2010)
16. Morbidi, F., Colaneri, P., Stanger, T.: Decentralized optimal control of a car platoon with guaranteed string stability. In: European Control Conference (ECC) 2013, Zürich, Switzerland, July 17-19 (2013)
17. UIC 556 2nd, Annex A - List of required information - Specification, Version 002.03 (2009)
18. Ochsner, R., et al.: ALP46 Comet V WTB Data Transfer Definition, NJT WTB/RDS Project Report (2002)

# Fair Preemption for Joint Delay Constrained and Best Effort Traffic Scheduling in Wireless Networks

Nicolas Gresset and Hervé Bonneville

Mitsubishi Electric R&D Centre Europe*, Rennes, France

**Abstract.** This paper proposes a preemptive scheduler that takes back resource previously allocated to best effort traffic users for minimizing the drop rate of delay constrained traffic users. An online implementation with low complexity is proposed, where the channel and QoS aware preemption metric takes into account the benefit for the drop rate of the delay constrained traffic and the cost on the fairness of the pre-allocated best effort traffic. By inverting the state of art order of the allocation of delay constrained and best effort traffic, we show that the fairness-throughput tradeoff curve of the best effort traffic is improved with no degradation on the drop rate of the delay constrained traffic. This scheduler is particularly relevant in cellular networks mixing safety-related and non-safety related (data) traffic, such as LTE for trains, tram, buses or cars.

## 1 Introduction

In the domain of Intelligent Transportation System (ITS), the communication infrastructure for safety applications are often isolated from other communication systems with a specific deployment. On the contrary, the most recent cellular networks provide a large panel of services to a multitude of users, with no strong guarantee of quality of service (QoS). A tram/bus operator might desire to cover a city with a cellular network, for example using the LTE technology, and to take the best benefit of this deployment by offering a large panel of services: safety related (data) traffic for the automatic tram control, CCTV, passenger information, infotainment, and even Internet access provisioning.

In order for the future ITS systems to propose new services to their customers, or for the cellular networks to host safety related services, a step forward must be made in terms of multi-user technologies with a strong guarantee of QoS. The scheduling of an heterogeneity of services with various quality of services is part of the radio resource management (RRM), which is an essential topic in cellular telecommunications (see [1] for a recent survey on RRM for LTE networks). A survey of the most common scheduling problems and technologies is given in [2]. Some multi QoS schedulers have been proposed for wireless networks [3][4], but they do not usually allow a low complexity implementation.

* This work was performed within project SYSTUF, which is subsidized by the French ministry of Industry in the framework of the AMI ITS program.

M. Kassab et al. (Eds.): Nets4Cars/Nets4Trains/Nets4Aircraft 2015, LNCS 9066, pp. 141–152, 2015.
DOI: 10.1007/978-3-319-17765-6_13

The choice of the metric to be optimized by the scheduler is crucial and usually divided into two families (see [2] for a complete overview of QoS oriented scheduler types):

- Delay-constrained metrics: the metrics consider the time to deadline of each packet with no considerations on the average transmission rate. This is particularly investigated when several data flows share the same channel.
- Channel-aware metrics: the metrics consider the channel capacity of each user, and optimize the system according to a sum-throughput/fairness trade-off. The scheduling can take benefit of the multi-user diversity, i.e., the statistical independence of fading realizations between resources and users (see, e.g., [5]).

Unlike most data traffics usually provided in cellular networks, the safety related traffic is most of the time periodical, with delay constraints below which the information is deprecated. If no packet is received during a given time window, emergency alarms are activated. For example, in an automatic train control environment, an emergency stop occurs. Thus, the drop rate is the main metric to be optimized and the challenge of the scheduler is to minimize it by allocating one user per resource (at most) by taking into account that each resource brings a different benefit to each user, leading to a channel and delay-aware scheduler. The safety related traffic can be seen as a delay-constrained traffic with very low drop rate requirements.

When all the safety users of the system have the same delay constraint (e.g., 50ms), the system performance is equal to the one of a system where all the packets transmission windows are aligned, which allows a per-block implementation of the scheduler. We will see in this paper that such a per-block definition of the problem naturally leads to converting the delay constraint into a rate constraint which further eases the channel awareness at the scheduler level, as discussed in Section 3. As a remark, the proposed solution also applies to non-equal delay constraints, but this is out of the scope of this paper. Such a goal has already been investigated in the literature [6], but usually arbitrarily combines Delay-constrained and Channel-aware metrics.

This paper is organized as follows: In section 2, we present general results on online utility-based and channel-aware schedulers, that will give the basis for our contribution presented in section 3 and 4. In section 3, we propose a new family of channel and delay aware online schedulers that optimize the drop rate of safety related traffic. In section 4, we propose a new scheduling strategy based on an initial allocation of the best effort traffic, followed by a fair preemption allocation of the safety related traffic, taking into account both the benefit of a resource selection in terms of drop rate and the cost on the best effort traffic. This approach is inspired from our previous work [4], the contribution of this paper allowing to drastically simplify the implementation of the scheduler while providing similar performance. Finally, in section 5, simulation results show the high gain provided by the proposed approach for best effort traffic, while keeping the drop rate of the delay-constrained traffic to its target.

# 2    Generalities on Multi-user Scheduling

We consider that the wireless system resource is divided into resource allocation blocks (that we will call *resources* in the rest of the paper) defining elementary square divisions of the frequency and time resource in an OFDM system. We assume that the multi-user scheduler works on a $n_t \times n_f$ time-frequency grid of resource allocation blocks where the total frequency bandwidth is $n_f$ times a resource allocation block bandwidth and the scheduling depth is $n_t$ times a resource allocation block length. Information can be transmitted at rate $r_k(i)$ in downlink to the $k$-th user on the $i$-th resource in the time-frequency grid. We assume that this rate can be estimated in advance by taking into account physical layer parameters, and more precisely from the link adaptation strategy, the link quality and the user mobility parameters.

## 2.1    Utility-Based Scheduling

Let us consider the problem of allocating an average rate $R_k$ to each user $k$. We focus on a sub-class of schedulers relying on utility functions of the rates, which solve the following optimization problem

$$\max_{\{R_k\}} \sum_k U_k(R_k), \quad s.t. \quad \{R_k\} \in \mathcal{C}$$

where $U_k(.)$ is a concave monotonically increasing function of the rate $R_k$ and $\mathcal{C}$ is the convex set of achievable rates, as defined by the system capacity limits. In other words, this limit can be defined by a resource sharing as follows: The rate of each user is defined as

$$R_k = \sum_{i \in \omega_k} r_k(i), \quad s.t. \quad \bigcup_k \omega_k \subset \Omega \tag{1}$$

where $\omega_k$ is the set of resource indexes allocated to user $k$, and $\Omega$ is the set of indexes of the system resources.

This defines a combinatorial optimization problem for which the exhaustive search is most often intractable, and for which many heuristics can be designed.

## 2.2    Online Scheduling

In this paper, we only address *online schedulers* that do not involve iterative decisions, i.e., we assume that one resource-user allocation is done at each step of the scheduling process. In other words, the rate of the $k$-th user evolves through the scheduling steps $n$. It is updated according to the scheduler decision of allocating the $\hat{i}_n$-th resource providing the rate $r_{\hat{k}_n}(\hat{i}_n)$ to the user $\hat{k}_n$, for example according to the averaging rule

$$\forall k, \quad R_k(n+1) = R_k(n) + \frac{1}{n}\left(\delta(\hat{k}_n, k)r_k(\hat{i}_n) - R_k(n)\right)$$

where $\delta(.,.)$ is the Kronecker's delta function indicating which user has been selected by the scheduler. It can be shown that under the utility-based and online scheduler assumption, and by using a Taylor expansion of the utility function $U_k(.)$ around $R_k(n)$, the optimization problem is equivalent to the resource-user selection

$$(\hat{k}_n, \hat{i}_n) = \arg \max_{k,i \in \Omega_n} U'_k(R_k(n))r_k(i) \tag{2}$$

where $\Omega_n$ is the set of free resources at the step $n$ of the scheduler, and where $U'_k(.)$ is the derivative of the utility function $U_k(.)$.

### 2.3 Channel Aware Scheduling

In the wireless communication domain, the most famous application of online schedulers targets best effort traffic under a full buffer assumption. In other words, the scheduler is resource-oriented and the goal is to find which user to be sent on each resource. In a case of throughput maximization, the user with the best rate should be allocated in each resource at the price of strongly degrading the throughput of the worst channel-quality users. Thus, a fairness metric allows to make a trade-off between the system spectral efficiency, related to the sum throughput, and each user experience. The $\alpha$-fair utility functions (see [7])

$$\begin{cases} f_\alpha(x) = \frac{x^{1-\alpha}}{1-\alpha}, & \alpha \geq 0, \alpha \neq 1 \\ f_\alpha(x) = \log(x), \alpha = 1 \\ f'_\alpha(x) = x^{-\alpha} \end{cases}$$

allow to define a family of schedulers with a good throughput/fairness tradeoff [5] by maximizing $\sum_k f_\alpha(R_k(n))$. The resource-user selection criterion of the online scheduler (2) becomes

$$(\hat{k}_n, \hat{i}_n) = \arg \max_{k,i \in \Omega_n} \frac{r_k(i)}{R_k(n)^\alpha} \tag{3}$$

where $\alpha = 1$ falls back to the well know *proportional fair* scheduler.

## 3    A Channel and Delay Aware Scheduling Metric

Let us consider that several packets are sent to several users, the $k$-th packet having a delay constraint of $\ell_k$ resource allocation blocks and a packet with a payload of $p_k$ bits. The definition of the delay constraint in number of resource allocation blocks is convenient but artificial, and can be computed as the time delay constraint divided by the time length of one resource allocation block and multiplied by the number of resource allocation blocks $n_f$ in the total frequency bandwidth. We consider that only one packet is destined to one user within the scheduling window, and multiple packets sent to one user can be seen as multiple packets sent to as many users. If the packet payload cannot be received within the delay constraint, we consider that the packet is not useful for the application and dropped. Thus, the metric of interest that characterizes the efficiency of the scheduler for allocating the delay constrained packets in time is the drop rate. This data traffic definition fits well with many safety related services. The minimal rate at which the packet must be sent for avoiding a drop event at the end of the delay window is $\rho_k = p_k / \ell_k$.

The ratio $R_k(n)/\rho_k$ gives an information whether the current average rate is beyond or behind the rate required for not dropping the packet. Thus, a conversion of the delay constraint into a minimal rate constraint is possible, as in [8]. Several *guaranteed bit rate* schedulers have already been investigated (see, e.g., [9]), but they do not optimize the drop rate of delay constrained users. When the system is overloaded, it is preferable to sacrifice few users for the others not to be dropped. This makes a main difference with the guaranteed bit rate criterion which tries to provide an acceptable rate to all users, that can be below the target rate. Thus, we intend to maximize the number of packets currently scheduled that will not be dropped by choosing the Drop Rate (DR)-related utility function

$$U_k^{(DR)}(R_k(n)) = \mathcal{I}\left(\frac{R_k(n)}{\rho_k}\right)$$

where $\mathcal{I}(.)$ is an indicator function such that $\mathcal{I}(x \geq 1) = 1$ and $\mathcal{I}(x < 1) = 0$. This conversion of the delay constraint into a rate constraint is particularly relevant in the safety scenario where all the safety packets are sent periodically with the same delay window. Additional criteria can be added when the delay windows are not aligned in order to boost the priority of packets close to the deadline (see many examples in [2]).

Advanced algorithms are required for solving the optimization problem (1) with the utility function $U_k^{(DR)}$. However, $U_k^{(DR)}$ being not concave, it cannot directly be applied to online schedulers (2). Thus, we propose to rely on the $\alpha$-fair utility functions which provide a good behavioral approximation of $\mathcal{I}(.)$. We call $\beta$ the fairness parameter for the delay constrained traffic, and the utility function $U_k(R_k(n)) = f_\beta(R_k(n)/\rho_k)$ results in the following resource and user selection

$$(\hat{k}_n, \hat{i}_n) = \arg \max_{k,i \in \Omega_n} \left(\frac{\rho_k}{R_k(n)}\right)^{\beta-1} \frac{r_k(i)}{R_k(n)} \tag{4}$$

which can be seen as the product of the proportional fair selection argument $r_k(i)/R_k(n)$ which relates to the channel usage of each user, and a fairness compression of $\rho_k/R_k(n)$ which is the inverse of the estimated packet transmission achievement $R_k(n)/\rho_k$, the priority of users with the lowest transmission achievement values being boosted. An other interpretation is that $\rho_k/R_k(n)$ is proportional to the estimated amount of resource needed until the packet transmission end, with a boost for the users requiring more resource.

When $\beta \to +\infty$, the optimization attempts to maximize the minimum of the transmission achievement $R_k(n)/\rho_k$, which will provide a very low drop rate if the free resource is high enough to schedule all users with their average rate (low load scenario). We observe that the resource and user selection is performed according to $\rho_k/R_k(n)$ which does not take the instantaneous rate $r_k(i)$ into account. We can expect that, as soon as the free amount of resource is not high enough, the drop rate will rise quickly to 100%. Indeed, such scheduler tends to equalize the transmission achievement rate of all users, which most probably results in all packets not reaching their full transmission achievement before deadline when the system is overloaded.

When $\beta = 1$, the selection criterion falls back to the proportional fair's one, which optimizes the resource usage but not the drop rate. However, when the system load is high, rejecting a user with high resource requirements can be beneficial for many others and for the average drop rate among users. This ultimately would be the strategy of the scheduler with $\beta = 0$, where the max-rate strategy is used for each resource allocation and shows the best performance at very high drop rate and system load regions, out of the scope of this paper.

Thus, this family of schedulers parametrized by $\beta$ allows for minimizing the drop rate according to the system load. The parameter $\beta$ can be for example chosen dynamically according to a target drop rate. Alternatively, several instances of the scheduler can be run in parallel with different $\beta$ values, and a selection can be made on the one providing a drop rate closest to the target. We will see in the simulation results section that a selection between two schedulers with parameters $\beta = 1$ and $\beta = 10$ is very representative of the optimized performance curve. For safety related traffic, the drop rate is usually small and a scheduler with $\beta = 10$ appropriate in all cases. As a remark, in [10], an arbitrary choice of the metric to be optimized has been proposed which is very similar to the $\beta = 2$ case.

## 4    Fair Preemption Strategy

We now consider that several delay-constrained (DC) users and best effort traffic (BET) users are sharing the same set of resources. In most state of art approaches, the highest priority is served first by a so-called preemptive scheduler, the lowest priority users being allocated on the remaining free resource. In the safety-related context, the DC users are of highest priority compared to the BET users.

In a previous work [4], we have proposed to allocate the BET users until no bottleneck on the resource arise for DC users, guarantying a low drop rate for DC users and maximizing the BET users throughput/fairness tradeoff. The bottleneck checking function can be of high complexity when the number of DC users is high. Also, a pre-processing step involves a segmentation of the DC packets, which introduces a sub-optimality for the BET throughput. Thus, we take a different approach in this paper that keeps the implementation complexity low and does not involve a packet segmentation step.

Let us now consider that a first round of scheduling has been made for the BET users according to the $\alpha$-fair scheduler with resource-user selection (3). As a result, the $j$-th resource is allocated to a BET user which gets the rate $v(j)$ on this resource. Then, at the end of the scheduling operation, the fairness metric is $\sum_{k'} f_\alpha(\sum_{j \in \omega'_{k'}} v(j))$, where $\omega'_{k'}$ is the set of resource indexes allocated to BET user $k'$.

In a second step, we perform the DC scheduler as described in section 3, and modify the resource-user selection by taking into account a cost experienced by the BET users when said resource is preempted by a DC user. We propose to define the cost $c(i)$ of the preemption of the resource $i$ previously allocated to the BET user $k'(i)$ as the loss on the fairness metric, where

$$c(i) = f_\alpha(\sum_{j\in\omega'_{k'(i)}} v(j)) - f_\alpha(\sum_{j\in\omega'_{k'(i)}} v(j) - v(i))$$

which leads to the following resource-user selection

$$(\hat{k}_n, \hat{i}_n) = \arg\max_{k,i\in\Omega_n} \frac{\left(\frac{\rho_k}{R_k(n)}\right)^{\beta-1} \frac{r_k(i)}{R_k(n)}}{c(i)} \tag{5}$$

This resource-user selection differs from the state of art, that usually combines arbitrarily resource-user selection criteria of QoS and channel aware schedulers (see many examples in [2]). Here, the pre-allocation of the BET traffic allows for precisely evaluating the impact of preemption on the global figure of merit.

## 5    Simulation Results

We perform static system level simulations of a multi-cell LTE cellular network with 10MHz bandwidth at 2GHz carrier frequency with nineteen 3-sectors base stations with an hexagonal deployment and 1732m inter-site distance. The antenna diagrams, transmitter and receiver parameters, as well as the path loss model are defined following the case 3 model of 3GPP (see A.2.1.1.1 in [11]). The users locations are selected at random and uniformly within the cell of interest, and Monte-Carlo simulations are performed on the user snapshots and channel realizations. In downlink, the OFDM modulation allows for dividing the time and frequency resource into 50 resource allocation blocks packed in the frequency domain, which are 180kHz-wide and 1ms-long and which carry 168 channel use (i.e., transmission of symbols over one sub-carrier in one OFDM symbol).

The small-scale fading follows an ITU 6-path Typical Urban channel model. We consider that one user is either subject to a *fast link adaptation* strategy where we assume that perfect Channel State Information is available at the transmitter, or to a *slow link adaptation* strategy where we assume that no Channel State Information is available at the transmitter. Fast link adaptation applies to low mobility users, while the slow link adaptation applies to high speed users. The rate obtained with a fast link adaptation on a given resource is estimated by the Shannon capacity limit according to the instantaneous signal to noise ratio experienced on each sub-carrier. The rate obtained with a slow link adaptation on a given resource is estimated by the highest value $R(1 - P_{out}(R, SINR))$, where $P_{out}(R, SINR)$ is the outage probability for a transmission on the given resource at rate $R$ with no channel state information knowledge at the transmitter but the long-term SINR (i.e, averaged over the fast fading). Usually, the long-term SINR is assumed constant in time and frequency, which involves that all the resources have the same rate for a given user.

We consider two classes of users. Firstly, the eNB scheduler receives *delay constrained (DC)* packets every 50ms with a fixed payload defined according to a given throughput. We assume for simplicity that all DC users/packets are received by the scheduler at the beginning of a 50ms-long window, which defines a scenario where a safety related server manages several users and wishes to send safety packets to each of them every $50ms$. Secondly, the eNB scheduler has buffers for data to be transmitted to *Best Effort Traffic (BET)* users, and we assume that the buffers always have enough data to serve said users (a.k.a. full buffer assumption). The scheduler works on blocks of $50 \times 50 = 2500$ resource allocation blocks in a block-wise fashion both for DC and BET users.

First, we evaluate the efficiency of the *Channel and delay aware scheduling* strategy proposed in Section 3. The number of DC users is 30 and no BET users are present in the system. All the DC users have the same throughput, and thus same packet payload. Fig. 1 shows the drop rate, i.e., the proportion of DC packets that could not be completely sent within the 50ms constraint length, as a function of each DC user throughput, when the DC users have a high or low mobility and subject to a slow or fast link adaptation, respectively. The performance of the proposed scheduler is shown for different parameters $\beta$. The simulation results confirm that larger $\beta$ values perform better for lower drop rates and smaller load (lower DC traffic user throughput). When the DC users have a high mobility, for $\beta \to +\infty$, a max-min scheduling decision is performed on the portion of payload already transmitted by each user, and provides the best performance at low load. This criterion does not take into account the instantaneous rate given by each resource. This is not detrimental in the slow link adaptation case since all the resource of the same user have the same rate, which is also the average rate playing a role in the portion of payload already transmitted. For $\beta = 1$, the scheduler falls back to a proportional fair scheduler that allows for providing a lower drop rate when the system is highly loaded. When the DC users have a low mobility, all the DC users have a sufficiently low speed to allow a fast link adaptation strategy. We observe the same behavior as for the high mobility, except for the $\beta \to +\infty$ performance, which is significantly worse than with $\beta = 10$ for relatively small values of the drop rate (around 1%). This is explained by the observation that the $\beta \to +\infty$ scheduler does not take into account the instantaneous rate of each resource, which varies because of the channel frequency selectivity and independence between users. Thus, it does not take benefit from the multi-user diversity which is one key gain factor for multi-user OFDM systems. Thus, a sufficiently large value $\beta$ (e.g., $\beta = 10$) takes into account both the delay constraint through the portion of payload already transmitted, and the channel-aware user fairness through the proportional fair metric (see (4)).

This paper targets safety related traffic with a low drop rate requirement. Thus, in the following, we set $\beta = 10$ as the parameter for scheduling the DC users. Admission control mechanisms can be used for controlling the system load and rejecting users that would endanger the QoS requirement of the DC users.

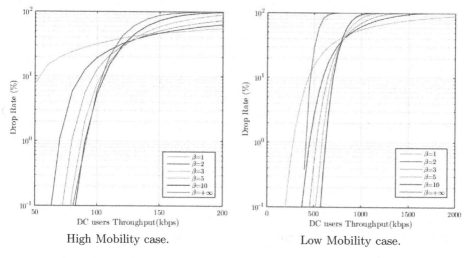

High Mobility case.                    Low Mobility case.

**Fig. 1.** Drop Rate as a function of each of the 30 DC users throughput for different values of the parameter $\beta$ of the channel and delay aware scheduler. The throughput is linearly related to the system load. Larger $\beta$ values provide lower drop rate when the system is close to full load.

Fig. 2 shows the compromise between the mean throughput and Jain's fairness index (see, e.g., [5]) for 30 BET users. High mobility and Low mobility are considered for 30 DC users. Their throughput is tuned to the limit that gives a quasi-null drop rate. The state of art approach is named *DC first, then BET*, and first allocates the DC traffic with an online scheduler using the metric (4). Then, it allocates the BET according to the metric (3) on the remaining free resource, with a variable parameter $\alpha$ that impacts the fairness-throughput compromise. The proposed approach is named *Fair Preemption* and first allocates the BET on all resources of the considered window of resource allocation blocks according to the metric (3) with a variable parameter $\alpha$; then allocates the DC traffic with an online scheduler using the metric (5). The *Fair Preemption* strategy highly improves the performance of BET users with no loss (null drop rate) for DC users. For the sake of comparison, we also have plotted the *Reservation and check* scheduler as presented in our previous work [4] comprising: a segmentation of the packets into smaller sub-packets according to the average user rate, a tagging of all resources that can carry each sub-packet, and an online BET scheduling with a check that no bottleneck occurs on the DC traffic. The packet segmentation and the high complexity of the checking function when many sub-packets are considered are the main drawbacks of this approach. For the simulations, we have limited the checking function to a random selection of 100 checks among the set of all possible checks, which explains that the throughput of BET for the *Reservation and check* can be outperformed by the *Fair Preemption*, especially for the high mobility scenario where all resources can carry the same rate. As a remark, the drop rate of *Reservation and check* is always equal to the one of

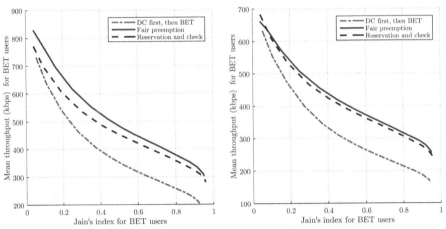

**Fig. 2.** Compromise between the mean throughput and Jain's fairness index for BET users. The 30 delay constrained users have a high (left figure) or low (right figure) mobility while the 30 BET users have a low mobility. The drop rate of DC users is null. The proposed scheduler with a fair preemption approach always outperforms the state of art approach. The parameter $\alpha$ is the fairness parameter used for the BET scheduling.

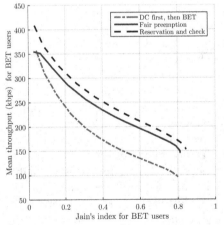
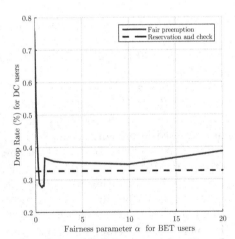

Compromise between the mean throughput and Jain's fairness index for BET users.

Drop Rate of DC users as a function of the fairness parameter used for the BET scheduling $\alpha$.

**Fig. 3.** The 30 delay constrained and 30 BET users have a low mobility. The throughput of DC users is 600kbps. The proposed scheduler with a fair preemption approach always provides improved BET performance with a similar drop rate for DC users.

*DC first, then BET.* The complexity of the proposed *Fair Preemption* is similar to the one of *DC first, then BET.*

In Fig. 3, in order to show that the drop rate and the BET throughput fairness are optimized altogether by our proposed scheduler, low mobility DC users are considered with a throughput of 600kbps that overloads the system for a portion of snapshots of users positions and leads to a non-null (yet low) drop rate. We observe that the drop rate is similar for the three strategies (the drop rate of *DC first, then BET* and *Reservation and check* are equal), while the *Fair Preemption* strategy highly improves the performance of BET users with respect to the *DC first, then BET*, with much lower complexity than *Reservation and check*. The same observation is made in Fig. 4, where the *DC* users have a high mobility and a throughput of 100*kbps* that leads to overloading for some snapshots, and for which the *Fair Preemption* marginally increases the drop rate with respect to the BET throughput improvement.

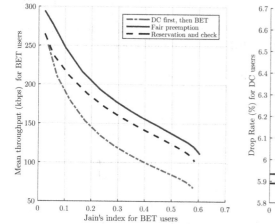

Compromise between the mean throughput and Jain's fairness index for BET users.

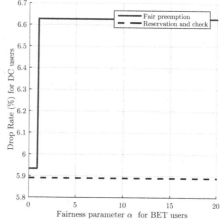

Drop Rate of DC users as a function of the fairness parameter used for the BET scheduling $\alpha$.

**Fig. 4.** The 30 delay constrained users have a high mobility. The throughput of DC users is 100kbps. The proposed scheduler with a fair preemption approach always provides improved BET performance with a similar drop rate for DC users.

## 6   Conclusion

In this paper, we have first proposed a channel and delay-aware scheduler that allows for optimizing the drop rate of safety related traffic, even when the wireless system is highly loaded. Then, we have presented a new preemption approach where the lowest priority (best effort) users are scheduled first, and some allocated resources taken back by a second step of high priority (delay constrained) scheduling, that takes into account both the delay constraints of the priority users and the throughput fairness of the best effort users. Future ITS networks mixing safety and non-safety services with an LTE-like wireless communication system will be particularly relevant applications of the results presented in this paper.

# References

1. Lee, Y.L., Chuah, T.C., Loo, J., Vinel, A.: Recent advances in radio resource management for heterogeneous lte/lte-a networks. IEEE Communications Surveys Tutorials 16(4), 2142–2180 (2014)
2. Capozzi, F., Piro, G., Grieco, L., Boggia, G., Camarda, P.: Downlink packet scheduling in lte cellular networks: Key design issues and a survey. IEEE Communications Surveys Tutorials 15(2), 678–700 (2013)
3. Zaki, Y., Weerawardane, T., Gorg, C., Timm-Giel, A.: Multi-qos-aware fair scheduling for lte. In: 2011 IEEE 73rd Vehicular Technology Conference (VTC Spring), pp. 1–5 (May 2011)
4. Gresset, N., Letessier, J., Bonneville, H.: A qoS-based multi-user scheduler applied to railway radio-communications. In: Berbineau, M., Jonsson, M., Bonnin, J.-M., Cherkaoui, S., Aguado, M., Rico-Garcia, C., Ghannoum, H., Mehmood, R., Vinel, A. (eds.) Nets4Trains 2013 and Nets4Cars 2013. LNCS, vol. 7865, pp. 31–45. Springer, Heidelberg (2013)
5. Schwarz, S., Mehlfuhrer, C., Rupp, M.: Throughput maximizing multiuser scheduling with adjustable fairness. In: 2011 IEEE International Conference on Communications (ICC), pp. 1–5 (June 2011)
6. Khattab, A.K.F., Elsayed, K.M.F.: Opportunistic scheduling of delay sensitive traffic in ofdma-based wireless networks. In: International Symposium on a World of Wireless, Mobile and Multimedia Networks, WoWMoM 2006, pp. 10–288 (2006)
7. Lan, T., Kao, D., Chiang, M., Sabharwal, A.: An axiomatic theory of fairness in network resource allocation. In: INFOCOM, 2010 Proceedings IEEE, pp. 1–9 (March 2010)
8. Svedman, P., Wilson, S.K., Ottersten, B.: A qos-aware proportional fair scheduler for opportunistic ofdm. In: 2004 IEEE 60th Vehicular Technology Conference, VTC2004-Fall, vol. 1, pp. 558–562 (September 2004)
9. Andrews, M., Qian, L., Stolyar, A.: Optimal utility based multi-user throughput allocation subject to throughput constraints. In: Proceedings IEEE 24th Annual Joint Conference of the IEEE Computer and Communications Societies, INFOCOM 2005, vol. 4, pp. 2415–2424 (March 2005)
10. Monghal, G., Pedersen, K.I., Kovacs, I.Z., Mogensen, P.E.: Qos oriented time and frequency domain packet schedulers for the utran long term evolution. In: IEEE Vehicular Technology Conference, VTC Spring 2008, pp. 2532–2536 (May 2008)
11. 3GPP, Further advancements for e-utra physical layer aspects, in TSG-RAN - E-UTRA, Tech. Rep. 36.814 (March 2010)

# Unleashing the Potential of LTE for Next Generation Railway Communications

Paula Fraga-Lamas, José Rodríguez-Piñeiro, José A. García-Naya, and Luis Castedo

Department of Electronics and Systems, University of A Coruña, Spain

**Abstract.** In an increasingly demanding marketplace that will put great strain on railway services, research on broadband wireless communication must continue to strive for improvement. Based on the mature narrowband GSM technology, Global System for Mobile Communications-Railways (GSM-R) has been deployed both for operational and voice communications. Although GSM-R fulfills the requirements of current railway services, it imposes limited capacity and high costs that restrict enhancements of operational efficiency, passenger security and transport quality. 4G Long Term Evolution (LTE) is expected to be the natural successor of GSM-R not only for its technical advantages and increasing performance, but also due to the current evolution of general-purpose communication systems. This paper examines the key features of LTE as well as its technical ability to support both the migration of current railway services and the provisioning of future ones.

**Keywords:** Railway applications, quality of service, LTE for railway, all-IP, VoLTE, interoperability, ProSe, GCSE, GSM-R.

## 1 Introduction

High-speed railway networks are extremely complex scenarios that have promoted many research initiatives primarily aiming to foster transportation quality. One of the strategic goals in high-speed rails focuses on the introduction of advanced broadband communication technologies allowing for improved services and coping with market needs in a rapidly changing landscape. Current railway communication technology was built in the beginning of the nineties considering readily available and well established mobile communication standards with great potential to fulfill the requirements of railway services at that time [1]. After a preliminary study on the usability of either Trans European Trunked RAdio (TETRA) or Global System for Mobile Communications (GSM), the latter was chosen because it was a proven technology in commercial use. Indeed, GSM Release 99 was standardized by European Telecommunications Standards Institute (ETSI) and it was well supported by its supplier association, the GSM Association (GSMA) Group. After extensive studies, GSM-R was finally standardized by the Union Internationale des Chemins de Fer (UIC) and the European Railways. The European Integrated Railway Radio Enhanced NEtwork (EIRENE) project was launched in 1992 as an alliance between

© Springer International Publishing Switzerland 2015
M. Kassab et al. (Eds.): Nets4Cars/Nets4Trains/Nets4Aircraft 2015, LNCS 9066, pp. 153–164, 2015.
DOI: 10.1007/978-3-319-17765-6_14

ETSI, railway operators and telecommunications manufacturers. EIRENE's aim was to specify the functional and technical requirements for railway mobile networks. Two leading working groups were established within EIRENE for this task: a functional group and a project team. The functional group defined the Functional Requirements Specification (FRS) which mainly describes the mandatory features to ensure interoperability across borders. The project team developed the System Requirements Specification (SRS) based on the functional requirements. This document defines the technical characteristics related to railway operation, thus identifying and specifying the additional Advanced Speech Call Items (ASCI) features [2].

A first draft of these EIRENE specifications was finalized in 1995 when the Mobile Radio for Railway Networks in Europe (MORANE) project was launched with the involvement of the UIC; the major railways in France, Italy and Germany; the European Commission, and a limited number of GSM suppliers. The aim was to specify, develop, test and validate prototypes of a new radio system, meeting both functional and system requirements specifications. In 1997, the UIC prepared a Memorandum of Understanding (MoU) to compel railway companies to only invest and cooperate in the implementation of GSM-R. This MoU was signed in 1998 by 32 railways all over Europe increasing up to 37 in 2009, including railways outside Europe. An Agreement on Implementation (AoI) came into effect in 2000 where the 17 signing railway companies have stated their intention to begin national GSM-R implementation by 2003 at the latest. From then on, GSM-R became the railway technology until now, when the rapid pace of commercial technologies are the driving force for further research on alternatives like LTE.

This paper provides an understanding of the progress of mobile technologies in railway domain since GSM-R. It describes the motivations for the different alternatives over time and the evolution of the railway requirements with its main specifications and recommendations. The aim of the study is to envision the potential contribution of LTE to provide additional features that GSM-R could never support.

The remainder of this article is structured as follows. Section 2 reviews GSM-R services. The aim is to identify what is required to roll-out LTE to address specific requirements for railway communication services. Next, Section 3 shows an overview of GSM-R shortcomings and LTE advantages. Current status of standardization is detailed in Section 4 in order to understand the evolution of the involved requirements and technologies. In Section 5, taking both the services and the associated operational requirements as a starting point, a formal analysis is introduced to study the feasibility of LTE for next generation railway networks. Next, the strategic roadmap to ensure a smooth migration is described in Section 6. Finally, the last section is devoted to the conclusions and future research lines.

## 2    GSM-R: Railway-Specific Services and Requirements

Based on GSM Phase 2 and Phase 2+ recommendations, GSM-R was analyzed to provide maximum redundancy and achieve maximum system availability. GSM-R provides two fundamental services: voice communication and transmission of European Train Control System (ETCS) messages. Both GSM-R and ETCS constitute the European Rail Traffic Management System (ERTMS) [3]. The UIC initiated the so-called ERTMS/GSM-R project to bring together existing and future implementers. Furthermore, ERTMS/GSM-R manages the UIC roll-out plan aiming to update the existing specifications of GSM-R. This common development has continued up to now, maintaining close cooperation with ETSI and the GSM-R industry.

The FRS version 7.4.0 [4] and SRS version 15.4.0 [5], designated as European Railway Agency (ERA) GSM-R Baseline 0 Release 4, were published in 2014 and represent the latest specifications. Such documents involve the description of mandatory requirements relevant to interoperability of the rail system within the European Community, according to the Directive 2008/57/EC [6], incorporating requirements for a major milestone towards an IP-based core network architecture [7].

The areas covered in the EIRENE SRS can be outlined as follows:

- GSM-R network configuration, applicable to ER-GSM band frequencies, provides a guidance to meet performance levels, GSM-R coverage, speed limitations, handover and cell selection, and call set-up time requirements. Broadcast and group call areas are also defined. The level of coverage should be at least 95% of the time over 95% of the designated coverage area for a radio installed in a vehicle with an external antenna.
- Mobile equipment specification distinguishes five types of mobile radios: Cab radio and the Human-Machine Interface (HMI) for transmission of voice and non-safety data; EIRENE-compliant general purpose radio; EIRENE-compliant operational radio with functions to support railway operations; shunting radio; and ETCS data-only radios.
- EIRENE numbering plan requirements and constraints, call routing and structure of Functional Numbers.
- Subscription management which handles the requirements for call priorities, encryption and authentication, broadcasts and Closed User Groups (CUGs).
- GSM-R operation modes: high-priority voice calls for operational emergencies (railway emergency calls); shunting mode, including the definition of user privileges; and an optional direct-mode communication providing short range fall-back communications between drivers and track-side personnel.

Some requirements are defined by individual railway companies [8]:

- Fixed network elements (links, switches, terminal equipment, etc) and their specifications with respect to Reliability, Availability, Maintainability and Safety (RAMS) (EN50126, EN50128, EN50129), network interconnections and capacity. The fixed network must also support a specified set of services to provide end-to-end functionality. The inter-working between the fixed and mobile side of the network must also be considered.

**Table 1.** Voice telephony services to be supported

| Voice-Call / Radio type | Cab | ETCS data only | General purpose | Operational | Shunting |
|---|---|---|---|---|---|
| Point-to-point | MI | NA | M | M | M |
| Public emergency | M | NA | M | M | M |
| Broadcast | M | NA | M | M | M |
| Group | MI | NA | M | M | M |
| Multi-party | MI | NA | O | O | M |

**Table 2.** Data services to be supported

| Data / Radio type | Cab | ETCS data only | General purpose | Operational | Shunting |
|---|---|---|---|---|---|
| Text message | MI | NA | M | M | M |
| General data applications | M | O | O | O | O |
| Automatic fax | O | NA | O | O | O |
| ETCS train control | NA | MI | NA | NA | NA |

- Requirements for signaling systems to be used within the fixed network.
- Non-mandatory specifications of controller equipment are provided by FRS, although details of such equipment and the interface between the equipment and the GSM-R network are assigned to the railway operator.
- System management functionality and platforms; in particular, the specification of fault, configuration, accounting, performance and security management requires various type of approvals to allow equipment to be connected to the network, i.e. safety approvals for each railway.
- Roaming on to a national public GSM network as part of a disaster recovery strategy in case of a loss of service.

According to the last EIRENE specifications, the railway integrated wireless network should meet the following general and functional requirements under the categories: Mandatory for Interoperability (MI), Mandatory for the System (M), Optional (O) or Not Applicable (NA), depending of the type of radio.

- Services: voice (Table 1), data (Table 2) and call related features. The required call set-up times shown in Table 3 shall be achieved for interoperability (MI) in 95% of cases and for 99% of cases shall not be more than 1.5 times the required call set-up time.
- Railway EIRENE-specific applications are summarized in Table 4.
- Direct mode facility for local set-to-set operation without network infrastructure.
- Railway specific features: set-up of urgent or frequent calls through single keystroke or similar, display of functional identity of calling/called party, fast and guaranteed call set-up, seamless communication support for train speeds up to 500 km/h, automatic and manual test modes with fault indications and control over mobile network selection and system configuration.

**Table 3.** GSM-R Call set-up time requirements

| Call type | Call set-up time |
|---|---|
| Railway emergency call | <2 s (MI) |
| Group calls between drivers in the same area | <5 s (MI) |
| All operational mobile-to-fixed calls not covered by the above | <5 s (O) |
| All operational fixed-to-mobile calls not covered by the above | <7 s (O) |
| All operational mobile-to-mobile calls not covered by the above | <10 s (O) |
| All low priority calls | <10 s (O) |

**Table 4.** Specific features to be supported

| Feature / Radio type | Cab | ETCS data only | General purpose | Operational | Shunting |
|---|---|---|---|---|---|
| Functional addressing | MI | NA | M | M | M |
| Location dependent addressing | MI | M | O | O | O |
| Direct mode | O | NA | NA | O | O |
| Shunting mode | MI | NA | NA | NA | M |
| Multiple communications within the train | MI | NA | NA | NA | NA |
| Railway emergency calls | MI | NA | O | M | M |

- Dedicated buttons that allow quick access to emergency call, Push-to-talk (PTT) and support for Link Assurance Signal (LAS) are required. Latest generation railway features such as Originator-To-Dispatcher-Information (OTDI), late entry, and frequency hopping in group call shall be considered. In addition, layouts for further features are presented: enhanced Presentation of Functional Number (ePFN), Driver's Safety Device alarm, Plain Text Messages, Presentation of the Functional Number (FN) of the initiator of a Railway Emergency Call (REC) and Alerting of a Controller.

A common minimum standard of performance is required to EIRENE compliant mobiles, although coverage and speed-limitations values are described in SRS, it should be noted that high-speed railway systems [9] (in operation, under construction and planned) have to cope with speeds of at least 250 km/h while enabling speeds over 300 km/h under appropriate circumstances. Generally, speeds around 200-220 km/h represent the threshold for upgraded conventional lines. Nevertheless stable wireless connections have to be ensured at the moving speed of 500 km/h or even more in the future [10].

Quality of Service (QoS) mechanisms shall ensure the priorization and pre-emption of critical services. Even though current wireless networks support various QoS policies depending on different traffic types, QoS for railway-critical communications and real-time applications shall be examined. QoS control is mandatory for resource management, safety, punctuality, efficiency and accident prevention of trains, to ensure immediate reaction to emergencies and on-time operations. Strict latency requirements are needed for the seamless transmission and reception of data regarding the train position and status, and Movement Authority (MA) permission between the in-service train and the control center, i.e. the transmission error probability over one train line should be less than 1% per hour and 99% of ETCS data should have a maximum latency of < 0.5 s [11,12]. QoS parameters with its percentage of availability are shown in Table 5.

**Table 5.** Summary of GSM-R QoS Requirements

| Requirements | Value |
|---|---|
| Connection Establishment Delay | $< 8.5\,s\ (95\%), \leq 10\,s\ (100\%)$ |
| Connection establishment error ratio | $< 10^{-2}\ (100\%)$ |
| Connection loss rate | $< 10^{-2}/h\ (100\%)$ |
| Transfer delay of user data frame | $\leq 0.5\,s\ (99\%)$ |
| Transmission interference period | $< 0.8\,s\ (95\%),\ < 1\,s\ (99\%)$ |
| Error-free period | $> 20\,s\ (95\%),\ > 7\,s\ (99\%)$ |
| Network registration delay | $\leq 30\,s\ (95\%),\ \leq 35\,s\ (99\%),\ \leq 40\,s\ (100\%)$ |
| Call setup time | $\leq 10\,s\ (100\ \%)$ |
| Emergency call setup time | $\leq 2\,s\ (100\ \%)$ |
| Duration of transmission failures | $< 1\,s\ (99\%)$ |

## 3    LTE: One Step Ahead

The most important GSM-R shortcoming is the limited support for data services derived from the lack of packet-switched transmissions. For example, to deliver bursty low-rate ETCS data messages, connections need to continuously occupy network resources despite they are not used. The maximum transmission rate per connection is limited to 9.6 kbit/s and the packet delay is about 400 ms, which is too high to for real-time applications. Thus, GSM-R [13] cannot support modern data services. Another major problem is the limited capacity of ETCS using GSM-R circuit-switched data services in high traffic areas, this can be solved with an LTE micro-cell deployment [14] or by using the ER-GSM band and changing to ETCS over packet-switched data using General Packet Radio Service (GPRS), Enhanced General Packet Radio Service (EGPRS) or Enhanced GPRS Phase 2 (EGPRS2) [15]. These shortcomings together with the commitment of the GSM-R Industry Group [16] members to the long-term support of GSM-R until 2025 are encouraging the switch to a different system architecture as the new bearer network for railways.

There is a growing recognition that railway telecommunications will have to evolve to keep up with and take advantage of rapid changes in technology. Hence, over the past few years, new technologies have been included by many railway operators such as Worldwide Interoperability for Microwave Access (WiMAX) in Train-to-Wayside Communication (TWC) deployments [17], primarily as a means to deliver best-effort passenger Internet services. In particular, the 802.16m has been backed up by market ecosystems. Wireless Local Area Network (WLAN)-based broadband capabilities have been used to deliver the most demanding train operation traffic but, until the amendment IEEE 802.11ac, the standard lacked QoS features such as end-to-end resource management, traffic admission and traffic policy enforcement capabilities.

The first major step in the evolution of LTE [18,19] occurred in March 2011 when LTE-Advanced (LTE-A) was issued as part of 3rd Generation Partnership Project (3GPP) Rel-10, which made LTE formally compliant with the International Telecommunication Union - Telecommunication Standardization (ITU-T) 4G technology definition known as IMT-Advanced. LTE also met the requirements set out by the mobile-operator-led alliance Next Generation Mobile

Networks (NGMN). Rel-10 extended the LTE radio access technology including the possibility of transmission bandwidths beyond 20 MHz, and improved spectrum flexibility by means of carrier aggregation.

Rel-11 includes basic functionality for Coordinated Multi-point (CoMP) transmission/reception as well as enhanced support for heterogeneous deployments [20]. Rel-12 (due out in December 2014) includes novel non-orthogonal waveforms to improve the performance of the Physical layer (PHY) layer, sparse signal processing that can decode bursty data traffic in an energy-efficient manner, robust systems that perform well under limited control channel bandwidth and imperfect channel knowledge, hence reducing the end-to-end delay of wireless links from 10 ms to around 1 ms to meet the requirements of new machine-to-machine services.

## 4   Current Status of Standardization

The UIC General Assembly held in Istanbul in 2008 announced that the advent of LTE was threatening the lifecycle of GSM technology. As a result, a technical report examining whether LTE communication systems would be applicable to the integrated railway wireless network [21] was published in 2009. The main outcomes were that LTE technology might be suitable for the future but noted that additional modifications would be required. Following this, a study on railways future mobile telecommunications systems was initiated.

In 2012, UIC envisioned the issue of next generation wireless communication standards at Paris World Conference. Future Railway Mobile Telecommunication System (FRMTS) project was officially launched in 2013 to conduct research on the definition of a new wireless communication system, frequency redistribution, additional features, new structure of a network, efficient conversion from GSM-R and railway signal transmission in a packet network. In particular, UIC has strengthen its cooperation with the 3GPP standard body to reflect the requirements of next-generation integrated wireless networks for railways in the LTE-based communication standards.

The American Research Innovation Technology Administration (RITA) envisions the future composite transportation network, taking as a whole the railway, the subway, and the road. For instance, the next-generation train-to-ground communication system for this composite scenario will be based on Wi-Fi and LTE-A systems. In an European level, with the aim of overcoming the existing fragmentation, the strategic vision for the European Union's long-term transport policy includes the completion of the Single European Railway Area (Directive 2012/34/EU).

On the other hand, LTE will be the baseline technology for next generation broadband public safety networks. Therefore, National Public Safety Telecommunications Council (NPSTC), TETRA + Critical Communications Association (TCCA) and Critical Communication Broadband Group (CCBG) [22] are contributing to the standardization processes. The current view is that this functionality could become available in products from circa 2016/17 onwards

**Table 6.** LTE specifications to address railway requirements

| Railway requirements | LTE implementation |
|---|---|
| Voice telephony services | • Point-to-point calls - VoLTE (GSMA IR. 92 v 7.0).<br>• Proximity-based services (ProSe); Stage 2 (3GPP TS 23.303).<br>  o  Service requirements for the Evolved Packet System (EPS) (3GPP TS 22.278).<br>  o  Architecture enhancements to support ProSe (3GPP TS 23.703).<br>  o  Security issues to support ProSe (3GPP TS 33.833).<br>  o  LTE device to device proximity services; Radio aspects (3GPP TR 36.843).<br>• 3GPP enablers for OMA; PoC services; Stage 2 (3GPP TR 23.979, OMA PoC V2.0 RD).<br>• Emergency calls - MS emergency sessions (3GPP TS 23.167).<br>  o  IP Multimedia Subsystem (IMS) emergency sessions (3GPP TS 23.167).<br>  o  Support for IP based IMS Emergency calls over GPRS and EPS (3GPP TR23.869).<br>• Group calls/Broadcast including emergency calls.<br>  o  GCSE_LTE (3GPP TS 22.468), GCSE_LTE; stage 2 (3GPP TS 23.468).<br>  o  Mission Critical Voice Communications Requirements for Public Safety, NPSTC BBWG.<br>  o  Public Safety Broadband High-Level Statement of Requirements for FirstNet Consideration, NPSTC Report Rev B.<br>  o  Service aspects; Service principles (3GPP TS 22.101).<br>  o  Architecture enhancements to support GCSE_LTE (3GPP TS 23.768).<br>• eMBMS (3GPP TS 23.246), MBMS; Protocols and codecs (3GPP TS 26.346). |
| eMLPP | • QoS concept and architecture (3GPP TS 23.107).<br>• Service-specific access control, Service accessibility (3GPP TS 22.011).<br>• E-UTRA; RRC; Protocol specification (3GPP TS 36.331).<br>• IMS multimedia telephony communication service and supplementary services (3GPP TS 24.173).<br>• AT command set for User Equipment (UE) (3GPP TS 27.007).<br>• Multimedia priority service (3GPP TS 22.153).<br>• Enhancements for Multimedia Priority Service (3GPP TR 23.854). |
| Call related features | • Call Forwarding supplementary services (3GPP TS 22.082).<br>• Call Waiting (CW) and Call Hold (HOLD) supplementary services (3GPP TS 22.083).<br>• Call Barring (CB) supplementary services (3GPP TS 22.088).<br>• Numbering, addressing and identification (3GPP TS 23.003). |
| LDA | • LTE Positioning Protocol (LPP) (3GPP TS 36.355) and Annex (3GPP TS 36.455).<br>• Functional stage 2 description of Location Services (LCS) (3GPP TS 23.271).<br>• Serving Mobile Location Centre (SMLC) Radio Resource LCS Protocol (RRLP) (3GPP TS 44.031). |

in LTE Rel-12 and 13. A new access technology might be defined in the Rel-14 and 15, while time frame for commercial deployment will be at the end of this decade.

## 5  Assessing LTE Potential for Railway Services

The maturity of LTE standards (up to Rel. 12) to address railway requirements is briefly summarized in the following paragraphs and in Table 6.

- **Point-to-Point Voice communications:** advanced voice communication is an essential functionality for railways. Different transmission strategies of voice call over LTE architecture have been considered: Circuit Switched FallBack (CSFB), SMS over SGs, and Voice over LTE (VoLTE). The latest has emerged as the favored solution by carriers and the GSMA has developed a profile [23] which defines the minimum set of features that a device and a network should implement to support a high quality IP Multimedia Subsystem (IMS)-based telephony services over LTE radio access.
- **Direct communication:** Proximity Services (ProSe) are designed to address both critical and commercial requirements for direct mode or

proximity, including discovery mechanisms and relay capabilities within and outside network coverage under continuous operator network control.

- **Location-based services:** in GSM-R, location services are used for addressing enhanced Location Dependent Addressing (eLDA) and route the call to the most appropriate Radio Block Centre (RBC). In LTE positioning, knowledge can be used in support of Radio Resource Management functions, as well as location-based services. ETSI TS 136.305 defines the E-UTRAN User Equipment (UE) entities and operations to support positioning methods. It provides support for DL and UL positioning, Enhanced Cell Id (ECID), and Assisted Global Navigation Satellite Systems (A-GNSS). LTE positioning services can be deployed through LTE Positioning Protocol (LPP). Furthermore, Open Mobile Alliance (OMA) LPP Extensions (LPPe) attempts to be bearer-independent as far as possible with respect to non-bearer associated position methods like A-GNSS and any terrestrial method applicable to a non-serving network. Although security, authentication, privacy and charging are out of scope of LPPe.

- **Point-to-Multipoint Voice communications:** the Voice Broadcast Service (VBS) (3GPP TS 43.069) will be similar to Voice Group Call Service (VGCS) (3GPP TS 42.068) with the restriction that only the originator of the call is allowed to speak. LTE Rel-9 provides Evolved Multimedia Broadcast Multicast Service (eMBMS) as a bearer service to deliver PTT over LTE and allows support for Dynamic Adaptive Streaming over HTTP (DASH) over broadcast and unicast reception in Multicast and Broadcast over Single Frequency Networks (MBSFN) subframes. MBSFN implies several advantages such as the reduction of interferences at the receiver, the increase of the signal level received at the edges of the cells, and diversity in the transmission. Rel-10 provides additional features such as Allocation and Retention Priority (ARP) which enables priority between eMBMS sessions. Rel-11 includes enhanced support of service continuity with MBMS, content schedule information included in User Service Description (USD) to save Power, Quality of Experience (QoE) metrics reports to optimize Forward Error Correction (FEC) configuration of File Delivery over Unidirectional Transport (FLUTE), and location filtering to allow UE to selectively receive a service, among others. Group Communication System Enablers for LTE (3GPP TS 22.468, 3GPP TS 23.468, 3GPP TS 23.768) provides an efficient mechanism to distribute the same content to multiple users in a controlled manner with an end-to-end latency lower than 150 ms.

- **Push-to-Talk over Cellular:** VGCS systems will be expected to evolve into the Push-to-Talk over Cellular (PoC) system (OMA PoC V2.0 RD) to offer wide improvement in the voice quality and much faster call establishment. In Rel-13, PTT is revised to support the mission-critical operation in LTE networks (3GPP TS 22.179), Mission Critical Push To Talk over LTE (MCPTT).

- **Emergency calls:** Enhanced Railway Emergency Call (eREC) is an improvement over REC to subdivide the area of the call to be set up only to the subscribers/lines that are directly affected, resulting in less production loss while maintaining safety levels. IMS emergency calls (3GPP TS 23.167, 3GPP TR 23.869) represent the replacement of GSM-R point-to-point railway emergency calls.

- **Priority management:** the priority to a point-to-point, VBS, or VGCS call is assigned by the enhanced Multi-Level Precedence and Pre-emption (eMLPP) function. eNodeB's also play a key role in the policy management performing UL and DL rate policing and radio resource scheduling. ARP is used to call admission control and priorization of bearers during its establishment. The eNodeB Medium Access Control layer (MAC) scheduler is responsible for scheduling radio resources and supporting the concept of radio bearer QoS. Transport resources are managed by Evolved Packet Core (EPC).

- **Multiservice IP support:** the railway domain clearly differentiates between non-critical and critical, and life safety systems for trains moving with the assignment of Safety Integrity Level (SIL). The features that IP transport networks must fulfill should be specified both at the level of communication standards and in their implementations in the upper functional layers. The migration to LTE technology implies the emergence of new security threats. As proposed by GSMA, Session Initiation Protocol (SIP) is the protocol used to register UE in the IMS server. Real-time Transport Protocol (RTP) and User Datagram Protocol (UDP) are the protocols recommended for voice transportation, and RTP Control Protocol (RTCP) for providing link aliveness information while the media are on hold.

- **Public Safety Networks Resiliency:** another important key technology is Self-Organizing Networks (SON) which allows managing, configuring, maintaining, and optimizing the LTE communication network, i.e. optimization of handover parameters in operations of heterogeneous networks.

Surplus capacity could be leased by public mobile operators to trigger new customer services and increase expectations on its delivery. 4-th Generation (4G) broadband will help to enhance its attractiveness giving it an advantage over other competing transport means (i.e. excellent coverage, information provision with real-time updates, live-streaming video, mobile ticketing), Fokum et al. [24] have already presented a comprehensive survey of approaches (TETRA, IEEE 802.11, satellite and so on) to deliver broadband internet access on trains. Railway safety can be improved with train diagnostics and driver advisory systems, i.e. on-board CCTV recordings transferred to a control center.

## 6    The Strategic Roadmap

In recent years, UIC has started the migration from GSM Phase 2+ to LTE while ensuring the life cycle of GSM-R will be extended with the unceasing progress of technologies. Authors emphasize the feasibility of a smooth evolution from GSM-R to LTE. LTE migration of metro and railway is envisaged to move at different paces. In the absence of a global standard for Communications Based Train Control (CBTC), metro trains are likely to adopt LTE relatively quickly, in particular on new lines. Nonetheless, on mainline railways where international standards determine transmission networks for safety-critical systems, migration is likely to occur in two steps. In the early stage of the deployment, the non-safety-critical applications that require broadband will be carried out by the LTE network, whereas safety-critical applications will be carried out by the legacy networks. This requires the right mechanisms and architecture in radio and core networks to guarantee QoS and achieve a seamless service experience for all services. Following the maturity of LTE, all the railway services will be then gradually transferred. When suppliers standardize ETCS on IP networks, LTE will replace GSM-R. Anyway, the coexistence of LTE and GSM-R will be required.

## 7   Conclusion

This paper examines the role of LTE for the next generation of railway wireless networks. A formal study regarding GSM-R operational requirements and services is previously presented in order to provide a fully understanding of future user needs. LTE Rel-11 adds the first feature for public safety, i.e. high-power UE. Nevertheless, starting from LTE Rel-12, the standard provides features for critical communications such as IMS emergency calls, ProSe, GCSE, PoC and eMBMS that will enable LTE to be used as part of a broadband public safety network. LTE Rel-13 introduces MCPTT, enhancements of ProSe and GCSE and the isolated E-UTRAN operation. In the railway environment, developing the new ecosystem will also require the design of a thorough migration strategy.

Novel concepts such as composite transportation, train-to-train communication, in-cab signalling, network topologies, vacuum maglev train techniques, security issues; the adoption of new paradigms such as Internet of Things (IoT), and the 5G wireless communications techniques are envisaged as innovative concerns and further research work in the near future.

**Acknowledgment.** This work has been funded by Xunta de Galicia, MINECO of Spain, and FEDER funds of the EU under grants 2012/287, TEC2013-47141-C4-1-R, IPT-2011-1034-370000 and FPU12/04139.

## References

1. Hofestadt, H.: GSM-R: Global System for Mobile radio communications for Railways. In: International Conference on Electric Railways in a United Europe, pp. 111–115 (March 1995)
2. Ljubic, I., Simunic, D.: Advanced Speech Call Items for GSM-Railway. In: 1st International Conference on Wireless Communication, Vehicular Technology, Information Theory and Aerospace Electronic Systems Technology, Wireless VITAE 2009, pp. 131–136 (May 2009)

3. Guiot, B., Winter, P., I. U. of Railways: Compendium on ERTMS: European Rail Traffic Management System. Eurail Press (2009)
4. Functional Requirements Specification Version 7.4.0, tech. rep., EIRENE (2014)
5. System Requirements Specification Version 15.4.0, tech. rep., EIRENE (2014)
6. Directive 2008/57/EC of the European Parliament and of the Council of 17 June 2008 on the interoperability of the rail system within the Community (2008)
7. ETSI TS 103 066 v1.1.2 (2012-04), Railways Telecommunications (RT); Rel-4 Core Network requirements for GSM-R, tech. rep., ETSI (2012)
8. Pushparatnam, L., Taylor, T.: GSM-R Implementation and Procurement Guide V 1.0-15.03 (March 2009)
9. High Speed lines in the World – UIC High Speed Department (September 2014)
10. Ai, B., Cheng, X., Kurner, T., Zhong, Z.-D., Guan, K., He, R.-S., Xiong, L., Matolak, D.W., Michelson, D.G., Briso-Rodriguez, C.: Challenges toward wireless communications for high-speed railway. IEEE Transactions on Intelligent Transportation Systems 15(5), 2143–2158 (2014)
11. Subset-093 issue 2.3.0 GSM-R Interfaces Class 1 Requirements, tech. rep. (2005)
12. REFERENCE O-2475 3.0 ERTMS/GSM-R Quality of Service Test Specification, tech. rep., UIC (2007)
13. Sniady, A., Soler, J.: An overview of GSM-R technology and its shortcomings. In: 12th International Conference on ITS Telecommunications (ITST), pp. 626–629 (November 2012)
14. Sniady, A., Kassab, M., Soler, J., Berbineau, M.: LTE micro-cell deployment for high-density railway areas. In: Sikora, A., Berbineau, M., Vinel, A., Jonsson, M., Pirovano, A., Aguado, M. (eds.) Nets4Cars/Nets4Trains 2014. LNCS, vol. 8435, pp. 143–155. Springer, Heidelberg (2014)
15. ETSI TR 103 134 V1.1.1 (2013-03) Railway Telecommunications (RT); GSM-R in support of EC Mandate M/486 EN on Urban Rail, tech. rep., ETSI (2013)
16. MoU between the EC, the ERA and the European Rail sector Associations concerning the strengthening of cooperation for the management of ERTMS (April 2012)
17. Aguado, M., Jacob, E., Higuero, M., Saiz, P.S., Berbineau, M.: Broadband communication in the high mobility scenario: the WiMAX opportunity (2009)
18. Sauter, M.: From GSM to LTE: An Introduction to Mobile Networks and Mobile Broadband. John Wiley & Sons, Ltd. (2010)
19. Sesia, S., Toufik, I., Baker, M.: LTE, The UMTS Long Term Evolution: From Theory to Practice. Wiley InterScience online books. Wiley (2009)
20. Lee, Y.L., Chuah, T.C., Loo, J., Vinel, A.: Recent advances in radio resource management for heterogeneous LTE/LTE-A networks. IEEE Communications Surveys & Tutorials 16, 2142–2180 (2014)
21. LTE / SAE - The Future Railway Mobile Radio System? A Future Railway Mobile Radio System v1.1, tech. rep., UIC (2009)
22. Mission Critical Mobile Broadband: Practical standardisation & roadmap considerations, tech. rep., TCCA CCBG (2013)
23. Permanent Reference Document (PRD) IP Multimedia Subsystem (IMS) profile for voice and SMS Version 8.0, tech. rep., GSM Association (GSMA) IR.92 (2014)
24. Fokum, D., Frost, V.: A Survey on Methods for Broadband Internet Access on Trains. IEEE Communications Surveys & Tutorials 12, 171–185 (2010)

# Broadband Internet Access on board High Speed Trains, A Technological Survey

Émilie Masson[1], Marion Berbineau[2], and Sébastien Lefebvre[1]

[1]Institut de Recherche Technologique Railenium, F-59300, Famars, France
[2] Univ Lille Nord de France, F-59000 Lille, IFSTTAR, COSYS, F-59650 Villeneuve d'Ascq

**Abstract.** Advances in information and communication technologies lead to the adoption of wireless communications in all sectors, including railway domain. Wireless communications for railway can be used for several applications, requiring safety, reliability, availability, high capacities, *etc.* Furthermore, wireless communications have been deeply integrated into people's life and current public telecommunication services increased the needs for mobility services. Railway domain is more and more competitive and it becomes crucial for railway operators to make additional revenue by offering more comfortable and pleasant travels thanks to new on board services. Thus, broadband Internet access on board trains has become, in recent years, an essential and highly expected service in the railway domain. This paper aims at presenting the different technologies that can bring an Internet access on board High Speed Trains.

## 1    Introduction

Broadband Internet access has become, in recent years, an essential and highly expected service, whatever the time of the day and regardless the location (home, office or public places, transportation). This expectation is even greater during phases of travel, including train, during which passengers want to transform their travelling time into a useful time. A business customer will prefer a train ride where he will enjoy services type "remote desktop" rather than air travel where the different phases (registration, flight and baggage claim) are not conducive to work. Other customer segments could enjoy the Quality of Service (QoS) of broadband Internet access for a variety of applications such as messaging, Video On Demand (VoD), Voice over IP (VoIP), TV, streaming, videoconferencing, *etc.* Ensuring broadband links between trains and infrastructure also allows considering, for network managers and railway operators, applications hitherto difficult to ensure such as real-time video surveillance from inside the carriages, or track inspection in direct link with the control center by data feedback of measurements and diagnosis.

The paper presents a review of all technological solutions allowing an Internet access on board High Speed Trains (HST). Section 2 presents the context of broadband Internet access on board trains. Section 3 is devoted to satellite solutions. Section 4 details all terrestrial solutions. Finally, Section 5 gives some conclusions on this work.

© Springer International Publishing Switzerland 2015
M. Kassab et al. (Eds.): Nets4Cars/Nets4Trains/Nets4Aircraft 2015, LNCS 9066, pp. 165–176, 2015.
DOI: 10.1007/978-3-319-17765-6_15

## 2    Introduction to Internet Access on Board Trains

Railway environment implies several complex factors to establish a wireless communication for broadband Internet access on board trains [1], [2]. The metallic structure of the train behaves as a Faraday cage causing important losses on transmission signals. Railway environment can be defined as a "high vibration" environment, which can require isolation of communication devices. Large temperature variations are observed and railway environment suffers of high electrical stresses (near high voltage lines, strong magnetic fields as for the MAGLEV trains, no stabilized power supply). Moreover, the presence of ground infrastructures may hinder the implementation of a communication system. The widespread use of tunnels is a constant barrier to seamless communications. Finally, railway companies constantly add or remove rail cars from trains, the communication networks have to discover this automatically.

The first solution for providing broadband Internet access on board trains could be that users directly connect their devices (smartphone, laptop, tablet, *etc.*) via their own mobile operator [2], [3]. However, this solution requires appropriate cells management and sufficient radio coverage along the railway line. In addition, as already mentioned, the metallic structure of carriages causes signal attenuation, which can reach 15 dB, and even 30 dB, in worst cases [3]. To overcome this problem, repeaters may be installed on board trains. However, installation and maintenance of theses repeaters involve significant costs. Furthermore, performance of these transponders depends closely on the quality of the radio coverage: the amplification of a weak signal causes a low Signal-to-Noise Ratio (SNR) and therefore a "bad quality" amplified signal. Some experiments testing a direct connection of a terminal in the train via High Speed Download Packet Access (HSDPA) were performed in 2007 by *Sauter* on a German Intercity Express (ICE) HST [4]. Peak throughputs of 1.5 Mbps and average throughputs of 850 kbps were observed. However, communication failures were often encountered. It is clear that other solutions need to be developed.

Many works performed on Internet access on board trains showed that a unique access terminal on the train, or "mobile router", represents the best technical solution to optimize performance and throughputs [2], [5], it is called the Train Access Terminal (TAT). The TAT can support many technology types. The antenna mounted on the outside of the train connects the TAT. The incoming signal from the TAT then fed access points in the carriages in train, as illustrated in Fig. 1. This architecture fixes then the problem of transmission loss due to the metallic structure of the train. The TAT can manage different types of technology, and then implement some smart agility to select the best means of communication and then to rise the obtained throughputs. Furthermore, such architecture reduces the handover of all passengers' connections into a single terminal handover, which aggregates all the traffic. Many researches stated that the TAT approach works better by combining a set of several wireless technologies to access the Internet [6], [7]. One technology is used to provide connectivity and a second one, so-called "gap-filler", is used when the first one is no more available. Such a mechanism implies a preferred technology to provide the connection [2]. Criteria to determine the technology to use are the quality of the connection (signal strength and errors), delays, throughputs and/or costs.

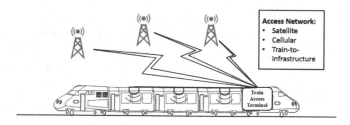

**Fig. 1.** TAT architecture for an Internet access on board trains

## 3     Satellite Solutions

### Description of the Technology

Communications based on satellites represent a first solution to enable broadband Internet access on board trains. The easy coverage of a large geographical area, the resistance to high velocity and the low capital expenditure (CAPEX) due to the absence of installation of a dedicated infrastructure on tracks represent the main advantages of the technology. Nevertheless, the use of satellites conducts to several constraints related to systems design, which have to be taken into account [3]. Line-Of-Sight (LOS) is required in order to obtain broadband connectivity. Any obstacle between the satellite and the receiving antenna (catenary, bridge, *etc.*) generates deep fadings or total loss of signal. Furthermore, high antenna gain and a very thin beamwidth are mandatory. It is then necessary to implement a precise and dynamic tracking of the satellite. Because of the several train movements, tracking solutions of the satellite have to be even more precise in order to avoid interferences with other satellites. Non Line-Of-Sight (NLOS) areas, such as tunnels, dense urban areas or stations, can lead to signal cut-off and require the combination with other technologies, so-called "gap-filler". Finally, the other railway constraints, such as electromagnetic compatibility with existing systems, interferences, installation and integration on rolling-stock, maintenance and space to install the antennas, have to be obviously taken into account. Railway constraints also impose a limitation on the size of the antennas with a consequence to the delivered throughputs. The satellite solutions rely on different satellite standards (S-UMTS, DVB-S2, DVB-SH, *etc.*) and mobile satellite systems (Inmarsat, Globalstar, Thuraya, *etc.*). Different criteria define a satellite system: frequency bands, PHY layer characteristics, multiple access techniques, orbit characteristics, *etc.* [8], [9]. Geostationary Earth Orbit (GEO) satellites are generally very attractive because they are able to cover a wide geographical area and provide broadband connectivity for mobile users. They are largely used in several existing communication and broadcasting systems. However, the use of GEO satellites leads to important propagation delays (around 400 ms), which is a problem in the case of highly interactive applications. Furthermore, GEO satellites being at equator level, north latitudes are then at weak elevation angles, that conducts to a reduced availability of satellites in case of obstacles. Finally, satellite systems lead to high operational expenditure (OPEX) due to the satellite capacity. Satellites in Ka band can represent a solution to this problem because of their high capacity, which induces a reduction of bandwidth costs (3 to 5 less expensive than the Ku band). Moreover, satellites in Ka band operate at higher frequencies, which allows reducing the size of the antenna. However, equipments in Ku and Ka bands are not compatible. Furthermore, signals in Ka band suffer of high attenuation in the case of bad atmospheric conditions (15 dB in worst cases [3]). Finally, the existing satellites in Ka band provide a coverage area of about 250-500 km$^2$ in order to allow a geographical reuse of frequency bands (and then an optimization of satellite capacity). Dynamic frequency allocation and horizontal handover have to be implemented to allow connectivity of the train from a cell to another. Global system is then more complex. A complete study of Ka band systems still have to be performed, such as investigation on mobility effects and cell changes.

### Existing Studies, Projects and Solutions

Several studies and projects were performed on satellite technologies. When the satellite link is blocked, the TAT switches to a terrestrial network. This solution of "gap-filler" was first introduced in the ROSIN project [9]. Works were pursued with the TrainCom [11] and FIFTH [12] projects. The solution was then integrated under the INTEGRAIL project [13], in the context of an intelligent integration of railway information system. Finally, the TrainIPSat project [14] aimed at defining, specifying and testing a technical solution to provide connectivity services for HST. The two main Companies that developed solutions relying on satellites are *Icomera* and *21Net*.

*Icomera* [15] developed a multi-technology platform using satellite technology for the downlink and cellular technology for the uplink, in order to provide broadband Internet access on trains with Wi-Fi access points deployed in the carriages. Initially, the system was based on the combination of a satellite link and a GSM link, allowing average throughputs of 0.5 Mbps. Then, several 3G/HSPA cellular networks were used at the same time (until 8) to increase performance. The system was recently updated to take advantage of 4G networks and reach 40 Mbps [16]. First tests of broadband on board trains in the world were performed in Sweden in 2002 with Scandinavian rail operator Linx, using *Icomera* platform. This one is also used in UK since 2004 by Intercity East Coast Railway franchise, since 2010 on board Irish Rail trains, since 2011 on the Chiltern Railway's mainline fleet and also on ScotRail trains running from Glasgow to Edinburgh. The Czech Railway Company provides also connection to passengers via Wi-Fi access points and additional entertainment options via infotainment system on board the Pendolino trains since 2011. Finally, a contract was won in October 2014 by *Icomera* to supply Wi-Fi to the fleet of vehicles operated by the Dutch transport Rotterdamse Elektrische Tram (RET). The installation of the complete information system and Internet on board was due for the end of 2014.

In 2004, *21Net* [17] performed trials with the RENFE demonstrating for the first time broadband Internet via a bi-directional antenna on a HST running at over 300 km/h, allowing throughputs up to 4 Mbps (downlink)/2 Mbps (uplink). The "gap-filler" relies on cellular solutions. An upgraded cellular solution is implemented since mid-2013 relying on a multi-operator and multi-SIM bonding that aggregates bandwidth across multiple channels simultaneously. Satellite solution was also upgraded in order to increase spectral efficiency and availability [18]. The system is deployed in the Thalys since 2008. Throughputs up to 4Mbps (downlink)/0.5 Mbps (uplink) are recorded. In November 2014, Thalys launched a trend to update its Internet on board service and raise throughputs 5 to 8 times [19]. *21Net* system's is also deployed in the NTV (Nuovo Trasporto Viaggiatori) HST since 2009 with integration into the design of the AGV (Automotrice à Grande Vitesse). Average throughputs recorded are 8 Mbps/0.5 Mbps. Currently, NTV is migrating from a satellite solution to a cellular one. *21Net* is responsible of the rollout, monitoring and integration of the new technology [20]. Finally, Indian Railways rely on the *21Net* system and provides broadband connectivity of 9 Mbps at 180 km [21]. The solution is scalable to Ka band systems and downlink throughputs up to 1.5 Gbps are announced.

Some other current or past solutions were also deployed around the world. The Canadian Company *PointShot Wireless* developed the *RailPoint* solution for broadband connectivity on board Vial Rail trains in Quebec. The Kazakh national Company equipped its Tulpar HST with an Internet access on board in 2011, with announced throughputs up to 2 Mbps. Finally, SNCF performed several tests [3], [22], [23], in order to provide a broadband Internet access on board HST. Solutions based on bi-directional satellite solutions were tested and a first Internet service was launched in 2010 on the TGV-East line, the "BoxTGX". The system relies on a bi-directional satellite solution on Ku band with a Wi-Fi and 3G coverage for NLOS areas. However, the system never found its profitability (high CAPEX and OPEX). In addition, technology could not be deployed on two levels trains due to high railway constraints, which leads to a poor legibility of the offer (offer not available on all trains). The solution was then stopped in late 2013. Others studies are currently on going.

## 4    Terrestrial Wireless Solutions

### Public Cellular Network Solutions

The public cellular network solutions are usually based on the use of several cellular networks deployed over landmasses. The TAT integrates several links (up to 8) with different mobile phone operators. Thereby, the TAT can manage the lack of coverage of one operator by supplying it with another one with better coverage. In the case of no coverage at all, a "gap-filler" solution can be used. *Nomad Digital* [24] is a specialist in on-vehicle Information and Communication Technologies (ICT), which provides wireless solutions to the transportation sector. The Company developed a wide range of solutions based on a scalable on board IP platform, allowing passenger Internet access on board via Wi-Fi, and local contents, such as passenger information, infotainment and displays. *Nomad Digital* provides solutions based on cellular networks only, and solutions based on the combination of cellular and WiMAX technologies. Many operators rely on the *Nomad Digital* solutions, such as the East Midland trains in UK, the DSB state-owned Danish rail operator, the NSB Norway's national rail Company, the NS Dutch Railways in Netherlands or the Queensland Rail in Australia. In [25], the author announces that Eurostar aims at bringing Wi-Fi on board its fleet using *Nomad Digital* solution. The *Nomad Digital*, relying on combination of cellular and WiMAX technologies, is also deployed in the Heathrow Express, the Southern Express and the Virgin trains in UK, and also in UTA trains in US and in Dubai's metro and future tramway. Other solutions, not based on *Nomad Digital* system, were also rolled out, such as the Via Rail in Canada, the Arriva's in Denmark, the trains of the Latvian Railway, the trains of the Swiss Federal Railways, the ICE trains of DB in Germany, the trains of the Gysev in Hungary, the Taiwan HST or the Amtrak trains in US. Thus, many rolled out solutions in the world rely on cellular solutions. It is quite difficult to obtain precise information on the performance of the systems, in terms of throughputs especially. At the TrainComms conference standing in London on June 2014, *Icomera*, which also provides cellular-based solutions, claimed that throughputs up to 250 Mbps can be reached relying on cellular-based solutions, depending on LTE deployment in the countries. Cellular-based allow low costs, relying on the use of existing infrastructures and no dedicated infrastructure deployed. However, minimum capacity requires multiple cells management. Moreover, base stations are not often near the tracks and antennas are not oriented for track coverage. Tunnel zones requires the deployment of a dedicated network. Finally, no control over QoS is provided, by depending on mobile network operators.

### Dedicated Train-to-infrastructure Solutions

**Technology Description.** The train-to-infrastructure solutions consist of the rolling out of a dedicated infrastructure on the ground, allowing connectivity to the TAT. This connectivity can be obtained with guided waves through leaky cables, with radio waves in free space via systems relying on Wi-Fi or WiMAX technologies for instance, or with optical signals, combining radio wave for the Radio-over-Fiber techniques, or full-optical for systems based on lasers or diodes. All these solutions are reviewed in this part. The train-to-infrastructure solutions allow meeting growing demand in terms of throughputs. However, these kinds of solutions rely on long, complex and expensive deployments of infrastructures along the track. In order to reduce costs, it is then essential to try to minimize the number of radio sites required to ensure radio coverage of the network. The radio coverage is thus one of the main features to be taken into account for the choice of the communication technology [26]. Furthermore, another key feature is the throughput that the system allows to reach. These two features are closely related and the best tradeoff between range and throughput has to be found to optimize the system. Other features have to be considered also, such as reliability, security and need for licensed radio spectrum. A model of train-to-infrastructure was first proposed in the FAMOUS architecture [27] and in the WIGWAM project [28]. The WIGWAM works were pursued by the deployment of the system in the Shanghai Transrapid, which will be presented thereafter.

**Leaky Coaxial Cables.** In Japan, some authors [29] demonstrated a broadband Internet access on board trains using leaky coaxial cables (LCX). Authors proposed a communication architecture for "bullet trains". The system was deployed on the Tokaido-Shinkansen in 2009. Theoretical throughputs up to 2 Mbps/1 Mbps can be reached. However, this kind of solution requires the deployment of the cable along the track, which leads obviously to high CAPEX and OPEX. Furthermore, a LCX system is non scalable, once a frequency is chosen, no modification can be brought.

**WiMAX.** The WiMAX's bandwidth capacity makes it suitable for providing high speed broadband Internet access. In the literature, few papers present experimental analysis using WiMAX technology in the railway domain. In [30], the authors present an architecture providing broadband wireless communication on trains, able to address the security, performance and communication needs, and enhancements in mobility management in the network. In [5], the SWiFT (Seamless Wireless Internet for Fast Trains) architecture is introduced. It is based on the deployment of WiMAX (IEEE 802.16m) base stations at the trackside and an optical backbone to link these base stations and the global Internet. In [31], a state of the art on handover mechanism for WiMAX is presented. It pointed out that while WiMAX is a promising technology (in terms of QoS, bandwidth and costs), there are still open issues about the handover management. A WiMAX solution is deployed in the Narita Express in Tokyo in Japan since 2009. It uses a WiMAX technology at 2.5 GHz bands. Maximum throughputs of 40 Mbps can be obtained for the downlink [32]. Since 2012, the same system equips the Super Hitachi trains. Solutions based on WiMAX are also currently studied for the Caltrain of Silicon Valley in US, relying on a *Nomad Digital* solution. No further technical details were found on this system.

**Wi-Fi.** Wi-Fi is an unlicensed and well-known technology allowing good performance and resistance to the high velocity. SNCF, in collaboration with Orange Labs, performed some experimental tests relying on Wi-Fi IEEE 802.11b and g [25]. The tested network was based on 4 access points located on bridges and pylons, covering an area of 13 km. Connectivity performance tests were performed showing a network able to support a traffic around 2 Mbps and handovers across the 4 access points. An extended network of 50 km was then deployed relying on 10 access points installed on 3G cellular radio sites. The results show some good performance in terms of throughputs. More recent experiments were performed in 2010 using the IEEE 802.11n [3], [28]. Two base stations were placed at 6.3 km from each other, close to the average distance between 2 consecutive GSM-R sites in France. Throughputs up to some tens of Mbps were achieved. To our knowledge, only one system was deployed for an Internet access on board train. Indeed, the Tsukuba express in Japan provides Internet connectivity in its trains since 2006, based on the Wi-Fi [33]. Throughputs up to 54 Mbps are indicated but no further information could be found.

**Radio-Over-Fiber.** Frequent handovers during the passage from a base station to another constitutes the main drawback of "classical" cellular networks. This leads to a significant decrease of throughputs. One solution to solve this problem is to deploy a system based on Radio-over-Fiber (RoF). In [34], the authors argue that broadband connectivity can be obtained by reducing the size of the cells. However, it leads to the rollout of a large number of base stations along the track. The authors propose then to use a RoF system, allowing feed base stations deployed along the track. Antennas fed by optical fiber are called Remote Antenna Units (RAU). The goal of a RoF system is to transfer complicated signal processing functions from the base stations along the railway to a centralized control station, and then to reduce costs deployment and frequency of handovers. For communications between the access network and the train, data are modulated at control station level and sent into optical format to each RAU, using multiplexing on wavelength, each RAU having a unique wavelength for communications. The antenna transforms the optical signal into a radio signal transmitted to the train. The RoF technology is used in the Shanghai Transrapid, which is a Magnetic Levitation (MAGLEV) train running up to 500 km/h. The system uses a communication system relying on fiber optic links and radio base stations deployed along the track [35]. Throughputs up to 16 Mbps can be reached in full duplex at 5.8 GHz [36].

**Other Proprietary Solutions.** In addition to wireless technologies such as Wi-Fi or WiMAX, other solutions can be used to provide Internet on board trains, such as proprietary solutions. Fluidmesh [37] aims at delivering fiber-like performance via unlicensed wireless spectrum, providing connectivity for transmission of video, voice, and data to sites and hard environments, such as high speed moving vehicles and trains. Fluidmesh developed a license-free trackside wireless system, operating in the 5 GHz band. Throughputs up to 100 Mbps on a train running up to 350 km/h are announced without service disruption and handoffs below 3 ms. The system relies on a 2x2 MIMO-based radio technology and dual-polarized trackside and on-board antennas. In June 2014, Amtrak announced its collaboration with Fluidmesh to install dedicated trackside technology on its HST line connecting Boston to Washington, D.C. Luceor [38] is a specialist in outdoor wireless networks developed for particular applications such as public transportations. The solution is based on the WiMESH technology, which is a routing and mesh technology based on IEEE 802.11n standard. Throughputs at UDP level up to 450 Mbps are announced, and mobility is supported until 350 km/h. Furthermore, a coverage from 100 m to 10 km is announced. RATP in France performed some tests in June 2014, based on this technology in the context of tunneling emergency situations, needing new generations of wireless transmission of video streams and voice in mobility and very high speed.

**Optical Solutions.** Optic Wireless Communications (OWC), also called Free Space Optics (FSO) represent an attractive technological solution in terms of throughput to obtain broadband Internet access on board trains. Indeed, FSO technologies offer large unregulated bandwidth allowing throughput up to Gbps, in addition to immunity to electromagnetic interferences and low Bit Error Rates (BER). Moreover, optical signals cannot penetrate walls and transmission can be completely secured. The Railway Technical Research Institute in Japan tested this technique, in collaboration with the Keio University [39]. Throughputs up to 700 Mbps are obtained at TCP level, for a speed of 130 km/h. The system is based on a "laser beam tracking" method for which the transmitter consists of a laser transmission device and a mobile mirror. It transmits laser beams towards the receiver. With a mobile mirror, the transmitter can follow the receiver and establish a continuous communication. Other works in UK were realized in order to evaluate performance of an OWC system for broadband Internet access on board trains [40]. These works are largely dominated by simulations and no measurement in real sites with railway constraints were performed yet.

**Summary on Dedicated Train-to-infrastructure Solutions.** Few existing solutions rely on a dedicated infrastructure, most of them based on WiMAX technology. However, this kind of solutions allow an entire control of the QoS, in terms of range and throughputs especially. Fluidmesh solution claims providing broadband connectivity up to 100 Mbps until 350 km/h. To our knowledge, the first passenger service that will use this solution is the Amtrak trains. The train-to-infrastructure solutions lead to high costs in terms of OPEX and CAPEX. A compromise has to be found between performance and costs (involved features are throughputs and coverage). Concerning optical solutions, promising throughputs up to several hundreds of Mbps were demonstrated in Japan. However, the major drawbacks remain the high CAPEX and OPEX and the performance dependence on atmospheric conditions.

### Zoom on Cognitive Radio and 5G

Among all the solutions presented, the aggregation of several available frequency bands is frequently used. This technique is used to increase the capacity of the systems and allows broadband communications. Another solution to optimize the use of the frequency spectrum and to reduce the deployment cost is the new concept called Cognitive Radios (CR). All the previous presented solutions lead to a common conclusion: the natural frequency spectrum is limited. It is necessary to operate at higher frequency bands in order to obtain wider spectrum allowing broadband communications. It becomes obvious that the current static frequency allocation schemes cannot accommodate the requirements of an increasing number of high throughput devices. CR concept, introduced by Mitola in [41], appears to be a tempting solution to the spectral congestion problem by using frequency bands not heavily occupied by licensed users. To our knowledge, only one paper deals with the CR in the Railway context [42]. Currently, the French project CORRIDOR (COgnitive Radio for RaIlway through Dynamic and Opportunistic spectrum Reuse), aims at validating cutting-edge opportunistic air interface technologies allowing robust low-latency links between HST and ground infrastructure [43]. Results will be demonstrated in July 2015.

Another emerging technology is 5G, which corresponds to the next phase of mobile telecommunications standards. It aims at providing throughputs up to several Gbps. 5G is not yet defined and official, it aims at emerging in 2020. Every big Telecommunication Companies take an interest in this new technology, in addition to the big institutions and the states. Several programs and groups were launched on 5G in Europe (5Gnow, IJoin, Tropic, METIS) and Asia (IMT-2020 (5G), 5GForum, 2020 and Beyond AdHoc group). For now, theoretical throughputs announced rely on the study of the downlink. The uplink still has to be explored.

## 5    Conclusion

Broadband Internet access on board HST represents a real challenge for railway operators, in a more and more competitive domain. Several solutions are deployed, especially in Europe and Asia. However, it remains difficult to reach QoS and low costs at the same time. Table 1 summarizes the different technologies that can be implemented. A combination of technologies can be applied, relying on a preferred technology and a "gap-filler". Cellular-based solutions are largely deployed because of the low costs in terms of investment. No dedicated infrastructure at the trackside has to be deployed and constraints due to railway context are limited. Finally, it is important to keep updated on future technologies, such as Cognitive Radio and 5G, which aim at providing high capacity systems.

**Table 1.** Summary of the different technologies to provide Internet on board trains

| | | | Dedicated infrastructure | | |
|---|---|---|---|---|---|
| | **Satellite** | **Cellular** | **Radio terminals** | **RoF** | **Optical** |
| **Through-puts** | > 10 Mbps | > 10 Mbps | > 100 Mbps | / | > 10 Gbps |
| **Latency** | > 400 ms | > 200 ms | > 100 ms | > 100 ms | > 50 ms |
| **Advantages** | Existing infrastructure | No infrastructure, low cost | Average throughputs, seamless communications | Low cost base stations, seamless communication | Very high throughputs, seamless communications |
| **Drawbacks** | Communication failures due to obstacles, limited throughputs | Possible limited coverage, limited throughputs | High costs | High costs | Heavy infrastructure, influence of atmospheric conditions, very high costs |

# References

1. Ai, B., Cheng, X., Kürner, T., Zhong, Z.D., Guan, K., He, R.S., Xiong, L., Matolak, D.W., Michelson, D.G., Briso-Rodriguez, C.: Challenges Toward Wireless Communications for High-Speed Railway. IEEE Transactions On Intelligent Transportation Systems 15(5) (October 2014)
2. Fokum, D.T., Frost, V.S.: A Survey on Methods for Broadband Internet Access on Trains. IEEE Communications Surveys & Tutorials 12(2), 171–185 (2010)
3. Ghannoum, H., Sanz, D.: Internet Onboard: technical analysis. In: 5th International Workshop on Communication Technologies for Vehicles, Nets4cars/Nets4trains, Lille, France (May 2013)
4. http://mobilesociety.typepad.com/mobile_life/2007/07/hsdpa-internet-.html
5. Kumar, R., Angolkar, P., Das, D., Ramalingam, R.: SWiFT: A Novel Architecture for Seamless Wireless Internet for Fast Trains. In: IEEE Vehicular Technology Conference (VTC Spring), Singapore, pp. 3011–3015 (May 2008)

6. Pareit, D., Van Brussel, W., Torfs, W., De Cleyn, P.: QoS-enabled Internet-on-train network architecture: inter-working by MMP-SCTP versus MIP. In: 7th International Conference on Intelligent Transportation Systems Telecommunications (ITST), Sophia-Antipolis, France, pp. 1–6 (June 2007)

7. Rodriguez, P., Chakravorty, R., Chesterfield, J., Pratt, I., Banerjee, S.: MAR: A Commuter Router Infrastructure for the Mobile Internet. In: 2nd International Conference on Mobile Systems, Applications, and Services (MobiSys), pp. 217–230 (June 2004)

8. Chini, P., Giambene, G., Kota, S.: A survey on mobile satellite systems. International Journal of Satellite Communications and Networking 28(1), 29–57 (2010)

9. Hu, Y., Li, V.O.: Satellite-based Internet: a tutorial. IEEE Communications Magazine 39(3), 154–162 (2001)

10. Fabri, A., Nieva, T., Umiliachi, P.: Use of the Internet for Remote Train Monitoring anc Control: the ROSIN Project. In: Rail Technology 1999, London, UK (September 1999)

11. Gatti, A.: Trains as Mobile devices: the TrainCom project. In: Wireless Design Conference, London, UK (May 2002)

12. Schena, V., Ceprani, F.: FIFTH Project solutions demonstrating new satellite broadband communication system for high speed train. In: IEEE 59th Vehicular Technology Conference, VTC-Spring, vol. 5, pp. 2831–2835 (2004)

13. Billion, J., Van den Abeele, D.: ICOM: A Communication Framework for Interoperable European Railways. In: 7th International Conference on Intelligent Transportation Systems Telecommunications (ITST), pp. 1–6. IEEE, Nice (2007)

14. Berbineau, M., Chennaoui, M., Gransart, C., Afifi, H., Bonnin, J.-M., Sanz, D., Duchange, D.: High Data Rate Transmissions for High Speed Trains, Dream or Reality? Technical state of the art and user requirements, Train-IPSAT Project - WP1. Tech. rep., Synthesis INRETS 51 (June 2006) ISBN 278-2-85782-643-5, ISSN 0769-0274

15. http://www.icomera.com

16. Wilson, D.: 10 Years of Wi-Fi on the East Coast Mainline. In: The WiFi on Trains Conference - Train Communications Systems, London, UK (June 2014)

17. http://www.21net.com

18. Thomson, H.H.: Challenges of Internet & Multimedia on Trains. The WiFi on Trains Conference - Train Communications Systems. London, UK (June 2014)

19. http://www.latribune.fr/entreprises-finance/services/transport-logistique/20141105trib5db4a0ea2/thalys-va-installer-un-wi-fi-plus-rapide-dans-ses-trains-sncf.html

20. NTV. NTV Presentation. The WiFi on Trains Conference - Train Communications Systems, London, UK (June 2014)

21. Niravkuamr, D.: 2nd Generation Of Secured Satellite Based Broadband System for efficient train operation and passenger Wi-Fi. In: The WiFi on Trains Conference - Train Communications Systems, London, UK (June 2014)

22. Sanz, D.: Satellite Technologies for Broadband Internet Access Onboard High Speed Trains. In: 7th World Congress on Railway Research, Montreal, Canada (June 2006)

23. Sanz, D., Pasquet, P., Mercier, P., Villeforceix, B., Duchange, D.: TGV Communicant Research Program: from research to industrialization of onboard, broadband Internet services for high-speed trains. In: 8th World Congress on Railway Research, Seoul, Korea (May 2008)

24. http://nomad-digital.com/

25. Brown, L.: Eurostar brings Wi-Fi on board. EURAILmag. 26, 189–190 (2014)

26. Ghannoum, H., Sanz, D., Villeforceix, B., Philippe, H., Mercier, P.: Delivering broadband Internet access for high speed trains passengers using the new WiFi standard 8802.11 for train-to-ground communications. In: 9th World Congress on Railway Research, Lille, France (May 2011)
27. De Greve, F., Lannoo, B., Peters, L., Leeuwen, T., Van Quickenborne, F., Colle, D., Demeester, P.: FAMOUS: A Network Architecture for Delivering Multimedia Services to FAst MOving USers. Wireless Personal Communications 33(3-4), 281–304 (2005)
28. Fettweis, G., Irmer, R.: WIGWAM: System concept development for 1 Gbit/s air interface. In: 14th Wireless World Research Forum (WWRF 2005) (July 2005)
29. Ishizu, K., Kuroda, M., Harada, H.: Bullet-train Network Architecture for Broadband and Real-time Access. In: IEEE Symposium on Computers and Communications, pp. 241–248. IEEE, Aveiro (2007)
30. Aguado, M., Onandi, O., Agustin, P.S., Higuero, M., Taquet, E.J.: WiMAX on Rails. VTC Magazine 3(3), 47–56 (2008)
31. Ray, S.K., Pawikowski, K., Sirisena, H.: Handover in Mobile WiMAX Networks: The State of Art and Research Issues. IEEE Communications and Surveys & Tutorials 12(3), 376–399 (2010)
32. Matsumoto, T.: Adding WiFi and Other Information Services to JR East Trains. In: The WiFi on Trains Conference - Train Communications Systems, London, UK (June 2014)
33. Yamada, K.: A High Speed Mobile Communication System Implementing Bicasting Architecture on the IP Layer, Technical report (2012)
34. Lannoo, B., Colle, D., Pickavet, M., Demeester, P.: Radio-over-fiber-based solution to provide broadband internet access to train passengers. IEEE Communications Magazine 45(2), 56–62 (2007)
35. Maureira, J.-C.: Internet on Rails. PhD thesis, University of Nice - Sophia-Antipolis (January 2011)
36. Schienbein, M., Dangelmeyr, J.: TrainCom radio system. Telefunken RACOMS (2009)
37. http://www.fluidmesh.com
38. http://www.luceor.com
39. Nakagawa, S., Matsubara, H., Nakamura, K., Tatsui, D., Haruyama, S., Teraoka, F.: Broadband Telecommunication System for Railways Using Laser Technology. In: 9th World Congress on Railway Research, Lille, France (May 2011)
40. Paudel, R., Ghassemlooy, Z., Le-Minh, H., Rajbhandari, S.: Modelling of free space optical link for ground-to-train communications using a Gaussian source. IET Optoelectronics 7(1), 1–8 (2013)
41. Mitola, J., Maguire, G.Q.: Cognitive Radio: Making Software Radios More Personal. IEEE Personal Communication Magazine 6(4), 13–18 (1999)
42. Amanna, A., Gadhiok, M., Price, M.J., Reed, J.H., Siriwongpairat, W.P., Himsoon, T.K.: Railway Cognitive Radio. IEEE Vehicular Technology Magazine 5(3), 82–89 (2010)
43. Berbineau, M., et al.: Cognitive Radio for High Speed Railway through Dynamic and Opportunistic spectrum Reuse, Transport Research Arena, Paris (April 2014)

# The Adoption of Public Telecom Services for the Evolution of the ERTMS-ETCS Train Control Systems: Challenges and Opportunities

Franco Mazzenga[1], Romeo Giuliano[2], Alessandro Neri[3], Francesco Rispoli[4], Agostino Ruggeri[5], Maurizio Salvitti[5], Emiliano Del Signore[1], and Valerio Fontana[4]

[1] Radiolabs/Dept. of Enterprise Engineering, Univ. of Rome Tor Vergata, Rome, Italy
[2] Dept. of Innov. Technologies and Processes, Univ. Guglielmo Marconi, Rome, Italy
[3] Radiolabs/Dept. Electronic Engineering, Univ. of ROMA TRE, Rome, Italy
[4] Ansaldo STS, Genova, Italy
[5] RadioLabs, Cons. Univ. Industria Laboratori di Telecomunicazioni, Rome, Italy

**Abstract.** The ERTMS-ETCS train control system relies on the GSM-R dedicated radio network for train to ground communications and on terrestrial dedicated network(s) for communications between the control center and the wayside equipments. However GSM-R technology will become obsolete in the next years, has limited capacity to accommodate growing traffic needs and is suffering from interference caused by the LTE. With the introduction of IP technology in the evolution path of the ERTMS-ETCS a number of possible alternatives are being analyzed and, among them we have studied an hybrid telecom system based on public networks (cellular + satellite). Although public cellular services are provided as best-effort, satellite can act as intelligent backup to complement the cellular networks and, all together, provide QoS in line with the ERTMS-ETCS requirements. This paper outlines the results of a specific test campaign to assess the performance of the cellular networks and satellite communications in a 300 km railways line for a cumulative 18,000 travelled Km in 21 days. These results, have been processed to estimate the achievable performance in the rail environment and to pave the way for realizing the multi-bearer solution. An economical assessment of the multi-bearer solution is presented making reference to the local and regional lines for which the deployment of a dedicated network is difficult to justify.

## 1 Introduction

In [EL1], [EL2] it is envisaged that future railway telecommunication systems will not be based on an unique modern or (futuristic) system, but it will integrate a variety of systems, each of them specialized/oriented to specific services. Services to passengers will be provided by one or more flexible radio systems

M. Kassab et al. (Eds.): Nets4Cars/Nets4Trains/Nets4Aircraft 2015, LNCS 9066, pp. 177–188, 2015.
DOI: 10.1007/978-3-319-17765-6_16

capable of evolving rapidly with the market demands and open to new and more advanced content-oriented applications. Instead, the communication platform for railway management will be oriented towards a unified infrastructure supporting real-time collaboration services. This allows to increase efficiency, speed-up the business processes, improve operational effectiveness, facilitate information exchange and improve the quality of decision making. Effective management of railway operation processes will require highly reliable and stable telecommunication platforms, supporting new operational modes enabling the increasing of the railway traffic capacity while ensuring high security and safety levels. The European Rail Agency (ERA) has already undertaken studies to evaluate possible options for the evolution of the GSM-R that will have to be replaced in the next years. In fact, GSM-R is suffering from technology obsolescence, electromagnetic compatibility with 4G-LTE networks operating in frequency bands close to those of GSM-R, and limited capacity. We observe that, concerning capacity, in addition to the ERTMS-ETCS needs, [SE1], wide-band passenger services (e.g. entertainment) and train equipment monitoring should be carefully considered. To enhance capacity, a first option would be the introduction of the GPRS, as done in the past for GSM. However, this option presents two major weaknesses: sustainability of capital costs associated to upgrades and extensions of the actual GSM-R radio network, especially for low traffic rail lines not yet covered by it, and interference issues. In the definition of a viable solution, two major challenges arise: to comply with the interoperability requirement, as done by the GSM-R today, and, from the train operator side, to protect the investments on the GSM-R. Nevertheless, a migration path to a fully IP-based telecom system is already started, and the incoming 5G could facilitate the evolution towards a full service-based system for all rail applications. Concerning cost reduction, a first breakthrough in economic sustainability is represented by the replacement of proprietary, dedicated networks with public networks, such as the cellular and satellite networks operated by commercial operators. This scenario implies a step-change in the liability process with the introduction of the guaranteed QoS as the most relevant Key Performance Indicator (KPI) in the provisioning of a mobile connectivity service package by a telecom operator(s), the starting point being the existing GSM-R specifications (see after). Considering that in the short term, each telecom bearer may provide best-effort services only, in the framework of the ESA ARTES 20 3InSat project we have investigated, by means of an experimental campaign, the possibility of achieving acceptable QoS on public networks. We consider QoS should be achieved by jointly using several best effort bearers managed by an on-board Multipath Router device (MAR: multiple access router). To further improve QoS we also propose the integration of a QoS guaranteed link provided by Satellite. This is helpful to improve quality in the case(s) of congested or unavailable terrestrial networks and/or to solve possible handover issues in the case of high speed trains. Due to limited space, experimental results presented and discussed in this paper are restricted to the case of terrestrial and, with integrated satellite communication used for transmitting standard signaling messages from train to ground and viceversa.

The test trials also included measurements for different types of communications services to/from train. Some of them have been designed to test the radio networks under very stressful conditions involving transmissions of data packets much longer than the typical signaling messages. As an example we have considered burst emissions of variable length packets even much longer than the standard SMS messaging used for typical signaling. We have also considered the case of the train control centre generating traffic having variable peak rates and characterized by different statistical distributions of the inter-arrival packet times such as the exponential one. Test activities have also included other two differentiated tests: the Radio Access Network end-to-end delay performance test directly performed by Vodafone-IT and the EuroRadio performance test performed by Ansaldo STS. The paper is organized as follows. In Section 2 we review the main issues related to the adoption of public land mobile radio network for supporting railway communication services. In Section 3 we describe the test scenario and we introduce the selected KPI. Results are presented and commented in Section 4 while a discussion on costs are presented in Section 5. Finally, Conclusions are drawn.

## 2   Main Issues for Railway Management Using Integrated Plmn/Satellite Networks

The adoption of PLMN/Satellite integrated radio networks for railway communications introduces some main concerns which are discussed in this Section.

### 2.1   Radio Coverage Issues

Design criteria of PLMNs are deeply different from those indicated in [EIR], and in general coverage requirements could be not guaranteed at all, outage probability could be over the prescribed limits and coverage holes could be present along the line. As indicated in [DSI] to improve coverage and link reliability and other performance parameters (see after) these two technical options could be considered.

1. **Multi-radio Technology (MRT):** on board equipment should be able to route messages/calls on any one of the terrestrial radio interface(s) available in the area (i.e. GSM, UMTS, LTE etc.) and/or on satellite. Routing decisions shall be taken on the basis of the current traffic load in the PLMN(s). The on board MAR should also be able to simultaneously select two (or more) radio interfaces for different communication services. As an example voice and/or data services could be routed on two distinct radio interfaces (e.g. GSM for signaling and UMTS for voice).
2. **Connecting to Multiple Radio Networks of Different Operators:** coverage could be improved by exploiting the simultaneous presence of networks of multiple mobile network operators (MNOs) in the same area[1]. In

---

[1] It should be noted that co-location of Base Stations of different operators works against improvement in radio coverage.

this case the on-board equipment should be able to switch among bearers of different operators and/or to setup and maintain multiple radio links with the different networks. Duplicates of messages have to be detected and discarded by applications used for train control. In this case the re-design of some parts of the Euroradio [ALC] protocol could be necessary, [DSI].

## 2.2   Handover and Cell-Reselection

Intense voice/data traffic originated by PLMN users may cause traffic congestions that may lead to (temporary) unavailability of radio bearers. This can have strong impact on the train Handover/Cell Reselection performance. To mitigate these problems, priority mechanisms for dropping one (or more) active calls, when the train is executing handover in presence of congestions, should be (possibly) negotiated with the telecom operator. The possibility of reserving radio channels for train communications only at some hours of the day, could be another option to meet handover/cell-reselection requirements.

## 2.3   Call Setup

In PLMN call setup delays can be related to cell load and could be difficult to control. Specifications in [EIR] consider priority levels in the call setup phase in relation to the call type. It seems difficult to relax call setup requirements even for regional and/or low traffic lines. The MRT and/or simultaneous usage of more than one telecom operator could be helpful to improve call setup objectives. Table 1 lists the main QoS requirements for the existing GSM-R system. We remark that the very demanding requirements in Table 1 refer to

**Table 1.** QoS parameters for GSM-R (ETCS)

| QoS Parameters | Demand Value |
|---|---|
| Call setup time | $\leq$ 10s ( 100%) |
| Connection establish failure probability | $\leq$ 1% (100%) |
| Data transmission delay | < 0.5s (99%) |
| Error rate | < 1%/h (100%) |
| Duration of transmission failures | < 1s (99%) |

high speed railway lines and they will be relaxed in the case of regional/low traffic lines[2]. However, the most important one is the time required for emergency call. In this case, the proposed adoption of Satellite is helpful to cope with congestion/unavailability of terrestrial network. In this perspective, the usage of integrated PLMN/satellite networks for railway communications can be seen as a valuable option.

---

[2] Requirements of radio systems supporting ERTSMS-ETCS over regional/low traffic lines are still under discussion.

# 3    Scenario and Test Trial

In this Section we present results from a test trial for the standard signaling service based on M2M service of the Vodafone IT public mobile radio network. The test scenario is represented in Figure 1. The trials were performed on the railway

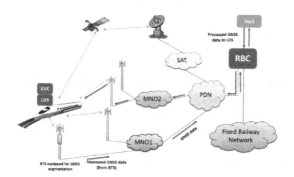

**Fig. 1.** Test scenario including augmentation sub-network

connecting the towns of Cagliari and Olbia in the Sardinia Island (Italy), in the framework of the ESA ARTES 20 3InSat Project, that foresees realization of a railway testbed for testing satellite navigation and communication technologies for rail applications, under real operational conditions. The line is about 300 km long and the maximum allowed train speed is 150 km/h, actually limited to 130 km/h (which is the maximum speed of the Minuetto Diesel traction trains used on the line). Tests and demonstrations have been performed reaching the maximum speed. During the 4 weeks of the test campaign, two trips per day each lasting 3:50 hours each way, have been performed. The GSM/GPS and satellite antennas were placed on the roof top of the train with unobstructed view to the sky. A power supply unit (PSU) of several batteries has been employed in the case of power outage. Tests have been executed by using the Vodafone 2G/3G public mobile access network, providing seamless handover even to the other mobile networks in case of lack of Vodafone coverage. The satellite link has been provided by Inmarsat Satellite (BGAN configuration). As shown in Figure 1 the on-board equipment includes the Euro Vital Computer (EVC) and a Location Determination System (LDS). Both EVC and LDS functionalities have been emulated by software running on a portable PC. The Radio Block Centre (RBC) emulator has been hosted by a server cluster located at TriaGnoSys lab facilities (Munich-Germany). The GPS antenna was placed on a windows sill outside the lab. To determine train position (train mileage with respect to the head station), the LDS uses data from GPS with differential corrections provided by a local augmentation network deployed along the line. The augmentation network includes two GPS measurement stations (one in Samasti and the other at Decimomannu) which acquire GPS data from satellites, pre-process them and send GPS observations by means of the wired network(s) to the Track Area LDS Server (TALS) in Monaco (see Figure 1). Data are processed by TALS to calculate corrections which are delivered to train using the terrestrial radio network.

### 3.1 Selected Key Performance Indicators

All data collected in the test trial, have been analysed to extract the following statistics:

1. End-to-End (E2E) delays vs train location (specified in terms of train mileage from the head of the track, in the reported plots illustrating the delay behaviour). The purpose of this statistics is to evidence the presence of (rare) anomalies in the E2E delay related to signal shadowing caused by rail-track infrastructures like tunnels, or coverage holes;
2. Cumulative Distributions of the E2E delay and of the corresponding Jitter;
3. Probability the E2E delay exceeds a threshold (Thr);
4. Packet Loss probability;
5. Mean and Standard deviation of the E2E delay computed using the data sets below the 90% percentile and below the 95% percentile[3].

## 4   Results

For brevity, only test results concerning the short messaging between train and the control centre are reported here. Test also considered the transmission of augmentation information from the control centre (i.e. TALS) and train. This first test was performed twice for a total duration of 184 min. The main characteristics of the generated traffic are detailed in Table 2. As shown in Table 2 traffic characteristics are different for forward (from Train to Ground) and reverse (from Ground to Train) links. The same tests have been repeated using the Satellite link.

**Table 2.** Test: traffic characteristics

| Stream type | Traffic Source | Traffic Destination | Traffic Type | Inter Departure | Payload Size (Bytes) |
|---|---|---|---|---|---|
| 1 | Ground/RBC | Cab/EVC | UDP | 0.33 pkts/sec | 300 |
| 2 | Cab/EVC | Ground/RBC | UDP | 0.25 pkts/sec | 50 |
| 3 | Ground/TALS | Cab/LDS | UDP | 1.0 pkts/sec | 135 |

---

[3] Rank order statistics filtering has been necessary to eliminate outliers that could seriously impair the calculation of statistics.

## 4.1   Terrestrial Network

In Figure 2 the average packet End-to-End Delay versus the train position (in terms of mileage from the head station) is plotted. The mileage has been quantized into bins, each one with a length of 250 meters. In each bin, we report the delays of packets that have been transmitted in the selected bin spatial interval. Purpose of this graph is to evidence the presence of anomalies in the estimated delay that can be related to the rail track characteristics. From analysis and

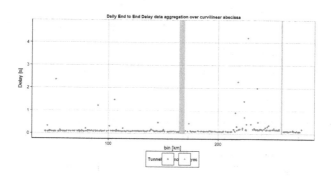

**Fig. 2.** Daily end-to-end delay versus train location - Terrestrial network, Stream 1

results in Figure 2 it is observed that large values of E2E delay are mainly due to tunnels and orography (physical barriers), causing poor service coverage areas along the rail track. This leads to significant variability of the available bit rate for transmission and/or to connection drops requiring re-setup. Another interesting phenomenon leading to an increase of the E2E delay was the delay in performing handover between different operators (roaming) or handover between 2G and 3G technologies and viceversa.

**Forward Link - Train to RBC.** The following Tables provide results on the percentiles of the packet E2E delay, jitter and on the probability that the packet E2E delay exceeds a threshold Thr (s). Results have been obtained by aggregating data obtained on the daily basis.   The computed Packet Loss is 2.1%. The

**Table 3.** Percentiles of End-to-End Delay and Jitter (s) - Stream 2

| No.Meas./Perc | 50 | 70 | 80 | 90 | 95 | 99 | 99,9 |
|---|---|---|---|---|---|---|---|
| **E2E Delay** | 0.11 | 0.14 | 0.19 | 0.47 | 0.68 | 5,33 | 36.00 |
| **E2E Jitter** | 0.00 | 0.01 | 0.019 | 0.08 | 0.28 | 2.03 | 12.68 |

mean and the standard deviation of the E2E delay obtained by excluding data above the 90 and 95 percentiles are: 0.16s and 0.13s for the 90-th percentile and 0.22s and 0.39s for the 95-th.

**Table 4.** Probability E2E delay exceeds (Thr)

| Dataset/Thr | 1 | 2 | 5 | 7 | 10 | 12 | 15 |
|---|---|---|---|---|---|---|---|
| Stream 2 | 2.87% | 1.98% | 1.03% | 0.77% | 0.51% | 0.44% | 0.33% |

**Table 5.** Percentiles of End-to-End Delay and Jitter (s) - Stream 1 and Stream 3

| No.Meas./Perc | 50 | 70 | 80 | 90 | 95 | 99 | 99.9 |
|---|---|---|---|---|---|---|---|
| E2E Delay - Stream 1 | 0.10 | 0.12 | 0.16 | 0.21 | 0.41 | 2.13 | 7.63 |
| E2E Jitter - Stream 1 | 0.00 | 0.01 | 0.011 | 0.03 | 0.13 | 1.19 | 5.75 |
| E2E Delay - Stream 3 | 0.1 | 0.11 | 0.16 | 0.19 | 0.35 | 2.15 | 8.15 |
| E2E Jitter - Stream 3 | 0.00 | 0.002 | 0.01 | 0.02 | 0.05 | 0.63 | 4.02 |

**Table 6.** Probability E2E delay exceeds (Thr)

| No.Meas./Thr. | 1 | 2 | 5 | 7 | 10 | 12 | 15 |
|---|---|---|---|---|---|---|---|
| Stream 1 | 2.06% | 1.04% | 0.28% | 0.17% | 0.06% | 0.03% | 0 |
| Stream 3 | 2.07% | 1.07% | 0.31% | 0.15% | 0.05% | 0.02% | 0% |

**RBC to Train - Reverse Link.** Similarly to the previous Section, the following Tables provide results on the percentiles of the packet E2E delay and jitter for Stream 1 and Stream 3 traffic types on the reverse link. Table 6 indicates the probability that E2E delay is greater than Thr. The packet loss for Stream 1 traffic is 3.40% and mean and standard deviation of the E2E delay computed on the 90 and 95 percentile datasets are: 0.12s, 0.05s (90-th) and 0.15s, 0.2s (95-th), respectively. Finally, the packet loss for Stream 3 is 3.40% and mean and standard deviation of the E2E delay computed on the 90 and 95 percentile datasets are: 0.11s, 0.04s (90-th) and 0.14s, 0.17s (95-th). Results for the two streams are not very different. In fact, signaling messages doesn't cause a significant increase in traffic in the terrestrial network. Table 7 summarizes the main results of the terrestrial network tests. The probability that E2E delay is larger than 2s has been evidenced. Results in Table 7 are taken from previous Tables for the three streams.

**Table 7.** Summary of test results - Terrestrial network

| Forward-Link (Train/EVC to Ground/RBC) | |
|---|---|
| Stream 2 - Probability E2E delay > 2 s | 1.98% |
| 95% Probability E2E max value | 679 ms |
| 95% Probability E2E mean value | 215 ms |
| 95% Probability E2E std dev. value | 390 ms |
| Packet Loss | 2.05% |
| | |
| Reverse-Link (Train/EVC to Ground/RBC) | |
| Stream 1 - Probability E2E delay > 2 s | 1.04% |
| 95% Probability E2E max value | 410 ms |
| 95% Probability E2E mean value | 147 ms |
| 95% Probability E2E std dev. value | 174 ms |
| Packet Loss | 3.40% |
| | |
| Stream 3 - Probability E2E delay > 2 s | 1.06% |
| 95% Probability E2E max value | 352 ms |
| 95% Probability E2E mean value | 141 ms |
| 95% Probability E2E std dev. value | 169 ms |
| Packet Loss | 3.40% |

## 4.2   Satellite Link

Tests with the satellite link have been repeated for 5 times for a total test duration of about 991 minutes. Figure 4.2 shows the measured packet E2E delay as a function of the train position. As expected E2E delay is increased with

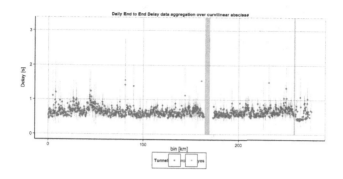

**Fig. 3.** Daily end-to-end delay as a function of the railway curvilinear abscissa - Integrated Satellite, Stream 1

respect to the terrestrial case, due to the additional (non negligible) propagation delay over the satellite link. Even in this case, significantly large E2E delays can be attributed to the presence of tunnels (in number of 2) and to orography, resulting in poor service coverage areas along the railtrack. When using satellite, we have experienced problems along the terrestrial interconnection path from the Inmarsat Gateway (England) and the control center (Ground/RBC in Munich) leading to an increase of delay from train-to-ground connection.

**Forward Link (from Train to Ground) - Satellite** The following Tables provide results on the percentiles of the packet E2E delay, jitter and on the probability the packet E2E delay is greater than Thr. As expected the probability that E2E delay is greater than 1s is significantly high due to both the additional satellite propagation delay and also to problems related to the terrestrial interconnection path from the Inmarsat Gateway (England) and the control center (Ground/RBC in Munich). The packet Loss is 1.02% and the mean and the standard deviation of packet delay evaluated by filtering data at 90 and 95 percentiles are: 1.09s, 0.43s (90-th) and 1.13s and 0.46 (95-th), respectively.

**Table 8.** Percentiles of End-to-End Delay and Jitter (s) - Stream 2, Satellite

| No.Meas./Perc | 50 | 70 | 80 | 90 | 95 | 99 | 99.9 |
|---|---|---|---|---|---|---|---|
| **E2E Delay** | 1.22 | 1.42 | 1.54 | 1.63 | 1.78 | 2.59 | 6.17 |
| **E2E Jitter** | -0.02 | 0.27 | 0.54 | 0.90 | 1.13 | 1.56 | 4.32 |

**Table 9.** Probability that delay exceeds (Thr), Satellite

| No.Meas./Thr. | 1 | 2 | 5 | 7 | 10 | 12 | 15 |
|---|---|---|---|---|---|---|---|
| Stream 2 | 67.8% | 3.1% | 0.14% | 0.08% | 0.05% | 0.04% | 0.03% |

**Table 10.** Percentiles of End-to-End Delay and Jitter (s) - Stream 1 and Stream 3. Satellite

| No.Meas./Perc | 50 | 70 | 80 | 90 | 95 | 99 | 99.9 |
|---|---|---|---|---|---|---|---|
| E2E Delay - Stream 1 | 0.56 | 0.69 | 0.80 | 0.98 | 1.16 | 1.69 | 4.34 |
| E2E Jitter - Stream 1 | 0.01 | 0.06 | 0.13 | 0.28 | 0.43 | 0.89 | 2.57 |
| E2E Delay - Stream 3 | 0.5619 | 0.7409 | 0.8525 | 1.019 | 1.148 | 1.707 | 4,43 |
| E2E Jitter - Stream 3 | 0.00 | 0.04 | 0.12 | 0.28 | 0.44 | 0.76 | 2.14 |

**Table 11.** Probability that delay exceeds (Thr)

| No.Meas./Thr. | 1 | 2 | 5 | 7 | 10 | 12 | 15 |
|---|---|---|---|---|---|---|---|
| Stream 1 | 9, 23% | 0.61% | 0.07% | 0.05% | 0.03% | 0.02% | 0.01% |
| Stream 3 | 10.52% | 0.71% | 0.08% | 0.05% | 0.03% | 0.02% | 0.01% |

**Reverse Link (from Ground to Train) - Satellite.** The following Tables provide results on the percentiles of the packet E2E delay and the corresponding jitter for stream 1 and stream 3 traffic used on the reverse link including satellite. In Table 6 we indicate the Probability that delay is greater than threshold (Thr). The packet loss for Stream 1 is 1.53% and the mean and the standard deviation of packet delay evaluated by filtering data at 90 and 95 percentiles are: 0.61s, 0.17s (90-th) and 0.64s, 0.23s (95-th), respectively. Instead, for Stream 3 packet loss is 1.76% and the mean and the standard deviation of packet delay evaluated by filtering data at 90 and 95 percentiles are: 0.62s, 0.19s and 0.65s, 0.24s, respectively. The main results of the tests for the integrated satellite link are summarized in Table 12. From previous results it can be observed that satellite

**Table 12.** Summary of test results - Integrated Satellite link

| Forward-Link (Train/EVC to Ground/RBC) | |
|---|---|
| Stream 2 - Probability E2E delay > 2 s | 3.06% |
| 95% Probability E2E max value | 1780 ms |
| 95% Probability E2E mean value | 1120 ms |
| 95% Probability E2E std dev. value | 463 ms |
| Packet Loss | 1.02% |
| | |
| Reverse-Link (Train/EVC to Ground/RBC) | |
| Stream 1 - Probability E2E delay > 2 s | 0.61% |
| 95% Probability E2E max value | 1160 ms |
| 95% Probability E2E mean value | 639 ms |
| 95% Probability E2E std dev. value | 223 ms |
| Packet Loss | 1.53% |
| | |
| Stream 3 - Probability E2E delay > 2 s | 1.06% |
| 95% Probability E2E max value | 1150 ms |
| 95% Probability E2E mean value | 650 ms |
| 95% Probability E2E std dev. value | 235 ms |
| Packet Loss | 1.76% |

integration has the (obvious) undesired effects of increasing the E2E delay but packet loss probability is significantly reduced in every case with respect to the terrestrial link. This is due to the increased availability, QoS and better coverage provided by the satellite.

## 5    Cost Assessment

Public telecommunication services represent a cost efficient solution for the economical sustainability of the ERTMS-ETCS platform on local and regional lines. To evaluate the costs of an hybrid (cellular-satellite) multi-bearer solution we have assumed the average price of cellular and satellite services offered by telecom operators and the cumulative data traffic exchanged between the train and the Radio Block Center according to the ETCS standard. The traffic is routed mainly through the cellular networks for approximately 80% of the time and the satellite is used, as a backup for the remaining 20% of the time. This share is arbitrary and results from a trade off on the availability of the cellular network in typical local and regional lines. A fleet of 100 trains (70 operating simultaneously) and an amortization period of 5 years have been considered to estimate the total operation costs incurred to ensure the service. Under these assumptions the average cost x train x month is about 900 euro and it includes the costs for equipping the trains with the multipath router, the satellite/cellular antennas, plus the communication fees for the providers of the telecom services. These costs are independent from the length of the rail line and vary only with the number of operational trains. Therefore the real benefits depend on the typology of the line, the number of operational trains and the line capacity. However for the local and low traffic lines (about 50% of the total European network length) this solution may be particularly convenient compared to traditional GSM-R networks that would imply up-front investments not economically sustainable for low traffic lines. Furthermore, the M2M based solutions are expected to grow exponentially in the near future and the cellular networks will improve their coverage and capacity with the incoming 5G standard. As a consequence the unitary cost for the transmission of ETCS messages is expected to drop. Similarly, the satellite communications networks will provide more bandwidth at lower cost and, most importantly, satellite operators can dedicate capacity for such services in order to guarantee the emergency call and group calls that, being the most demanding in terms of set up time, cannot be guaranteed with the best-effort services of the cellular networks.

## 6    Conclusions

We have investigated the performance of cellular and satellite public networks in the railways environment for supporting an hybrid telecom solution as candidate alternative to the GSM-R for the ERTMS-ETCS evolution. The proposed solution consists of a multi-bearer system making use of a combined cellular-satellite system with on board intelligent routing to select the bearer and guarantee the

Quality of the Service that is required by the ERTMS-ETCS. The case of the regional/low traffic lines has been analyzed and resulted attractive from the economical point of view since the investments to deploy a dedicated GSM-R network can be avoided. This solution could accelerate the modernization of these lines most of which are obsolete and costly to operate. The test campaign has been carried out along a 300 Km line crossing big cities, rural areas, tunnels and bridges and the tests have been repeated for 21 days totaling some18 thousands km travelled distance. The data have been processed to derive the most important parameters and the results in terms of packet loss and E2E delays are encouraging. Further work is on progress to develop and validate the multi-bearer routing algorithms and to define the process for homologation and certification a service-based solution in the frame of the ERTMS-ETCS evolution.

**Acknowledgments.** This work has been done in the frame of the 3InSat project [3SAT]; Radiolabs has been responsible for the Telecom test campaign. Authors wish to thank RFI, Trenitalia, Vodafone Italia, Telespazio, Triagnosys and DLR.

# References

EL1.    Elia, M.: What is the future of telecommunications in rail? In: RAILTEL Europe 2012, Hilton Vienna, Austria, February 27-29 (2012)

EL2.    Elia M. M.: CCS & Operation Sector Plenary, Paris (March 15, 2012)

EIR.    GSM-R Operators Group, EIRENE System and Functional Requirements Specification, V15.3.0. (2012)

GSMR.   GSM-R Industry Group, GSM-R the only approved world telecom standard for railways

SE1.    Senesi, F., Marzilli, E.: European train control system. In: CIFI (2007)

ALC.    Alcatel, Alstom, Ansaldo Signal et. al.: Euroradio FIS, subset-037, v. 2.3.0 (October 14, 2005)

DSI.    Del Signore, E., Giuliano, R., Mazzenga, F., Petracca, M., Vari, M., Vatalaro, F., Neri, A., Rispoli, F.: On the Suitability of Public Mobile Networks for Supporting Train Control/Management Systems. In: IEEE Wireless and Networking Conference (WCNC) 2014, Instanbul, Turkey (April 2014)

3SAT.   3inSat EU project, description avaialble online at http://iap.esa.int/projects/transport/3insat

# Air

# Towards a Deterministic Mixed Criticality High Availability Seamless Redundancy (HSR) Ring

Peter Heise[1,2], Fabien Geyer[1], Alexandros Elefsiniotis[1],
and Roman Obermaisser[2]

[1] Airbus Group Innovations, 81663 Munich, Germany
[2] University of Siegen, 57068 Siegen, Germany
peter.heise@airbus.com, roman.obermaisser@uni-siegen.de

**Abstract.** There is a growing trend for real-time Ethernet in nearly all industrial branches. While each industry has its own Ethernet-based protocols in networks, the High Availability Seamless Redundancy (HSR) network is currently of interest to the automation industry. A key factor and main benefit of HSR is its built-in fault-tolerance against the failure of a single communication link. However, it lacks mechanisms to guarantee certain bandwidth to applications. In this paper we propose a mechanism to guarantee packet arrival within a certain time while still offering best-effort traffic in order to support for mixed criticality traffic. Furthermore, a mathematical model is developed, that describes the upper latency limit of the proposed mechanism. We compare HSR with and without the proposed extension using an OMNeT++ simulation and show its advantages and weaknesses.

## 1   Introduction

Critical systems need to work even in case of failures and offer a maximum of safety, reliability and security. While safety translates to having no critical failure of the system, critical systems also need to have a guarantee on a network level, that packets are delivered in all cases. Therefore, the network must ensure that packets are delivered before a deadline. When speaking about deadline guarantee for packets, often the term deterministic is used. For a network architecture to be called deterministic, it must fulfill the following points: (a) formal verification of maximum end-to-end latencies and (b) mechanisms in the network to guarantee that ill-behaved end-systems will not interfere with well-behaved end-systems. This is generally achieved by the definition of a contract on the flows of the network, which defines how an end-system must send its packets on the network.

The easiest way to achieve redundancy on network level is to have two parallel networks by duplication of all hardware and thus also costs. An example for this is the Avionics Full Duplex Ethernet[4] (AFDX) network, that is commonly used in avionics. A redundancy solution on system level without device duplication is used in High-Availability Seamless Redundancy[7] (HSR) as standardized in IEC 62439-3 Clause 5. In HSR, nodes are connected with 2 interfaces to a ring network and packets are transmitted twice in opposite directions across that

© Springer International Publishing Switzerland 2015
M. Kassab et al. (Eds.): Nets4Cars/Nets4Trains/Nets4Aircraft 2015, LNCS 9066, pp. 191–202, 2015.
DOI: 10.1007/978-3-319-17765-6_17

ring. Therefore, the system can survive a fault as long as the second path is still in operation.

Similar as seen in the IEEE Time-Sensitive Networking Task Group[6] 802.1 Qbv project working on Enhancements for Scheduled Traffic, we also propose a time-aware mechanism to achieve determinism and traffic limitation in one step. Unlike a global TDMA-like schedule that has to be known by every switch, we introduce a decentralized time-aware scheme that simplifies configuration of the network nodes as they only need to know their own schedule. The contribution of this paper is two-fold. We present a mechanism to introduce determinism for HSR ring networks and give an analytical model to give its upper latency bound. Further, we extend both the mechanism and the model to support multiple time-triggered flows per node. The next section will present some related work that has been done on the field, then the problem statement and contribution is presented in detail. After his, the mathematical model is introduced for multiple cases. Before concluding, the last two sections present the simulation environment and the comparison of simulation to model results.

## 2    Related Work

Deterministic networks are widely available in literature and practice. A typical example for such a network in avionics is AFDX, which offers real time guarantees through statistical multiplexing. Traffic is segregated into virtual links (VL), each of which defines a unidirectional stream from one end-system to one or several other end-systems. Each stream is characterized by a Bandwidth Allocation Gap (BAG) and a maximum and minimum frame size effectively limiting its bandwidth. Switches enforce compliance to this traffic description and can thus offer guaranteed service. In typical applications, the network is laid out twice with duplicated hardware to establish redundancy and enable fault-tolerance.

In order to avoid duplicated hardware, as described above, a ring network is introduced. One current state-of-the-art ring network is HSR[7]. Its main goal is to provide seamless redundancy at an affordable cost, while being compatible with Ethernet. Packets coming from a node are duplicated before being sent out on two disjunctive paths across the network. This behavior ensures that if one packet is lost, the second packet can still reach its destination. HSR uses the ring topology where packets are transmitted in opposing directions. No mechanism for traffic policing is specified in the current version leaving the network vulnerable to flooding. Several works are available on traffic policing in HSR; Nsaif and Rhee[9] introduce a quick remove approach, that stops forwarding packets when the packet has been seen on the opposing link already. In the same paper, they describe on how to use VLANs to minimize traffic on other network, e.g. coupled rings. They later extended their work with RURT[10] to minimize traffic in scenarios with coupled rings. While both works focus on minimizing traffic within the network, it does not offer any guarantees or traffic shaping. Lee et al.[8] propose design methods for more reliable networks when using such coupled rings.

Another deterministic network is *Time-Triggered Ethernet* (TTEthernet)[11] as standardized in SAE AS6802. TTEthernet offers support for time-triggered, rate-constrained and best-effort messages. Rate-constraint traffic works like in AFDX, whereas the time-triggered messages work on a global TDMA like schedule. Abuteir et al.[3] propose a TTEthernet based ring solution with selective fault-tolerance and support for mixed-criticality. Unlike in TTEthernet, the approach in this paper only needs configuration of the local node and not all nodes. Furthermore, in our approach we support multiple time-triggered classes with different schedules per node.

To the best of the authors knowledge, there is no further work in the field of deterministic HSR networks.

# 3  Problem Statement

While HSR has means to offer redundancy at system level, it lacks real-time mechanisms to guarantee timely packet arrival. Therefore, a traffic policing mechanism is introduced in this section being a main contribution of this paper and not covered by the HSR standard.

## 3.1  Delay Variability

In HSR, packets are always sent twice, therefore for determining a maximum latency both paths have to be considered. If always this maximum case is considered, no difference will be seen in case of a failure compared to the fault-free scenario. The worst case will thus be created, when a direct neighbor is addressed: a short path with a hop count of 0 and a long path across the whole ring. The time between the arrival of both packets is called *delay variability* V. In order to minimize the maximum latency, the delay variability time has to be minimized. This can be done by relaxing (or maximizing) the short path while at

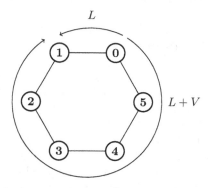

**Fig. 1.** Delay variability on a ring network

the same time prioritizing the longer path. An illustration of this can be seen in Fig. 1. While the short path latency allows for several strategies, a minimization of the longer path is achieved by giving priority to packets that are already on the ring. Following some initial simulations, we therefore opt for the ring-first scheduling strategy as it is easy to implement in hardware and keeps buffering of packets on a ring to the minimum.

### 3.2   Time-Aware Queue

To police incoming traffic and keep latency to a minimum, we propose the use of *time-aware queues* (TAQ). A TAQ is a normal FIFO queue that is enabled by a time-based schedule. Its schedule works on a global time-base and allows the dequeuing of packets from its queue only when the schedule allows for it. We introduce one or more time-aware queues connected along with several normal queues to a *strict priority scheduler* (SPQ). The SPQ gives the highest priority to the TAQs; the second highest priority to the incoming ring traffic and the lowest priority to local best-effort traffic. As the TAQs will never send at the same time, their priority can be considered to be the same. An illustration of this can be seen in Fig. 2. Because nodes only need to know their local schedule and treat other ring traffic in normal queues, this mechanism is enabling a decentralized TDMA while the ring traffic is still going first.

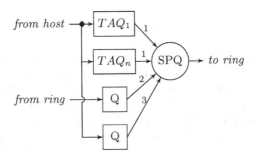

**Fig. 2.** Time-aware queues (TAQ) in each node port

## 4   Mathematical Model

In this section, we develop a mathematical model to describe upper limits of traffic latencies for the proposed architecture in section 3. It is based on synchronization of queues which, however, in a worst case can be lost. While TSN[6] and TTEthernet[11] try to prevent such failure mode by using redundant clock masters, the HSR standard does not cover such mechanisms and is as such vulnerable to synchronization loss. Therefore, the model aims to give an upper bound in a synchronized condition as well as under clock failure.

We introduce the following naming conventions, following the definitions in RFC 1242. An exemplary path in Fig. 1 from node 0 to node 1 can take two paths. The first path with the lesser amounts of hops is called the *short path* and has in this example a hop count of 0. The longer path is called *redundant path* and has a hop-count of 4 in the example. We assume a static processing delay in each hop of $T_{switching}$.

## 4.1 One TAQ per Node

In engineered networks, network designers specify a refresh time that describes how often an information needs to be updated. We call this time $T_{cycle}$ and it is assumed to be given by the scenario. Also, the designers specify how much data D needs to be transferred. Therefore, the slot per data-flow is given by $T_{slot} = \frac{D}{BW}$.

Each time a packet is transmitted, the physical line might already be in use causing a delay of $T_{cross} = \frac{D_{Cross}}{BW}$ called *head-of-line blocking*. Because we want to allow mixed criticality and thus best-effort traffic, we have to assume $D_{Cross}$ to be the maximum allowed Ethernet packet size and therefore have a static $T_{Cross}$ depending only on the used transmission speed $BW$.

While the TAQ is sending according to its schedule, the local application in the node is not aware of the time synchronization. Therefore, the host sends packets at an arbitrary point in time down to the network card where it will be transmitted when the schedule permits. This value is expressed by $T_{\text{local}}$:

$$T_{\text{local}}^N = T_{switching} + T_{Cross} + T_{Cycle}^N \tag{1}$$

$T_{\text{local}}$ denotes the maximum latency that it takes a packet to be transmitted from the node N into the ring. The worst-case is created, when the packets arrived at the network card right after the slot has ended and has to wait a whole cycle before it can send thus $T_{cycle} - T_{slot}$. The transmission of the packet itself takes another $T_{slot}$ so that it can be removed from the equation. Time lost at each additional host resembles to the interfering slots and head-of-line blocking and is expressed with $T_{\text{perhop}}$ for a node N:

$$T_{\text{perhop}}^N = T_{switching} + T_{Cross} + T_{Slot}^N \tag{2}$$

The maximum end-to-end delay E from a node N across the ring going through the hops on its path. All hops on the path are added to the set PATH. The end-to-end delay E is then given by equation (3). $T_{Slot}^N$ is added to follow RFC 1242 definition of latency.

$$E^{N \rightarrow \text{PATH}} = T_{\text{local}}^N + \sum_{A \in \text{PATH}} (T_{\text{perhop}}^A + T_{Slot}^N) \tag{3}$$

While equation (3) describes the case that happens under untimely scheduled cross-traffic, $T_{Slot}^A$ will not interfere at each hop if synchronization is working. Therefore, E can be simplified to the following form.

$$E_{\text{synchronized}}^{N \rightarrow \text{PATH}} = \underbrace{T_{switching} + T_{Cross}}_{T_{\text{local}}^N} + \text{size(PATH)} \cdot (\underbrace{T_{switching} + T_{Cross}}_{T_{\text{perhop}}^A} + T_{Slot}^N)$$

$$\tag{4}$$

## 4.2   Multiple TAQs per Node

To allow multiple applications per node, it is likely different schedules are needed as each application might have their own transmission cycles. Therefore, we introduce support for multiple TAQs per node each with its own schedule. The schedules have to be globally synchronized so that no collisions occur.

We extend the previous formulas with an additional argument i indicating the TAQ on the node, denoted by $T_{Cycle}^{N,i}$ and $T_{Slot}^{N,i}$. Formula (1) is extended as follows for a given TAQ i on a node N:

$$T_{local}^{N,i} = T_{switching} + T_{Cross} + T_{Cycle}^{N,i} \tag{5}$$

Again $T_{local}^{N,i}$ denotes the maximum latency that it takes a packet to be transmitted from the local node into the ring. As the schedules for parallel queues have to be configured collision-free, other queues don't influence this value.

$$T_{perhop}^{N} = T_{switching} + T_{Cross} + \sum_{i=0}^{\#\text{TAQs of N}} T_{Slot}^{N,i} \tag{6}$$

This bound could be lowered if only consecutive slots are considered and not all of the nodes'. Following equations (5) and (6), the maximum end-to-end delay E across a set PATH containing all nodes on the path.

$$E^{N,i \rightarrow \text{PATH}} = T_{local}^{N,i} + \sum_{A \in \text{PATH}} (T_{perhop}^{A} + T_{Slot}^{N,i}) \tag{7}$$

For a $E_{synchronized}^{N,i \rightarrow \text{PATH}}$ the same simplifications as before can be made leaving only a dependence of $T_{switching}$, $T_{Cross}$ and $T_{Slot}^{N,i}$ and is therefore omitted.

## 4.3   Specifics to High Availability Seamless Redundancy (HSR)

In a HSR ring with all nodes n $\in$ NODES, the packets always take two paths. Therefore we can specify a HSR end-to-end latency H for the short path, which is usually taken, and the redundant path, which has to be considered in case of link failure.

$$H^{N \rightarrow \text{PATH}} = \begin{cases} E^{N \rightarrow \text{PATH}} & \text{Short Path} \\ E^{N \rightarrow NODES \setminus \{\text{PATH} \cup N\}} & \text{Redundant Path} \end{cases} \tag{8}$$

Following the assumption of being able to handle one failure per containment region, the maximum latency is equal to the link down case. As the packets in HSR take two different path, the two HSR copies take different times to arrive at the destination. The maximum packet end-to-end delay variability V of those two copies is described in the following equation. PATH represents here the short path's hops.

$$V^{N \rightarrow \text{PATH}} = E^{N \rightarrow NODES \setminus \{\text{PATH} \cup N\}} - E_{synchronized}^{N \rightarrow \text{PATH}} \tag{9}$$

## 4.4 Gain of Time-Aware Queues Compared to Normal Traffic Policing

To make up for the complexity of time-awareness a major advantage should be enabled. As a reference for comparison we use a non-synchronized network like HSR in combination with a simple traffic shaper. The resulting latency is highly dependent on cross-traffic. Best-effort cross-traffic will have the same effect on both mechanisms and is as such not neglected in the following.

*Non-synchronized scheduling* : An established way to calculate latency bounds is the use of *network calculus* (NC). Initial NC developments were first used for providing reservations across the internet and later adapted also for the use in AFDX style networks[5]. The calculated bounds are usually too pessimistic, however, provide an upper limit which then can be used for certification, as done in Airbus' A380 airplane. In NC each switch is modeled with a service curve $\beta_{R,T}(t) = R\lceil t - T\rceil^+$ with R being the bandwidth and T the static switching delay. AFDX flows are modeled using a token-bucket model $\gamma_{r,b}(t) = (rt + b)$ for $t > 0$ with $r = \frac{s_{max}}{BAG}$ and $b = s_{max}$. Using network calculus, we can calculate the latency of the HSR node in a non-synchronized way.

*HSR model* : We use equation (5) to compare it to the non-synchronized mechanism. While the formula gives a dependence on the cycle, it also limits the amount of slots that can be inserted.

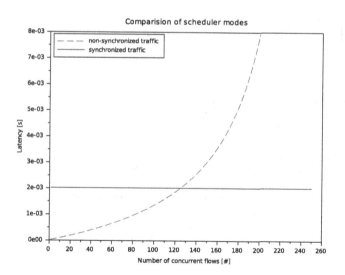

**Fig. 3.** Comparison of non-synchronized and synchronized traffic
packet size = 100byte, transmission speed = 100Mbps, switching time = $20\mu s$, cycle time = 2ms

In Fig. 3 it can be seen, that non-synchronized flows can send right away but have an increasing latency with each additional flow being added. This gives an advantage to the time-aware architecture, where the network card needs to wait for the cycle. For the scheduled traffic, however, the resulting latency is then not dependent on other flows. Further it is giving a better performance above a certain threshold. However, only a certain number of slots can be assigned to a slot. If more flows are to be added, the cycle time needs to be selected larger giving a larger latency.

## 5 Simulation

To simulate the proposed solution and have a means to compare it to our analytical model we developed a simulation model of HSR. We implemented HSR in version of IEC 62439-3:2012 in a simulation environment including its main features of packet duplication and deduplication. The simulator used is OMNeT++ [2] with the INET extension[1].

Also specified in the HSR standard is a profile for the *Precision Time Protocol* (PTP). PTP is a time synchronization protocol, that achieves sub-microsecond accuracy between clocks. For PTP no communication model has been implemented, however, a clock model is introduced following the accuracy descriptions demanded in the standard with an accuracy of 50ppm and a maximum drift of 1ppm/s. An example node and network implementation can be seen in Fig. 4.

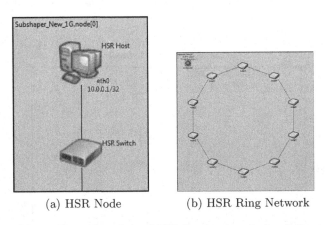

(a) HSR Node            (b) HSR Ring Network

**Fig. 4.** Examples of the OMNeT++ network simulation

## 6 Comparison of Mathematical Model and Simulation Results

In this section we show some of the simulation results that have been generated with the simulation from section 5 and compare it to the analytical model. In the following all nodes are configured the same way. Each node has one time-triggered stream and a variable amount of best-effort traffic to random destinations across the ring. The topology used is a simple single ring with 10 nodes as seen in Fig. 4b. Further the parameters from Table 1 were used in the simulation.

**Table 1.** Simulation parameters for the OMNeT++ network simulation

| Abbr. | Parameter Description | Value |
|---|---|---|
| N | Number of nodes in the network | 10 |
| $T_{switching}$ | Static switching delay | $0\mu s$ |
| $T_{cross}$ | Best-effort cross traffic | $12\mu s$ |
| $T_{slot}$ | Slot length for each node | $5\mu s$ |
| $T_{cycle}$ | Cycle length for each node | $1000\mu s$ |
| BW | Transmission speed | $1Gbps$ |
| Load | Node's use of bandwidth for BE (1 equal to: $1 \cdot \frac{BW}{N}$ ) | 1 |

## 6.1 Normal Working Mode without Failure

In a first step we simulated a working HSR ring without any failure modes. It can be seen in Fig. 5a, that in normal operating mode the network behaves as expected. Messages that have to cross more hops have a higher latency. Further, it can be seen that synchronized traffic experiences a lower latency than best-effort traffic. Best-effort traffic achieved on average also a fair latency, mainly dependent on the selected strategy that packets once on the ring get forwarded and the ring not yet being at it's full capacity limit.

## 6.2 Single Link Failure Case

In a next step we looked at HSR's main feature and the resilience against link failures. Therefore, the shortest path was broken so that the slower redundant message needs to be waited for. In Fig. 5b it can be seen, that messages on the previous shortest path to a direct neighbor now take about 8 times longer to arrive than before. Messages that have to cross 4 hopes like before in the working case experience around the same latency. The load factor on the ring itself does not increase as the same messages are transmitted in case of normal and failure operation.

## 6.3 Loss of Time Synchronization

One failure mode that can appear is the loss of time synchronization. Therefore, we manually construct a worst case with a maximum of cross-traffic and check if the model holds. In Fig. 6 it can be seen, that the cycle-miss time is higher than even a link failure on the same path. Exemplary we show here the calculation for the time-sync loss case. The model predicts:

$$E^{8\to\{7,6,5,4,3,2,1\}} = T_{local}^8 + \sum_{A\in\{7,6,5,4,3,2,1\}} (T_{perhop}^A + T_{Slot}^8)$$

$$= T_{Cycle}^8 + T_{Cross} + 7 \cdot (T_{Cross} + T_{Slot}^8)$$

$$= 1000\mu s + 12\mu s + 7 \cdot (12\mu s + 5\mu s) = 1131\mu s$$

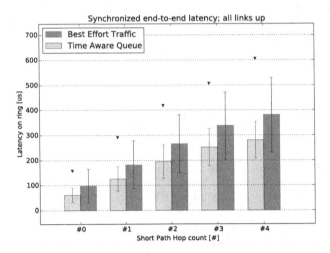

(a) All links running end-to-end latency

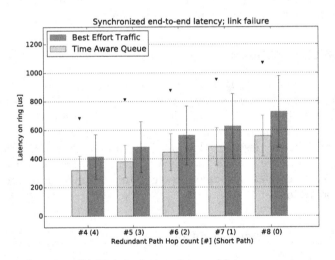

(b) Link broken end-to-end latency

**Fig. 5.** Simulation results for running and failure case
(black arrow indicating maximum value for synchronized traffic)

The maximum value in the simulation is given by $1048\mu s$ and is thus bound by the model. The difference can be explained by not perfectly aligned traffic that would take up all $12\mu s$. The model also holds if packets on the short path are lost due to, for example, link failure.

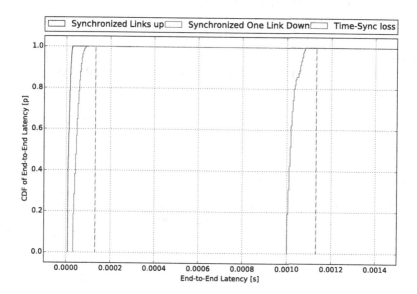

**Fig. 6.** Cumulative distribution function (CDF) of latency of in normal, link fail and time-sync loss case (dashed line represents model bounds)

## 7    Conclusion

In this paper an OMNeT++ network simulation of HSR has been presented. A mechanism to guarantee packet arrival was developed and implemented in the network simulation. Further, a mathematical model for the mechanism has been developed and compared with the simulation results. It was shown, that time-awareness offers better latency in higher load scenarios. However, it was also shown that the loss of time-awareness increases the latency significantly and it has to be carefully evaluated, if such a step is to be done.

### 7.1    Open Problems and Future Work

One failure mode that has to be considered during certification is the babbling idiot case of a switch. A crashed switch would be stopped by HSR's deduplication mechanism: ring nodes shall dispose duplicates of packets that arrived with the same sequence-number and source mac. However, as the address space for MAC-addresses is quite large, hardware implementations usually do some kind of hash-table look-up which might proof hard to certify. Another problem exists in avionics, where one design guideline is to always have a second line of defense, meaning a second mechanism independent of the first to stop such behavior.

In a next step the model could be extended to cover a scenario with multiple coupled rings and as such bringing up more than two paths. Probabilities could be assigned failure modes like link failure and then assigned to the model bounds, thereby giving probabilistic latency boundaries.

**Acknowledgment.** This work was supported in part by the German Federal Ministry of Economics and Technology (BMWi) under the *KASI* project (support codes 20K1306B).

# References

1. INET Framework, http://inet.omnetpp.org/
2. OMNeT++, http://www.omnetpp.org/
3. Abuteir, M., Obermaisser, R.: Mixed-Criticality Systems Based on Time-Triggered Ethernet with Multiple Ring Topologies. In: 2014 9th IEEE International Symposium on Industrial Embedded Systems (SIES) (2014)
4. Aeronautical Radio Incorporated: Aircraft Data Network, Part 7: Avionics Full Duplex Switched Ethernet (AFDX) (2006)
5. Grieu, J.: Analyse et évaluation de techniques de commutation Ethernet pour l'interconnexion des systèmes avioniques. Ph.D. thesis, Institut National Polytechnique de Toulouse (2004)
6. IEEE 802.1 Working Group: Time Sensitive Networks, http://www.ieee802.org/1/pages/tsn.html
7. International Electrotechnical Commission: IEC 62439-3 High Availability Automation Networks - PRP & HSR (2012)
8. Lee, K., Lee, Y., Kim, Y., Rhee, J.K.K.: Efficient Network Design for Highly Available Smart Grid Communications. In: Opto-Electronics and Communications Conference (OECC), pp. 121–122 (July 2012)
9. Nsaif, S.A., Rhee, J.M.: Improvement of High-availability Seamless Redundancy (HSR) Traffic Performance. In: 2012 14th International Conference on Advanced Communication Technology (ICACT), vol. 14, pp. 814–819 (2012)
10. Nsaif, S.A., Rhee, J.M.: RURT: A novel approach for removing the unnecessary redundant traffic in any HSR closed-loop network type. In: 2013 International Conference on ICT Convergence (ICTC), pp. 1003–1008 (October 2013)
11. SAE International: SAE AS6802 Time-Triggered Ethernet (2011)

# A Review on Collision Avoidance Systems for Unmanned Aerial Vehicles

Imen Mahjri[1], Amine Dhraief[1], and Abdelfettah Belghith[1,2]

[1] HANA Research Laboratory, University of Manouba, Tunisia
[2] College of Computer and Information Sciences, King Saud University,
Saudi Arabia
{imen.mahjri,amine.dhraief}@hanalab.org, abelghith@ksu.edu.sa

**Abstract.** Unmanned Aerial Vehicles (UAVs) have seen an important growth in various military and civilian applications including surveillance, reconnaissance, homeland security and forest fire monitoring. Currently, UAVs are limited in their access to the civil airspace. The chief barrier confronting the routine and safe integration of UAVs into the civil airspace is their lack of an effective and standardized collision avoidance system. This paper presents a survey on collision avoidance systems for UAVs. We analyze the fundamental functions conducted by a collision avoidance system and review significant recent researches treating each function.

**Keywords:** Unmanned Aerial Vehicle (UAVs), collision avoidance system, sensing technologies, conflict detection, conflict resolution.

## 1 Introduction

Recently, there has been intense worldwide interest in Unmanned Aerial Vehicles (UAVs). The rising popularity of UAVs is notably attributed to their reduced cost and the acceptance of high risk missions that cannot be performed by manned airplanes. UAVs are mostly used in military applications. However, they are also considered as viable future solutions for civil, scientific research, and commercial applications such as homeland security, search and rescue, sea ice flow observations, crop monitoring and aerial advertising. Indeed, there are several UAVs models with different capabilities and characteristics responding to different user needs [1]. Current unmanned aircraft can be remotely controlled, semi-autonomous or autonomous with different sizes, cruise speeds, operating altitudes, endurances and payload capabilities.

The most significant barrier to the use of UAVs in several actual civil and commercial applications is the lack of access to civil airspace. Currently, UAVs missions are limited to secluded areas or are restricted in their access by a cumbersome authorization process [2]. Obtaining such an authorization can take weeks to months depending on the region where the mission will take place. A fundamental consideration in the authorization process is the UAV collision avoidance capability. The UAV must demonstrate its aptitude to sense and safely avoid collisions with other airplanes, the ground, or other obstacles.

© Springer International Publishing Switzerland 2015
M. Kassab et al. (Eds.): Nets4Cars/Nets4Trains/Nets4Aircraft 2015, LNCS 9066, pp. 203–214, 2015.
DOI: 10.1007/978-3-319-17765-6_18

Therefore, UAVs are required to have an effective standardized collision avoidance system in order to routinely and safely integrate the civil airspace. An effective collision avoidance system must guarantee that the UAV can identify and be identified within the shared airspace and avoid risks to both the surrounding traffic as well as persons on the ground.

Because of its potential for disastrous impacts, collision avoidance has become the focus of several studies by industrial and research communities, including the Defense Advance Research Project Agency (DARPA), the Air Force Research Lab (AFRL) and the Technical Analysis and Application Center (TAAC). So far, numerous methods addressing the collision avoidance problem for manned and unmanned aircraft have been proposed. However, there have been little comprehensive surveys and discussions about these methods. In [3], Kuchar and Yang provided a summary and a comparative evaluation of the collision detection and avoidance methods for manned aircraft. [4] reviews the UAVs collision avoidance technologies and discusses the associated challenges from a civil aviation perspective. Albaker and Rahim provided in [5] an up-to-date review and discussion of major approaches addressing unmanned aircraft collision avoidance. Recently, in [6] Kendoul has proposed a framework for the assessment of the autonomy and the technology readiness of unmanned aircraft systems.

Unlike the majority of collision avoidance reviews that were restricted to the categorization and the comparison between the different methods, we address in this paper the complete functional architecture of a collision avoidance system. We analyze the fundamental functions conducted by a collision avoidance system and point out significant recent researches treating each function. We also provide some recommendations on required actions permitting the harmonized and routine integration of UAVs into the shared civil airspace. The rest of this paper is organized as follows: section 2 outlines the overall goal and the generic main functions of a collision avoidance system. A collision avoidance system is generally organized into three major functions: the sensing function, the detection function and the resolution function. Section 3 details the sensing function and reviews the sensing technologies used by the current operating UAVs. Section 4 details the detection function, reviews the corresponding up to date works and discusses the measures of reliability of these works. Section 5 details the resolution function, categorizes the corresponding researches based on four design aspects and argues the advantages and disadvantage of each category. Section 6 concludes the paper and gives some useful recommendations on the integration of UAVs into the civil airspace.

## 2   Collision Avoidance System

The overall goal of the collision avoidance system is to enable UAVs to safely fly within a shared airspace. In a shared airspace, an UAV comes across many encounters including other aircraft and obstacles that would endanger its mission. During its cruise, an UAV may be fully autonomous, semi autonomous or completely guided by an operator at a remote control station. Depending on the autonomy level of the UAV, the role of a collision avoidance system may range from the simple conflict detection and warning to the fully autonomous conflict detection and resolution. A conflict occurs when at least two encounters come within a distance less than a minimum desired separation distance.

Fig.1 shows the functional architecture of the collision avoidance system of a fully autonomous UAV. A collision avoidance system is generally organized into three fundamental functions: the sensing function, the detection function and the resolution function. The sensing function represents the capability of the system to perceive its surrounding environment and collect current state information for encounters. Using the appropriate communication equipments and sensors such as cameras and radars, an UAV can have an estimation of the current traffic situation (e.g., nearby airplanes positions and velocities). The detecting function enables UAVs to discover future conflict risks. First, state information is projected into the near future. Current and future state information are then combined to extract conflict metrics (e.g., closest point of approach). Using conflict metrics, a decision is finally made as to whether an actual risk of conflict exists and if an avoidance manoeuvre is needed. When a near future conflict is detected, the conflict resolution function may be invoked. The main role of the resolution function is to avoid a possible collision with an encounter by determining how and which manoeuvres should be performed. Generally, a conflict situation can be resolved by a horizontal, vertical or a speed change manoeuvre. Once the collision risk has been mitigated by the appropriate avoidance actions, the UAV can return back to its original course path. The conflict detection unit should usually detect future conflicting traffic in a sufficient time beforehand. Thus, the resolution unit will have enough time to determine and perform avoidance manoeuvres so as not to create collisions.

In the following sections we will detail the three functional units of the collision avoidance system: the sensing unit, the detection unit and the resolution unit.

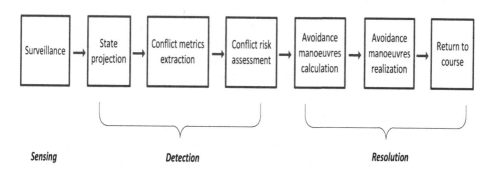

**Fig. 1.** Fully autonomous collision avoidance system

# 3    Sensing Technologies

Surveillance for collision avoidance can be achieved by using a wide variety of sensors that can be divided into two main categories: cooperative and non-cooperative sensors. Cooperative sensors comprise all communication equipments that enable UAVs to exchange their flight data. UAVs not fitted with such communication equipment may instead rely on non-cooperative sensors. In this case other surrounding airplanes are directly sensed, irrespective of their desire to be sensed.

## 3.1    Cooperative Sensors

Cooperative collision avoidance systems rely on a set of devises permitting information exchange, such as position, heading, speed and waypoints, between UAVS.

The Air Traffic Control (ATC) transponder is the primary used cooperative sensing equipment. A transponder is an electronic device that transmits a specific reply when it receives a specific radio frequency interrogation. This method performs well in a controlled airspace where all airplanes are fitted with transponders. However, it does not permit the sensing of non-transponding targets, so such targets have to be sensed via other means. As they are usually sold for powered airplanes, most transponders freely use a large amount of power. They consequently can't be used in battery-powered UAVs.

The Automatic Dependent Surveillance  Broadcast (ADS-B) is a relatively new technology that allows UAVs to detect other similarly equipped aircraft with much more precision than transponders. In ADS-B, an UAV determines its precise 3D position using the Global Navigation Satellite System (GNSS). The UAV's position, along with other information such as its unique identifier, speed and heading intent are periodically updated and broadcasted via data links. The resulting periodic and widely available position feedback enables accurate monitoring of the UAV by both ground stations and other airplanes in its surrounding airspace. ADS-B heavily depends on the integrity of the UAV navigation system. The failure of this system prevents the UAV from broadcasting its accurate position. Another drawback of the ADS-B is that it is relatively easy to simulate non-existent traffic by sending fraudulent messages.

## 3.2    Non Cooperative Sensors

Non cooperative sensors are promising technologies for UAVs. Indeed, unlike cooperative sensors, these technologies do not require the coordination with other similarly equipped aircraft. Moreover they benefit from the fact that they can be used to detect both moving and stationary obstacles. Non cooperative sensors can be divided into two categories: active or passive sensors. Active sensors diffuse signals to discover obstacles in the flight path while passive sensors rely on the signals emitted by the obstacles themselves.

Examples of active sensors are the laser range finder and the radar. Laser range finder is a device that uses laser energy to estimate the distance to an object. A laser pulse is first sent in a narrow beam towards the target. Then, the propagation time of the pulse to the target and back is measured to determine the source-target distance. Most laser range finders are planar. That is obstacles below or above the measurement plane are not detectable. Alternatively, radar systems can be used to detect any enclosing object. A radar uses radio waves to estimate the position and the speed of an object. It is able to detect airplanes, guided missiles, terrains and even weather formations (rain, snow, hail, etc). A radar has a transmitter that emits either radio waves or microwaves that are reflected by any object in their path and detected by a receiver. This technique is ideal in bad optical vision conditions such as stormy, foggy and night times. However, it is not used in small UAVs because of its large weight and size. Moreover radar systems are considered costly.

Passive sensors mainly include acoustic sensors, Electro-Optical (EO) cameras and Infra-Red (IR) cameras. Acoustic sensors are used for detecting and tracking objects only by their emitted sounds. They generally involve a simple and light hardware and cover only a short range. EO and IR cameras are the most used sensors in UAVs. EO cameras provide UAVs with day-light visions by recording the reflected light. IR cameras produce night visions by detecting the objects heats. Cameras are small, light and inexpensive and therefore suit UAVs requirements especially small ones.

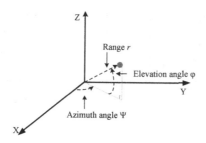

**Fig. 2.** Main sensing information

Table 1 summarizes the above mentioned sensing technologies and presents examples of developed UAVs using the corresponding technologies. Essentially, a sensor needs to acquire the range, the azimuth and the elevation (Fig.2) of the objects of interest [4]. Most of the cooperative sensing techniques are able to accurately provide these information, but they are only capable of surveying alike equipped airplanes. Non cooperative sensing techniques can detect both cooperative and non cooperatives objects. However, they usually operate over a much shorter distance than cooperative sensors. Distant objects can't be correctly sensed. Besides, some non cooperative sensors, such as cameras and lasers, are only capable of providing either range or azimuth and elevation information but not both. The ability to detect obstacles at night and in bad weather conditions are also important attributes evaluating the sensing technology. All the mentioned sensing techniques, except the EO cameras, are capable of detecting obstacles day and night. However, only transponders, ADS-B and radars are effective in bad weather conditions. All the considered sensing technologies, except for ADS-B, are operating on many UAVs in various countries around the world. ADS-B technology is yet in a demonstration phase of development. On march 2012, an ADS-B devise was tested on NASA's MQ-9 Ikhana UAV. Then, on august 2012, General Atomics Aeronautical Systems, the U.S. Department of Homeland Security, Customs and Border Protection and the Federal Aviation Administration cooperatively tested an ADS-B based surveillance system on a Guardian RPA UAV.

Due to the restrictions in each sensing mode, a single sensor cannot assure a complete monitoring. Multiple sensors are required to provide an exhaustive solution. Thus, the weakness of a sensor can be compensated by the strength of another.

**Table 1.** Sensing technologies for unmanned aerial vehicles

| Technology | Category | Range | Azimuth | Elevation | Day & Night | Bad Weather | Example systems |
|---|---|---|---|---|---|---|---|
| Transponder | Cooperative | Yes | Yes | Yes | Yes | Yes | XPV-2 Mako Dakota |
| ADS-B | Cooperative | Yes | Yes | Yes | Yes | Yes | |
| Laser | Non-Cooperative (Active) | Yes | No | No | Yes | No | GoldenEye Vulture |
| Radar | Non-Cooperative (Active) | Yes | Yes | Yes | Yes | Yes | RQ-4 Global Hawk MQ-9 Predator B |
| Acoustic | Non-Cooperative (Passive) | Yes | Yes | Yes | Yes | No | Hornet MK-V Nishan TJ-1000 |
| EO camera | Non-Cooperative (Passive) | No | Yes | Yes | No | No | Carcara RPH 2A |
| IR camera | Non-Cooperative (Passive) | No | Yes | Yes | Yes | No | ScanEagle GoldenEye |

## 4    Conflict Detection

We define a conflict as a situation in which two or more airplanes experience a loss of minimum separation [3]. That is, a conflict occurs when the distance between two or more airplanes is less than a minimum required separation distance. This separation requirement defines a protected zone surrounding each airplane that should not be infiltrated by any other airplane.

We also define conflict detection as the process of detecting future conflicting traffic. Hence, conflict detection process permits to decide when intrusions of the protected zones will occur. Conflict detection unit must issue conflict alerts early enough that avoidance manoeuvres can be performed, but not very early that nuisance warnings occur. The conflict detection approaches mainly differ by the considered state information, state projection method and alerting metrics. In followings, we first discuss each of these factors and then define the primary metrics that quantify the reliability of a conflict detection approach.

## 4.1    State Information

State information provides an estimate of the current traffic situation. It may be composed by one or many state variables such as the range $r$, the azimuth angle $\psi$, the elevation angle $\phi$, the speed $v$, the acceleration $a$, the position vector $\mathbf{x}$ and the velocity vector $\mathbf{v}$. Depending on the used sensing technology, this information can be acquired directly or indirectly and may cover the two dimensional vertical plane ($2D_V$), the two dimensional horizontal plane ($2D_H$), or the three dimensional plane ($3D$). Most of the proposed conflict detection systems use either $3D$ or $2D_H$ position and velocity vectors to describe the surrounding environment [7].

## 4.2    State Projection

State projection shows how the current states are projected into the future. There are mainly three projection methods : nominal, worst case and probabilistic [3].

In the nominal projection method [8], the current states are propagated into the future along a single trajectory (i.g, straight trajectory). It completely ignores uncertainties in the state projections. The nominal projection is simple but it is only applicable when aircraft trajectories are very predictable or when the propagation period is very short. Indeed, this approach does not take into account the fact that an encounter may not behave as predicted, an aspect that is very probable in a long propagation period.

In the worst case projection [9], the system examines a whole range of possible future manoeuvres. If any one of these manoeuvres could cause a conflict, then a conflict alert is triggered. This approach detects collision risks even in worst case scenarios however, it is far from providing optimal solutions. It should be limited to a short propagation period to reduce the computation requirement and avoid excessive false alerting (i.e., issued alerts without subsequent conflicts).

The probabilistic projection [10,11] considers uncertainties in airplanes futures trajectories. This uncertainty can be modelled either by adding position errors to the nominal trajectories and then deriving conflict probability or by building a full spectrum of future trajectories and assigning a probability of occurring to each one (e.g, using a probability density function). A conflict alert is issued if the conflict probability is above a given threshold. The nominal and the worst case are subsets of the probabilistic approach: in the nominal case the UAV follows a single trajectory with probability one; in the worst case the UAV may follow any trajectory with equal probability. The probabilistic projection causes less missed alarms (i.e., conflicts with no prior issued alerts) than the nominal projection and less false alarms than the worst case projection. Nevertheless, methods using this approach usually require heavy processing. It may also be difficult to model the probabilities of future trajectories.

The projection may be based only on current state information or may also use additional information such as a flight plan [12,13]. The flight plan describes the UAV future waypoints along its flight path. This intent information can be used to ameliorate future trajectory estimation and consequently enhances the alerting decisions.

### 4.3   Conflict Metrics

Conflict metrics are the parameters derived from current and predicted states to make alerting decisions. Unlike the state projection that can be separately performed for each airplane, conflict metrics extraction necessitates the aggregation of the states of the different involved airplanes. The minimum separation distance, the time to the closest point of approach [14], the number of available avoidance manoeuvres, the conflict probability and the collision rate [15] are the most used conflict metrics in traditional conflict detection systems. Some new approaches use more complex and direct metrics than physical metrics. In [16] the authors propose an alternate approach where alerting decisions are based directly on computed values of performance metrics such as false alarms probability.

Based on the derived metrics, a decision is made on whether an avoidance manoeuvre is needed to avoid the collision menace. This decision is usually made by comparing conflict metrics with one or more threshold values. The threshold values depend on many parameters such as the surrounding environment, the UAV's state, characteristics and performances. Ideally, the conflict detection system should dynamically adapt the threshold values to the specific monitored situation.

### 4.4   Measures of Reliability

The reliability of a conflict detection approach can be mainly measured in terms of false alarms and missed alarms. A false alarm is an issued alert without a subsequent conflict. Conversely, a missed alarm is a conflict with no prior issued alert. Missed alarms are considered as an extreme hazard leading to perilous aircraft collisions while false alarms are considered as nuisance alarms resulting in unnecessary escape manoeuvres. Hence, minimizing false alarms and eliminating missed alarms is a crucial design requirement for conflict detection algorithms.

## 5   Conflict Resolution

The conflict resolution function should be invoked once a near future conflict is detected. We define the conflict resolution as the process that specifies how a particular conflicting situation can be resolved in order to avoid an imminent collision. Conflict resolution techniques can be mainly categorized based on four design aspects which are: the used resolution manoeuvre, the considered resolution approach, the handling of multiple aircraft conflicts and the assumption of coordination or non coordination between UAVs. In this section, we explain each of these aspects as well as the key measures of effectiveness of a conflict resolution technique.

## 5.1  Resolution Manoeuvres

The resolution manoeuvres are the set of actions used to resolve a conflict. Basic manoeuvres include speed change (speedup or slowdown), horizontal manoeuvre (turn left or right) and vertical manoeuvres (climb or descend). In some cases a single basic manoeuvre is sufficient to avoid a collision. In others a combination of basic manoeuvres is required. The combined manoeuvres may be performed simultaneously or sequentially.

## 5.2  Resolution Approach

Resolution approaches are the methods by which resolution manoeuvres are generated. There are three major resolution approaches categories: rule based, force field and optimized.

In the rule based approaches [17,18] conflicts are resolved based on a set of pre-defined rules. In[17], when a conflict alert is issued, the threatened aircraft is assumed to perform a fixed climbing turn avoidance manoeuvre to turn away from a parallel flying intruder. Rule based approaches are generally easy to implement and simple to understand which reduces the response time to conflict alerts. However, they usually do not appropriately account for unexpected events in the environment. For example, in [17] the climbing manoeuvre provides a vertical separation between the threatened airplane and the intruder. If the intruder unexpectedly climbs, this vertical separation would be reduced or even eliminated resulting in an additional conflict.

Force field approaches [19,20] consider airplanes as charged particles evolving in a force field and use the repulsive forces between them to generate escape manoeuvres. The force field approaches use relatively simple electrostatic equations to resolve conflicts, but the feasibility of the computed solutions is not guaranteed due to UAVs dynamic limitations. A force filed solution may for example require a sharp variation of UAVs direction or speed which is physically very difficult or infeasible.

Optimized approaches produce resolution manoeuvres that minimize a certain cost function such as flight time, energy consumption, deviation from the original trajectory or workload. Optimization approaches include different sub-categories that differ in the method by which the resolution decision is derived. Main sub-categories include game theory based methods, genetic based methods and optimal control theory methods. In game theory based methods, the conflict resolution problem is formulated as a cooperative [21] or a non-cooperative [9] game. Genetic based methods [22] generate optimized resolution manoeuvres using techniques inspired by natural evolution such as crossing, mutation and selection. In optimal control theory methods [23] the airplanes dynamics, the constraints and the cost functions are defined and an optimal resolution is determined. Optimized approaches seem attractive since they minimize costs. Nevertheless, the complexity of the used functions can make these approaches difficult to understand and computationally intensive.

### 5.3   Management of Multiple Aircraft Conflicts

There are two approaches by which a conflict resolution system can handle conflicts between more than two aircraft: pairwise or global. In the pairwise approach conflicts are addressed sequentially in pairs. In the global approach the whole situation is assessed simultaneously and the conflict is resolved at once. This is usually done by grouping all the airplanes involved in the conflict in a cluster. Although the pairwise approach is much simpler than the global approach, it may, in some situations, lead to unsafe or ambiguous situations. Global approaches may offer more robust solutions than the pairwise approaches, however they require a lot of computational complexity.

### 5.4   Coordination

Assumed coordination or non-coordination between conflicting airplanes is one of the important design factors effecting the conflict resolution process. In coordinated conflict resolution, involved airplanes cooperatively agree on a set of manoeuvres in order to resolve conflicts. In non-coordinated conflict resolution, each airplane exclusively manoeuvres without taking into consideration the other involved airplanes eventual manoeuvres.

Several coordination strategies have been proposed. Some strategies applied multi-agent systems theory [24], others used rule based [25], code number or token allocation methods. Coordination helps reduce manoeuvring cost and avoid manoeuvres that would intensify or extend the conflict. However, coordination may be interrupted in case of data links failure or data exchange interference. Thus, a conflict resolution system with assumed coordination should also be able to handle cases in which coordination is impossible.

### 5.5   Measures of Effectiveness

The number of near misses and the resolution cost are generally used as the primary metrics to quantify the performance of conflict resolution algorithms. From a safety point of view, any conflict resolution algorithm is required to maintain a minimum separation distance between airplanes. Any violation of this safe separation results in a near miss. Conflict resolution algorithms should ensure as few near misses as possible. The resolution cost evaluates the loss produced by the resolution manoeuvres. Usually, a set of basic cost parameters are combined to generate a cost function estimating the loss yielded for the airplane. The basic cost parameters essentially include the additional energy consumption, the delays at planned waypoints, the number of necessary resolution manoeuvres, the total altitude changes and the total heading changes.

# 6  Conclusion and Recommendations

In this paper we discussed in details the functional architecture of UAVs collision avoidance system. A collision avoidance system is usually organized into three basic functions: the sensing, the detection and the resolution function. We explored each of these functions and reviewed the most noteworthy technologies and approaches treating each function.

It is clear from this review that there is a wide variety of models and technologies that can be used to develop an efficient collision avoidance system. However, although much has been accomplished, there remain several issues that need to be treated to assure a full, harmonized and standardized integration of UAVs into the civil airspace. First, UAVs civil operations require new secure and effective data links. So far, in the civil airspace, there are no reserved frequencies bands for this purpose. A set of UAVs reserved frequencies need consequently to be agreed with the international community. Second, in the shared civil airspace, UAVs will be expected to interact with the current air traffic systems. Hence, UAVs new communication and surveillance systems need to fluidly interoperate with these existing systems. Finally, there are yet no common regulations on UAVs systems and operations. Standard regulations addressing UAVs systems and operations are highly required in order to facilitate UAVs worldwide integration.

# References

1. Austin, R.: Unmanned aircraft systems: UAVS design, development and deployment, vol. 54. John Wiley & Sons (2011)
2. Dalamagkidis, K., Valavanis, K., Piegl, L.A.: On integrating unmanned aircraft systems into the national airspace system: issues, challenges, operational restrictions, certification, and recommendations, vol. 54. Springer Science & Business Media (2011)
3. Kuchar, J.K., Yang, L.C.: A review of conflict detection and resolution modeling methods. IEEE Transactions on Intelligent Transportation Systems 1(4), 179–189 (2000)
4. Lacher, A.R., Maroney, D.R., Zeitlin, A.D.: Unmanned aircraft collision avoidance–technology assessment and evaluation methods. In: 7th Air Traffic Managemtent Research & Development Seminar (2007)
5. Albaker, B., Rahim, N.: A Conceptual Framework and a Review of Conflict Sensing, Detection, Awareness and Escape Maneuvering Methods for UAVs. INTECH Open Access Publisher (2011)
6. Kendoul, F.: Towards a unified framework for uas autonomy and technology readiness assessment (atra). In: Autonomous Control Systems and Vehicles, pp. 55–71. Springer (2013)
7. Munoz, C., Narkawicz, A., Chamberlain, J.: A tcas-ii resolution advisory detection algorithm. In: AIAA Guidance, Navigation and Control Conference, pp. 19–22 (2013)
8. Albaker, B., Rahim, N.: Straight projection conflict detection and cooperative avoidance for autonomous unmanned aircraft systems. In: 4th IEEE Conference on Industrial Electronics and Applications, pp. 1965–1969. IEEE (2009)

9. Tomlin, C., Pappas, G.J., Sastry, S.: Conflict resolution for air traffic management: A study in multiagent hybrid systems. IEEE Transactions on Automatic Control 43(4), 509–521 (1998)
10. Hu, J., Prandini, M., Sastry, S.: Aircraft conflict prediction in the presence of a spatially correlated wind field. IEEE Transactions on Intelligent Transportation Systems 6(3), 326–340 (2005)
11. Liu, W., Hwang, I.: Probabilistic 4d trajectory prediction and conflict detection for air traffic control. In: 49th IEEE Conference on Decision and Control, pp. 1183–1188. IEEE (2010)
12. Yepes, J.L., Hwang, I., Rotea, M.: New algorithms for aircraft intent inference and trajectory prediction. Journal of Guidance, Control, and Dynamics 30(2), 370–382 (2007)
13. Hwang, I., Seah, C.E.: Intent-based probabilistic conflict detection for the next generation air transportation system. Proceedings of the IEEE 96(12), 2040–2059 (2008)
14. Munoz, C.A., Narkawicz, A.J.: Time of closest approach in three-dimensional airspace. Tech. rep., National Aeronautics and Space Administration, Langley Research Center (2010)
15. Leven, S., Zufferey, J.C., Floreano, D.: Dealing with midair collisions in dense collective aerial systems. Journal of Field Robotics 28(3), 405–423 (2011)
16. Yang, L.C., Kuchar, J.K.: Performance metric alerting: A new design approach for complex alerting problems. IEEE Transactions on Systems, Man and Cybernetics, Part A: Systems and Humans 32(1), 123–134 (2002)
17. Carpenter, B., Kuchar, J.K.: Probability-based collision alerting logic for closely-spaced parallel approach. In: AIAA 35th Aerospace Sciences Meeting and Exhibit, Reno, pp. 97–0222 (1997)
18. Pallottino, L., Scordio, V.G., Bicchi, A., Frazzoli, E.: Decentralized cooperative policy for conflict resolution in multivehicle systems. IEEE Transactions on Robotics 23(6), 1170–1183 (2007)
19. Chang, D.E., Shadden, S.C., Marsden, J.E., Olfati-Saber, R.: Collision avoidance for multiple agent systems. In: 42nd IEEE Conference on Decision and Control, vol. 1, pp. 539–543. IEEE (2003)
20. Wang, S., Schaub, H.: Spacecraft collision avoidance using coulomb forces with separation distance and rate feedback. Journal of Guidance, Control, and Dynamics 31(3), 740–750 (2008)
21. Archibald, J.K., Hill, J.C., Jepsen, N.A., Stirling, W.C., Frost, R.L.: A satisficing approach to aircraft conflict resolution. IEEE Transactions on Systems, Man, and Cybernetics, Part C: Applications and Reviews 38(4), 510–521 (2008)
22. Mondoloni, S., Conway, S.: An airborne conflict resolution approach using a genetic algorithm. In: AIAA Guidance, Navigation, and Control Conference (2001)
23. Hoffmann, G.M., Tomlin, C.J.: Decentralized cooperative collision avoidance for acceleration constrained vehicles. In: 47th IEEE Conference on Decision and Control, pp. 4357–4363. IEEE (2008)
24. Sislak, D., Volf, P., Komenda, A., Samek, J., Pechoucek, M.: Agent-based multi-layer collision avoidance to unmanned aerial vehicles. In: International Conference on Integration of Knowledge Intensive Multi-Agent Systems, pp. 365–370. IEEE (2007)
25. Dowek, G., Munoz, C., Carreno, V.A.: Provably safe coordinated strategy for distributed conflict resolution. In: AIAA Guidance Navigation, and Control Conference and Exhibit (2005)

# Performance of Context-Aware Publish/Subscribe Systems for AANET

Mickaël Royer, Alain Pirovano, and Fabien Garcia

ENAC Toulouse, France

**Abstract.** AANET (Aeronautical Ad hoc NETworks) are a subclass of Vehicular Ad-Hoc Networks (VANET). They are a very promising solution in order to answer to new air-ground communication needs. The Publish / Subscribe communication paradigm enjoys wide applicability in AANET where resources are limited. Many Publish / Subscribe systems exist for wired networks, however, these solutions are not fully adapted to mobile networks like AANET or VANET composed of cars. For the second category, the research community investigated and proposed some solutions. The aim of this article is to evaluate the performance of typical Publish / Subscribe systems suitable for VANET with cars on AANET with a realistic scenario based on commercial aircraft traffic. We show that some approaches suitable for VANET do not give good results in this case.

**Keywords:** Vehicular Ad Hoc Network (VANET), Aeronautical Ad Hoc Network (AANET), Publish / Subscribe communication systems.

## 1 Introduction

Mobile Ad-Hoc Networks (MANET) are self-configuring networks of mobile nodes connected by wireless links without a fixed infrastructure. Vehicular Ad-Hoc Networks (VANET) are a subclass of MANET in which nodes are vehicle (cars, trains...). This sub-category shows a lot of specific characteristics, the most important being the high mobility of nodes and the predictability of movements. As detailed in [1], AANET (Aeronautical Ad hoc NETworks, which consist in aircraft acting as nodes of a MANET) can be seen as a subcategory of VANET. In a context of increasing air traffic and new needs in term of air ground communication systems, AANET represents a relevant solution as explained in [2]. Content-based information dissemination enjoys wide applicability in AANET where resources (like bandwidth) are limited. Notification of dangerous weather events to aircraft which will navigate close to the concerned geographical area or important messages from airline operational center to aircraft belonging to the company are good examples. Indeed, this approach allows a space decoupling between source and recipients since the sender of a message does not know which nodes will receive it. The aim of the network is then to find the recipients, based on the message's content. To accomplish content-based routing in a network, the Publish / Subscribe communication paradigm is the most widespread

M. Kassab et al. (Eds.): Nets4Cars/Nets4Trains/Nets4Aircraft 2015, LNCS 9066, pp. 215–226, 2015.
DOI: 10.1007/978-3-319-17765-6_19

solution. In this model, *event* distribution from *publisher* (event producer) to *subscriber* (event consumer) is based on the subscriber interest and the event's content. Many Publish / Subscribe systems exist for wired network ([3], [4]) but are not suitable for MANET with low bandwidth and frequent network partition. Moreover, the applications described above need two extra features compared to classical Publish / Subscribe systems. The first one is the persistence of events in the network to reduce the problem of network partitions (similar principle as Delay Tolerant Networks, [5]). The second is the introduction of node context to reduce the scope of events/subscriptions and use more efficiently the network resources. As explained in [1], this context can be assimilated to a location context (an area or just a position). For example, with a classical Publish / Subscribe solution, aircraft can subscribe to "dangerous weather situation". However, this subscription will be too wide and will lead to the reception of useless events since aircraft are interested especially by "dangerous weather situation *close to my position or route*".

In the past years, some solutions have been proposed by the research community to provide Publish / Subscribe systems adapted to VANET (especially for cars), introducing the persistence of events and the use of node context in event delivery decision process. The aim of this article is to evaluate some solutions using different approaches against a typical scenario (notification of weather events) in a realistic AANET based on real traffic of commercial aircraft.

The next section presents a brief state of the art on Context-Aware Publish/Subscribe systems adapted for VANET. Section 3 compares some existing solutions based on a typical use case for AANET. The scenario and all implementation choices made to simulate aircraft mobility and Publish / Subscribe systems are explained in this section. Finally, section 4 concludes this article and introduces further work on this topic.

## 2  Context-Aware Publish/Subscribe Solutions in VANET

As explained in [1], existing Context-Aware Publish/Subscribe systems that are adapted for VANET can be classified in three categories: geographic routing, proximity routing and overlay network based solutions.

Geographic routing based solutions like [6] or [7] are based on the assumption that each event / subscription is linked to a geographical area. The publish / subscribe system uses a geographic routing protocol to dispatch events from the publisher to the subscribers. Actually, an event is sent to the nodes located in the geographical area defined as the context of the event. In the same way, a subscription is sent to the geographical area defined in the context. Then, as described in figure 1a, when a subscription matches with an event, nodes located at the intersection can act as middleman between publisher and subscribers.

Proximity routing based solutions like [8] or [9] provide many likeness with the previous solution. The main difference relates to the area where events and subscriptions are sent. This kind of solutions disseminate events/subscriptions only within a radius close to the sender (see figure 1b).

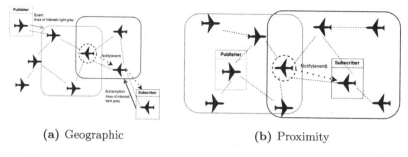

(a) Geographic                           (b) Proximity

**Fig. 1.** Principle of geographic and proximity routing based P/S

Overlay network based solutions introduce a new component in P/S architecture, *the broker*. Brokers are responsible for dispatching events from publishers to subscribers. They are interconnected and thus form an overlay network. In most of these solutions, like [10], brokers form an acyclic graph. Subscriptions are thus sent to all brokers of the graph (or just a part of it if context is used to filter recipient brokers). Based on these subscriptions, they can populate the table used to forward events to interested subscribers.

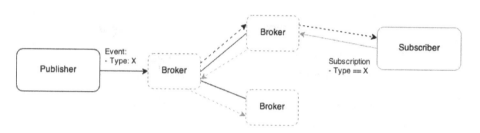

**Fig. 2.** principle of overlay network based P/S

## 3    Solution Comparison

After a brief description of existing context-aware P/S solutions, this section studies the performance of these solutions. Section A describes the scenario used to compare the solutions. This application relies on an AANET. Section B explains all the choices made during the implementation of the scenario and the P/S solution in a simulation model. The last section explains the results obtained for each solutions.

### 3.1    Scenario

The scenario used to compare publish/subscribe solutions is a common problematic for civil aviation: how to inform aircraft of new weather situation ? Indeed, some phenomena like storm or wind shear are very dangerous and thus aircraft must be aware of these phenomena. Nowadays, these information are broadcasted by ground entities (like Air Traffic controller or airlines operational center) using radio, VDL (VHF Data Link) or SATCOM means.

A new approach to solve this problem can be found with the use of a context aware P/S system over an AANET composed of commercial aircraft. In this scenario, aircraft aware of a dangerous phenomena, using its weather radar for example, sends an event over the network to announce the new weather situation. This event contains at least the type of event and the estimated duration of the event. The context associated to this event will be the geographical area cover by the weather phenomena. Meanwhile, aircraft know their short term trajectory and then can subscribe to weather events which happen near their route. The context associated to this subscription will be a geographical area that covers a part of the trajectory (see Figure 3).

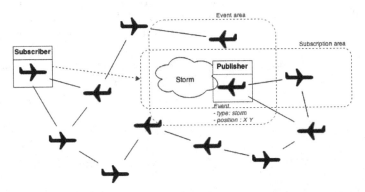

**Fig. 3.** principle of subscription to weather events

### 3.2    Simulation/Implementation Choices

All the simulations have been performed with Omnet++ ([11]). This paragraph deals with all the implementation choices that has been made to simulate the scenario and the Publish / Subscribe systems with Omnet++.

**Mobility.** The mobility model used for the simulations is based on real traffic traces from the French civil aviation authority and Eurocontrol based on either radar data or position report from the aircraft itself. Concretely, for a given day of the year, all position reports of commercial flights around the world (in spherical coordinate with an interval of 30min) can be obtained in a file following a specific format.

This file is then parsed by a tool developed at the ENAC, *acparse*. It offers many options to filter aircraft, interpolate trajectories and export the result to common format. In our case, acparse is used to get an XML file which contains two parts for each aircraft. The first one (surround by the tag *mobility*) contains position reports with an interval of 1 minute (thanks to the interpolation that `acparse` offers) and is used by a new homemade mobility module for Omnet++. The second one (surrounded by the tag *plan*) can be assimilated to a *flight plan*. In the simulation model, this flight plan is used by nodes in order to subscribe to weather event close to their short term trajectory.

Due to logistical limitations, it was difficult to simulate all the world traffic in reasonable time. As AANET is especially interesting for area where no ground infrastructures are available, as over oceans, we choose to reduce the scope to the transatlantic traffic. That is why our simulations are taking into account aircraft whose latitude belongs to the interval [23,5° - 70°] and the longitude belongs to the interval [-90° - 10°].

**Physical/Mac Layer.** Studies presented in this article deal with Publish / Subscribe service and not with the AANET feasibility which has been demonstrated in other studies like [2]. That's why it is not mandatory to have realistic physical and MAC layer. We choose to use `IdealWireless` module provided by the `inet` library [12], which simulates a simple physical and MAC layer. When a node sends a message, all nodes whose distance from the sender is below the parameter `transmissionRange` receive the message. In the same way, bit rate is a configurable constant. All messages are sent at this bit rate. However the values used for the simulations are deduced from a previous studies evaluating the feasibility of AANET built with commercial aircraft. In particular, [13] evaluates the use of CDMA as the layer 2 to interconnect aircraft and obtains an available bit rate of several Mbits/s for a transmission range of several hundred of kilometers.

**Events/Subscriptions.** The generation of events meets the following rules. We fix the number of simultaneous events at the beginning of the simulation. We choose to keep this number low due to the size of the simulated AANET (limited to the transatlantic traffic). Each event occurs close to a randomly chosen aircraft. These events are then published by the aircraft close to it through the Publish / Subscribe system. When an event ends, a new event is created close to another aircraft and so on until the end of the simulation. The geographical area linked to an event is a cylinder which starts at the ground and finishes at an altitude of 20km (the cruising altitude for a commercial aircraft is around 10km). The cylinder radius is a parameter of the simulation. The generation of subscriptions by aircraft is based on flight plan described in the section 3.2. This flight plan can be broken up to segments. Each segment fit 10 minutes of a flight and a subscription is generated for each segment. The time period associated to this subscription is the time interval between two position reports that form the segment. The geographical area linked to the subscription is the segment itself. Consequently, a subscription matches with an event if two conditions are verified. Firstly, the time period of the event fits the subscription's one. Secondly, the segment associated to the subscription intersects or is inside the cylinder which represents the geographical area of the event.

**P/S Systems.** Three Publish / Subscribe systems have been simulated. The first one is the most simple. Events are disseminated to all nodes of the network. Subscriptions never leave the source node and are recorded in a table. When an event is received by a node, the event is checked against recorded subscriptions. If one matches, the event is forwarded to the application. This solution serves as a reference to compare performance of P/S solutions and will be called "broadcast event solution" in the rest of this article. Intuitively, this solution gives the best result in term of delivery since all events are received by every node but is not resource efficient since even nodes that are not interested by an event receive it anyway.

The second one is a geographic routing based solution. LBM (Location Based Multicast) [14] is the geographical routing protocol used to dispatch events and subscriptions. LBM allows to send a packet to all nodes within a target geographic area (called a multicast region). In this way, the sender of the message defines a forwarding area according to his position and the multicast region. Only nodes within the forwarding area retransmit the message. Thus, the size of the forwarding area has a direct effect on the delivery ratio of the protocol (better with a large region) and the resulting load on the network (lower with a small region). The home-made implementation of LBM offers two options to define this forwarding region. The first one is explained in [14] and is based on the distance. A node $A$ forwards the message received from node $B$ for the region $R$ if $dist(A, R) < dist(B, R) + \delta$ where $dist(A, R)$ is the distance from $A$ to $R$ and $\delta$ is a parameter of the protocol. The second option is a *conic* approach. In this case, $A$ forwards the message if $A \in cone(B, R, \alpha))$ where $cone(B, R, \alpha)$ is a cone whose the vertex is $B$, the axis is defined by the points $B$ and the center of the region $R$, $\alpha$ is the opening angle. This family of Publish / Subscribe solutions also requires a unicast protocol in order to send an event from the node used as an intermediary to subscribers interested by the event. In our case, we choose AODV [15] (Ad hoc On-Demand Distance Vector). This choice was motivated by the nature of the network (hundreds of highly mobile nodes) and the quality of service expected by the application. Our main objective is to be as efficient as possible in order to save bandwidth, furthermore, in this scenario, the delay to disseminate event to all subscribers is not a performance criteria. Thus a reactive routing protocol seems adequate and AODV is the reference in this category.

The third one is a proximity routing based solution. For each event/ subscription, a proximity perimeter is defined (parameter of the simulation). The message is sent to all nodes inside this area. As with previous solution, when a node receives an event from which it knows subscribers, AODV is used to send this event to recipients.

## 3.3    Results

For all the results introduced in this section, the table 1 gathers the value of main parameters used for the simulations. The transmission range and bit rate chosen for the simulations are coherent with previous studies on AANET like [16].

For each simulation, two results will be observed:

- *Delivery ratio*, for each event

$$Ratio = \frac{\text{Number of subscribers that received the event}}{\text{Total number of subscribers}}$$

- *Total cost of network*, which is the total number of bytes sent in the network (including control message) to dispatch events to subscribers. It is calculated as the sum of sent bytes (at the level of MAC layer) for all nodes of the network.

**Table 1.** Common parameter values for all simulations

| Duration of the simulation | 24h |
|---|---|
| Day | 2012/12/25 |
| Transmission range | 300 km |
| Physical layer bit rate | 1 Mb/s |
| Duration of an event | uniform(1800s, 3600s) |
| Duration of subscriptions | 30 min |
| Size of zone covered by an event | 250km |
| Size of a subscription message | 32 Bytes |
| Size of a event message | 4096 Bytes |
| Number of simultaneous events | 5 |

The first paragraph details some general results, valid for all the simulations and useful to understand other results. The three following paragraphs show and explain results for each simulated pub/sub solution.

**General Results.** Table 2 lists the number of events and subscriptions generated during the simulation. We observe there is far more subscriptions message than event. This is the consequence of the chosen scenario. Indeed, only one event is active at a given time, then few events have been generated during the simulation. On the other hand, aircraft generate subscription every 10 minutes. As there are hundreds of aircraft flying for several hours, the result is more than 20000 generated subscriptions.

**Table 2.** Number of events and subscriptions

| Number of events | 150 |
|---|---|
| Number of subscriptions | 23978 |

Figure 4 shows the number of flying aircraft in the targeted area during the simulated day. This number has a direct impact on the network connectivity and thus on the delivery ratio possible by the pub/sub solution. We see number of aircraft during a part of the night is low compared to rest of the day. Consequently, it is difficult to obtain a delivery ratio close to 100% since it seems obvious that during this period, network partition exists. Previous studies on AANET like [2] found a reachable packet delivery ratio around 90%. It appears to be the maximum possible value of delivery ratio reachable with a publish / subscribe solution.

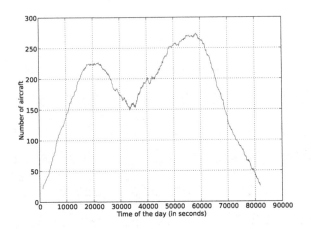

**Fig. 4.** Number of simultaneous aircraft during the day

**Broadcast Event Solution.** This paragraph deals with results obtained with the event based dissemination solution. The table 3 shows the delivery ratio and the network load obtained with this solution.

**Table 3.** Standard broadcast event solution

| Delivery ratio | 64,02% |
|---|---|
| Network load | $3,70 \cdot 10^{7}$ |

The observed result is not as good as estimated. However, it can be easily explained. The event has been disseminated in the network just after its creation. As the life of the event is between 30 and 60 min, it is possible that an aircraft appears after the generation of the event but it is interested by it anyway. With the implemented solution, it can never received the event.

Figure 5 highlights this phenomena. We introduced a new parameter in the simulation: *retransmiTime*. If its value is strictly higher than 0, it allows the retransmission of the event every *retransmiTime* seconds. The graphs show the obtained delivery ratio and network load depending on the retransmit time. We see delivery ratio can be increased up to 25 percent if the retransmit time is short (less than 600 seconds). The counter part is the exponential increase of the network load. As expected, this solution can give decent results at the cost of important network load which is not acceptable for AANET where bandwidth resources are very limited.

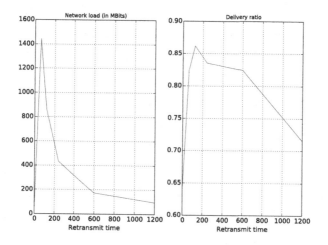

**Fig. 5.** Broadcast event solution depending on retransmit time

**Geographic Routing Protocol Based Solution.** Results shown in this paragraph follow from simulations where LBM has been configured to use forwarding region based on the distance with $\delta = 20km$. Table 4 gives first results obtained with this solution. They are worse than expected. The delivery ratio appears lower than with the broadcast solution and most importantly the network load is higher. In conclusion, the *broadcast event* solution is more efficient than this one.

**Table 4.** Standard geographic routing based solution

| Delivery ratio | 30,66% |
| --- | --- |
| Network load | $7,16 \cdot 10^8$ |

Several reasons can explain this result. Firstly, events and subscriptions are only sent to nodes belonging to the area defined with the geographical context. In our case, it corresponds to the cylinder which represents the weather region for events and a cylinder that surrounds the aircraft trajectory for subscriptions. These regions are small thus few or no aircraft are present to act as middleman between publishers and subscribers. To highlight this problem, the model has been modified to extend geographic context area thanks to a new parameter, *proximitySize* which defines the radius of cylinder used as context region, the center being the center of the weather situation for events and the center of the segment for subscriptions. Figure 6 shows obtained results according to *proximitySize*'s value. We see delivery ratio can be increased if the proximity size is extended but stays below 50% and thus this solution is far less efficient than the broadcast. The high network load can be explained by the characteristic of the application using the Publish / Subscribe service. As seen in section 3.3, aircraft send far more subscriptions than events and this solution forwards subscriptions compared to the previous one. Thus, even if subscriptions' size is lower than events' one, the important number of subscriptions increases substantially the load of the network.

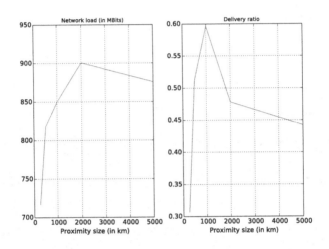

**Fig. 6.** Geographic routing based solution

**Proximity Routing Based Solution.** Table 5 gives first results obtained with the proximity routing based solution (the perimeter has been set to 250km). These results are consistent with those obtained in the previous section. The delivery ratio is lower than with the geographic solution and the network load is roughly equivalent.

**Table 5.** Standard proximity routing based solution

| Delivery ratio | 19,66% |
|---|---|
| Network load | $4,54 \cdot 10^8$ |

In the same way than the geographic solution, we verify the influence of the delivery perimeter on the performance of the solution. Figure 7 shows results according to size of proximity area. As expected, the delivery ratio and the network load increase with the size of the proximity region. The maximum delivery ratio obtained is close to the one obtained with the broadcast event solution. However, the network load is higher. The reason is the same as earlier with the dissemination of subscriptions in the network.

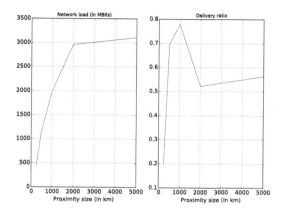

**Fig. 7.** Proximity routing based solution

## 4   Conclusion

In this article, after a brief survey about context aware Publish / Subscribe solutions adapted for VANET, we compare some solutions on AANET based on real commercial traffic, especially with a typical application for this type of network. We show that interesting approaches for VANET like geographical routing protocol are not suitable in this situation and lead to worse results than a basic approach based on the broadcast of the event in the network. Proximity based solution gives better results in terms of delivery ratio but with higher load of the network, which is not acceptable for AANET with low bandwidth resources.

Further work will concentrate on two axes. Firstly, this article shows that the development of a new publish / subscribe system is necessary to be suited to AANET and specific applications used on it. A promising approach is based on the definition of cluster in the network with different forwarding strategy inside and outside cluster groups. For example, we can imagine a solution where subscriptions are broadcasted inside a cluster group and events are sent to all cluster heads. It allows to take into account applications which generate far more subscriptions than events (as the one described in this article). The second axes is the research and the simulation of new application for which content based routing will be interesting. For example, in civil aviation domain, some research team studies ways to build real-time wind map and use of a Publish / Subscribe service over an AANET is a very promising solution to support this application.

## References

1. Royer, M., Pirovano, A., Garcia, F.: Survey on Context-Aware Publish/Subscribe Systems for VANET. In: Berbineau, M., et al. (eds.) Nets4Trains 2013 and Nets4Cars 2013. LNCS, vol. 7865, pp. 46–58. Springer, Heidelberg (2013)
2. Besse, F., Garcia, F., Pirovano, A., Radzic, J.: Wireless Ad Hoc Networks Access For Aeronautical Communications. In: AIAA 28th International Communications Satellite Systems Conference (2010)

3. Rowstron, A., Kermarrec, A.-M., Druschel, P.: SCRIBE: The Design of a Large-Scale Event Notification Infrastructure. In: Crowcroft, J., Hofmann, M. (eds.) NGC 2001. LNCS, vol. 2233, pp. 30–43. Springer, Heidelberg (2001)

4. Pietzuch, P.R., Bacon, J.M.: Hermes: A distributed event-based middleware architecture. In: Proceedings of the 22nd International Conference on Distributed Computing Systems Workshops, pp. 611–618 (2002)

5. Zhang, Z.: Routing in intermittently connected mobile ad hoc networks and delay tolerant networks: overview and challenges. IEEE Communications Surveys Tutorials 8(1), 24–37 (2006)

6. Leontiadis, I., Costa, P., Mascolo, C.: Persistent content-based information dissemination in hybrid vehicular networks. In: IEEE International Conference on Pervasive Computing and Communications, PerCom 2009, pp. 1–10 (March 2009)

7. Frey, D., Roman, G.-C.: Context-aware publish subscribe in mobile ad hoc networks. In: Murphy, A.L., Vitek, J. (eds.) COORDINATION 2007. LNCS, vol. 4467, pp. 37–55. Springer, Heidelberg (2007)

8. Meier, R., Cahill, V.: STEAM: event-based middleware for wireless ad hoc networks. In: Proceedings of the 22nd International Conference on Distributed Computing Systems Workshops, pp. 639–644 (2002)

9. Eugster, P., Garbinato, B., Holzer, A.: Design and Implementation of the Pervaho Middleware for Mobile Context-Aware Applications. In: International MCETECH Conference on, e-Technologies, 2008, pp. 125–135 (January 2008)

10. Cugola, G., Picco, G.P.: REDS: A reconfigurable dispatching system. In: Proceedings of the 6th International Workshop on Software Engineering and Middleware, SEM 2006, pp. 9–16. ACM, New York (2006)

11. Varga, A., Hornig, R.: An overview of the OMNeT++ simulation environment. In: Simutools 2008: Proceedings of the 1st International Conference on Simulation tools and Techniques for Communications, Networks and Systems & Workshops, pp. 1–10. ICST (Institute for Computer Sciences, Social-Informatics and Telecommunications Engineering), Brussels

12. http://inet.omnetpp.org/

13. Besse, F., Pirovano, A., Garcia, F., Radzik, J.: Interference estimation in an aeronautical ad hoc network. In: 2011 IEEE/AIAA 30th Digital Avionics Systems Conference (DASC), pp. 4C6–1–4C6–11 (2011)

14. Ko, Y.-B., Vaidya, N.H.: Geocasting in mobile ad hoc networks: Location-based multicast algotithms. In: Proc. of the IEEE Workshop on Mobile Computing Systems and Applications (WM-CSA) (1999)

15. Perkins, C., Belding-Royer, E., Das, S.: Ad hoc On-Demand Distance Vector (AODV) Routing. RFC 3561 (Experimental) (July 2003)

16. Vey, Q., Pirovano, A., Radzik, J., Garcia, F.: nautical Ad Hoc Network for Civil Aviation. In: Sikora, A., Berbineau, M., Vinel, A., Jonsson, M., Pirovano, A., Aguado, M. (eds.) Nets4Cars/Nets4Trains 2014. LNCS, vol. 8435, pp. 81–93. Springer, Heidelberg (2014)

# Emulation-Based Performance Evaluation of Routing Protocols for Uaanets

Jean-Aimé Maxa[1,2], Gilles Roudiere[1], and Nicolas Larrieu[1]

[1] ENAC, TELECOM/Resco, F-31055 Toulouse, France
[2] Univ de Toulouse, F-31400 Toulouse, France
maxa@recherche.enac.fr, {gilles.roudiere,nicolas.larrieu}@enac.fr

**Abstract.** UAV Ad hoc NETwork (UAANET) is a subset of the well-known Mobile Ad-hoc NETworks (MANETs). It consists of forming an ad hoc network with multiple small Unmanned Aerial Vehicles (UAVs) and the Ground Control Station (GCS). Similar to MANETs, the UAANET communication architecture is infrastructure-less and self-configuring network of several nodes forwarding data packets. However, it also has some specific features that brings challenges on network connectivity. Consequently, an adapted routing protocol is needed to exchange data packets within UAANETs. In this paper, we introduce a new hybrid experimental system that can evaluate different types of adhoc routing protocols under a realistic UAANET scenario. It is based on virtual machines and the Virtualmesh [1] framework to emulate physical aspects. We evaluated AODV, DSR and OLSR efficiency in a realistic scenario with three UAVs scanning an area. Our results show that AODV outperformed OLSR and DSR.

**Keywords:** UAV Ad hoc Network, Ad hoc Routing Protocol, VirtualMesh, Emulation, Simulation

## 1  Introduction

An Unmanned Aerial Vehicle (UAV) is a pilotless aerial vehicle that can be either controlled by an on-board computer or remotely piloted by a distant operator. As almost all of them are equipped with a wireless communication system, UAVs can be used to create a self-organizing and multi-hop network called UAV Ad-hoc NETwork (UAANET). This network architecture shares some common features with the well-known Mobile Ad-hoc NETwork (MANET), but also face distinctive issues. For instance, the relatively low number of nodes in UAANETs and their fast mobility leads to new challenges towards connectivity. Another challenge is also the QoS constraints of data traffic. UAVs missions often involve real-time data transmissions (video, real-time measurement), therefore, a certain QoS must be ensured to exploit the received information.

Furthermore, a routing protocol is needed to route data traffics through the multiple UAVs within UAANETs. Due to the several features of UAANETs (detailed section II), an adaptive routing protocol is needed to properly exchange

M. Kassab et al. (Eds.): Nets4Cars/Nets4Trains/Nets4Aircraft 2015, LNCS 9066, pp. 227–240, 2015.
DOI: 10.1007/978-3-319-17765-6_20

data traffics within UAANETs. To create such protocol, a possibility is either to create a routing protocol from scratch or to use an existing routing protocol proposed in the literature for MANETs and adapt them based on UAANETs requirements. The second case has particularly drawn our attention since it takes less effort and also because we would like to further concentrate on security aspect in our future work.

With this intention, a performance evaluation of the several MANETs routing protocols under UAANET scenarios must be carried out. In fact, there are only few studies that have been conducted to measure routing protocols for UAANETs [2] [3]. These studies are simulation-based and as such do not consider the linux kernel networking stack and a realistic mobility model. Indeed, simulation-based implementations might hide several important parameters (e.g, protocol implementations, background traffic, real time execution) due to the lack of OS-based implementations. These limitations could induce significant differences between simulations and real test-bed results.

Our emulation-based implementation allows to combine the low cost of a simulation with the accuracy of a real protocol stack. The traces used to generate UAVs mobility patterns were extracted from real traces so that physical related factors could be as realistic as possible. This article will present this testbed which could be used by the network community to carry out experimental evaluations of different types of Ad-Hoc Networks (e.g, VANET). It is also possible to evaluate different type of network protocols.

In the first part of this paper, we describe the different features of a UAANET architecture. The second part is dedicated to our experimental test protocol and results. Finally, the last part details the different software components of the testbed. Please note the entire framework is freely available and can be used by the research community.

## 2   UAANETs Characteristics

Similar to MANETs, the UAANETs architecture is an infrastructure-less network which uses multiple UAVs to forward data packets. It shares some similarities with standard mobile ad hoc networks such as self-organized pattern, self-managed information and communication between nodes without a centralized authority. However, UAANETs also have specific features that can be listed as [4].

- **Number of Nodes:** when an UAV deployed in a given mission has a relatively high speed, it can be sufficient to cover a restricted mission area. Then, the need for a large number of UAVs is not justified in such a case. Usually, UAV mission involves an average of 3 to 4 UAVs [5] [6] [7] [8] [9]. This has the advantage of reducing the impact of scalability issues which affects several MANET architectures.

- **Topology Variability:** as the medium is shared between multiple agents, collisions can occur, and loss rate can raise on high load. Moreover, distance between UAVs can make them loose connectivity between each other. These issues impact how critical information (i.e. control packets) has to be managed in the network.
- **Mobility:** UAV mobility patterns are a lot different from any other vehicle. An UAV movement is above all 3D based. This brings a whole set of challenges on the physical layer, the antenna behaviors and the security aspect(e.g, misbehavior detection). Furthermore, UAVs are used for specific missions that can include several different mobility patterns like area scanning, reaching a way-point, staying at a position or even patrol around a circuit. Accordingly, an innovative approach has been proposed in [10] where the author provided a mobility pattern for UAVs based on real traces. The diversity of UAV moves leads to very varied connectivity patterns.
- **Energy:** energy and computing power are limited in UAANETs but not as much as in sensor networks. This issue is usually not considered as a determining factor in UAANETs. Indeed, the energy needed to move the UAV is much greater than the energy needed to compute data.
- **Propagation Model:** in MANETs networks, nodes usually move close to the ground (like in VANETs or sensors networks). UAANETs are rather different as it is composed of flying node moving in large free space. Consequently, the free-space path loss model is often used to model the physical layer. Nevertheless it is advisable to take into account factors like large obstacles, ground reflections or weather conditions which can affect connectivity between UAVs.
- **QoS Constraints:** UAVs mission usually need real-time services, from aerial video and photography to real-time monitoring. Consequently, delay constraints are stronger in UAANETs. Also, some control/command traffic should be guaranteed as high-priority traffic to avoid control losses.

## 3   Routing Protocols for UAANETs

Several dynamic routing mechanisms are available for UAANETs. As exposed in [11], topology-based mechanisms, such as proactive, reactive or hybrid routing are the basis of numerous protocols. Nonetheless geographical routing, as surveyed in [12], could also be efficient in specific contexts.

**Proactive Routing:** A proactive routing mechanism tries to establish a route from one node to another before it is needed. Each node in the ad-hoc network sends control messages at a fixed rate. They usually contain the node routing table and relayed information from other nodes. Step by step, routing information is relayed from the destination node to the source node, and a route can be established. As proactive routing protocols we can cite OLSR [13] and its extensions (like DOLSR [14], M-OLSR [15] or CE-OLSR [16]), DSDV [17] and B.A.T.M.A.N [18].

**Reactive Routing:** In contrast with proactive protocols, reactive protocols establish a route when it is necessary. When a node wants to send a packet to a destination node, it first sends a route request packet which will be flooded through the whole network. When a node receives the route request packet, it adds its address to the list of the nodes that the packet went through. When one (or several) route request packets reach the destination node, a route response packet is sent back to the source using the shortest route discovered. The source uses this route to reach the destination. Several reactive protocols have been proposed in the literature : AODV [19] and its extensions (like AODVSEC [20], Time-slotted on-demand routing [37], or MAODV [21]) or DSR [22].

**Geographical Routing:** Geographical routing uses the nodes positions to find the best route from a source to a destination. Usually, it uses two distinct mechanisms: greedy forwarding and a backup mechanism in case where the former failed. The greedy forwarding consist of selecting as a next hop the closest node from the source node position. Alternatively, in case where no node within range closer to the destination is found, a backup mechanism is automatically launched. We can cite as an example "Face Routing" used by GFG [23], a mechanism which consists in creating a planar graph of the network connections, then using the *right hand rule* [24] to reach the destination. Several geographical routing protocols have been proposed: GPSR [25], GPMOR [26], USMP [27] or MPGR [28].

**Hybrid Routing:** Hybrid routing is a generic term referring to a combination of two routing mechanisms. As an example, we could cite RGR [29], which is a reactive protocol using greedy forwarding as a backup mechanism.

### 3.1  Previous Comparison Studies

In [2], AODV, GPSR and OLSR has been compared with simulated systems. This study showed that with a large number of nodes (more than 50), GPSR outperformed AODV an OLSR in terms of delay and packet delivery ratio. AODV has slightly better performances than OLSR in terms of packet delivery ratio, but can create higher delays at a low workload. In [30], protocols are compared with a set of 19 nodes. In this situation, AODV performs better than other topology-based protocols, having a slightly better overall throughput and a lower end-to-end delay. However, it is important to underline that these evaluations are based on simulations and do not consider real systems related issues. Also, they usually consider a large number of nodes in an unrealistic mission scenario and based on inadequate mobility patterns. These limitations led us to create our own experimental test protocol, which is detailed in the following part.

**Table 1.** Comparison of different kind of testbeds [1]

| Simulation | Real Word | Emulation |
|---|---|---|
| + / − Variable experiment duration | = Real experiment duration | = Real experiment duration |
| + Scalable | − Not easily scalable | + Scalable |
| + Mobility easy to set up | − Mobility difficult to set up | + Mobility easy to set up |
| + Reproducibility | − No reproducibility | = Reproducibility for physical factors |
| + Mastered environment | − Undesirable interferences | + Mastered environment |
| − Simulation specific implementation | + Operating system implementation | + Operating system implementation |
| − Whole system approximation | + Real system | = Physical environment approximation |

## 4    Emulation-Based Performance Evaluation of Routing Protocols for UAANET

### 4.1    Using Emulation for Protocols Evaluation

Some studies have already approached the comparison of routing protocols for UAANETs but they are usually based either on simulation or real flights experiments. Table 1 shows a comparison of each solution. Our proposal fits between these two solutions, it aims to evaluate protocol implementations compatible with a standard operating system without a need to perform a real environment test. We propose to use a real-time simulated physical environment in combination with virtual machines.

The main advantages of our hybrid experimental systems are:

- To perform a complete implementation of the different routing protocols that we want to analyse. Indeed, when a routing protocol is modelled inside a simulator, there is a need to simplify some parts of the behaviors and it is not obvious to predict that the obtained results will be consistant in real world. With the virtual machines implementation in this testbed, we can deal with the entire complexity of an Operating System such as Linux.
- To exchange information with a high number of nodes following a realistic flight plan. Indeed, it is expensive to gather enough UAVs, enough pilots and enough free space for the operation field. By using the *OMNeT++* [31] simulator, we can simulate a high number of nodes (each one being realistic thanks to the Linux virtual machine that we run). Furthermore, we have introduced real UAVs mobility pattern[1] into the OMNET simulation tool to be as close as possible to the UAANET outdoor experiments.

### 4.2    Experimental Test Implementation

The system we used to evaluate protocols is divided in several parts. It includes a set of tools that can fit to several scenarios : An hypervisor to run the virtual

---

[1] provided by Delair Tech company, see http://www.delair-tech.com for more details about this company.

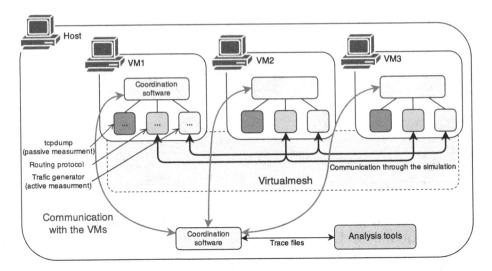

**Fig. 1.** Testbed implementation

machines, a measurement tools and a framework to allow virtual machines to communicate through a virtual wireless medium. An illustration of this system is on Figure 1.

**Virtualization:** We chose to use *VirtualBox*[32] as a virtualisation tool because it is an easy-to-use and efficient hypervisor. The virtualized system is a 11.04 version Ubuntu, working with the 2.6.38 version of the Linux kernel. This version were chosen because it is the same than the one used on the development system. A higher linux kernel can be used for improvement purposes.

**Traffic Measure and Analysis**

*Evaluated Parameters:* we decided to measure 3 parameters to evaluate routing protocols performances. First, the extra traffic generated by each protocol is evaluated. This overhead is caused by the control packets. This parameter impacts how much bandwidth can be allocated to applications. Secondly, we chose to evaluate the end-to-end delay for each protocol, even if with a low number of node this parameter becomes less interesting. Finally, the routing protocols abilities to find a new route after a route loss is evaluated. This is a really important matter in a high mobility context.

*Active and Passive Measurement:* due to Virtual Machines (VM) implementations, we could use any software to generate real traffic. However, for measurement purposes, we created our own tool written in Python. This script is able to generate a realistic traffic (as described in 4.3) overloaded with a short header including an ID -incremented for each packet sent- and a timestamp.

On the other hand, to get accurate data on the traffic going through the network during the test, we also used passive measurement tools. They aim at capturing traffic going through any interface without modifying the traffic. The tool used is the well-known *tcpdump*. Furthermore, *Wireshark* is used to analyse and extract several metrics (e.g, overhead) from the traces.

**The Virtualmesh Framework:** the *Virtualmesh* framework has been proposed by [1]. It is a framework that interfaces a Linux-based system with an *OMNeT++* [31] simulation. *Omnet++* is a powerful network simulator which simulate several systems and normalized protocols. Using *Virtualmesh* could be summed up in these simple steps :

1. A virtual wireless interface is created on the Linux system we want to include in the simulation;
2. We launch the *OMNet++* simulation (which has to include some modules supplied by the framework);
3. The framework links the Linux virtual interface to the simulation. This uses UDP sockets, so we can use either real or emulated Linux systems.

Once these steps are complete, a new node appears in the simulation. Any packet sent through the virtual interface is encapsulated in a UDP packet and sent to the simulation, which relays the packets depending on physical simulation parameters : nodes transmission range, signal attenuation, emission power, etc... Conversely, a packet received by an agent in the simulation is relayed to the virtual interface. An illustration of this system is exposed in Figure 2.

### 4.3    Test Scenario

**Realistic Mission Scenario:** to evaluate our routing protocols, we chose to create our experimental test protocol according to what could be a real UAV swarm mission. The scenario selected to evaluate protocols performances has been proposed by the Delair-Tech company based on their expertise in this field. It consists of three drones scanning an area for video surveillance purposes. We suppose that an obstacle blocks the traffic between two UAVs and the ground station, so a third one is deployed to be responsible for relaying data packets. This scenario is illustrated in Figure 3.

### Protocols Implementations

*Chosen Protocols Implementations:* we selected three implementations to test our protocols :

OLSR  As a well maintained implementation of OLSR, we chose OLSRd [34]. It is an implementation compatible with several Linux version and is available in Ubuntu's packages repositories.

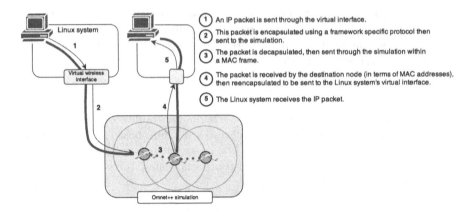

**Fig. 2.** The virtualmesh functionning

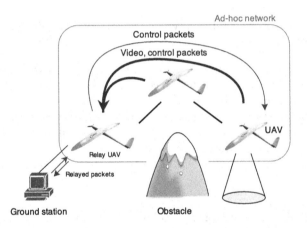

**Fig. 3.** Our video surveillance scenario

AODV We used AODV-uu [35] as the implementation of AODV. This is the only one we could find that is compatible with Linux. Nevertheless, it has been necessary to modify this version for it to be compatible with our Linux kernel version (2.6.38).

DSR As a Linux-compatible DSR implementation we used Piconet 2, as proposed in [36]. Unfortunately, this implementation was also not compatible with our kernel, and we chose to modify it to make it compatible with our kernel.

These implementations are parametrized according to the corresponding RFC recommended values.

**Geographical Protocols:** Concerning geographical protocols, their mechanisms are usually based on the following assertion : each node, to choose the next hop to the destination node, has to know the position of its close neighbours and the position of the destination. Thus, to deploy completely geographical protocols, we would have to implement an additional mechanism to exchange the different node positions through the Ad-Hoc Network (otherwise we would have to use an other communication medium, which is in our case not available). The main existing position sharing mechanisms are detailed in [33]. We did not choose to implement such a mechanism given that the evaluation of the routing protocol would have been deeply impacted by the specific additional mechanism we have selected. As future works, it could be interesting to analyse the different position sharing mechanisms available in the literature and implement one that is the most efficient to enhance this study.

**Realistic Traffic Generation:** To test protocols performances, we generate a realist traffic. This is achieved by using real traces supplied by Delair-Tech, from a mission with only one UAV. We extracted control traffic characteristics and extrapolate these informations to a three UAVs mission. As a result, we have been able to recreate a realistic traffic scenario. As we supposed a video surveillance mission, we considered that a HD video would be the main applicative traffic from UAVs to the ground station. The used codec is the H264 for being a popular codec for this kind of video quality. We supposed a 4 Mbits throughput for a full HD image (1920x1080 pixels) at 30 images per seconds. H264 being a variable rate codec, we decided to include an arbitrary value of 50% variability for each image sent and separated in 1,000 bytes packet to avoid fragmentation. These different results are described in Table 2.

**Table 2.** Generated traffic

| Type | Source→Destination | Paquet size | Rate |
|------|--------------------|-------------|------|
| Tick | 1→2,1→3 | 64 bytes | 1.0 packet/s |
| Georef | 2→1,3→1 | 64 bytes | 1.8 packet/s |
| Command | 1→2,1→3 | 64 bytes | 0.034 packet/s |
| Video | 2→1,3→1 | | 4 Mbits/s |

## 4.4 Results and Analysis

### Connectivity

*Connectivity analysis:* we extracted disconnected states on the links 3→1 and 2→1, as being the most loaded traffics they allow an acurate active measurement. To prevent short unstable states to disturb the measurement, two losses that are too close in time (less than 0.1s) are merged. We performed the same mobility scenario with each protocol, so that the connectivity patterns would be similar. Thus, we synchronised each measurement on the first long loss (higher than

**Table 3.** Connectivity results for a 3 hours test

|  | AODV | DSR | OLSR |
|---|---|---|---|
| **Test duration** (from the first to the last disconnection) | 2h 57min 3s | | |
| Disconnected state / Test duration | 61.52 % | 61.0 % | 58.8 % |
| **Unstable states / Test duration** | 3.78% (6 min 41s) | | |
| Connectivity during unstable states | 88.5 % | 66.7 % | 15.3 % |

Traffic 3→1

|  | AODV | DSR | OLSR |
|---|---|---|---|
| **Test duration** (from the first to the last disconnection) | 2h 58min 44s | | |
| Disconnected state / Test duration | 62.9 % | 61.7 % | 60.4 % |
| **Unstable states / Test duration** | 3.79% (6 min 46s) | | |
| Connectivity during unstable states | 90.65 % | 58.2 % | 24.1 % |

Traffic 2→1

15s) to evaluate differences between each connectivity result. From this data, we extracted what we called "unstable states" which corresponds to states when all protocols do not behave the same way. By acting this way, we took away states during which connectivity, or non-connectivity, were stable for each protocol. This unstable states extraction is shown in Figure 4. We obtained the results exposed in Table 3. As we can see, the total connection time is slightly better for reactive protocols. In unstable states, AODV stand out from the others making able connectivity up to 90%. This means that AODV is the most reactive routing protocol to topology changes.

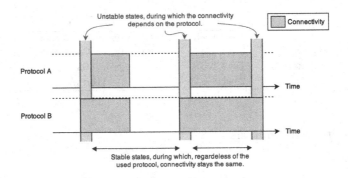

**Fig. 4.** "Unstable states" extracted from the measurement

**Overhead:** we performed a one-hour test to evaluate the overhead created for each protocol and obtained the results exposed in Table 4. As we can see, OLSR is slightly better than AODV, but they both outperform DSR that has a really high overhead.

**Table 4.** Protocol overhead over a one-hour test (captured from the interface of UAV 1)

|  | AODV | DSR | OLSR |
|---|---|---|---|
| Control packets | 501 kB | 759,99 kB | 438 kB |
| Traffic % (bytes) | 0.034% | 4.393% | 0.027% |
| Headers added to data packets | 0 | 26,723 kB | 0 |
| Average header length | 0 | 17.8 B | 0 |

**Delays:** concerning delays introduced by each protocol (exposed in Table 5), we notice that delays are really low. However we can see that DSR introduces a slightly higher delay than the other protocols but this is probably due to the DSR implementation. The fact that DSR needs to modify data packets by introducing a header, and that it uses acknowledgements for each packets sent, can also affect its performance.

**Table 5.** Average and maximum delays over a one hour test (captured from the interface of UAV 1)

|  | AODV | DSR | OLSR |
|---|---|---|---|
| Average delay | 5.32 ms | 10.15 ms | 5.91 ms |
| Maximum delay | 100.0 ms | 100.0 ms | 99.8 ms |

**Conclusion:** as AODV being the protocol the most reactive to topology changes and having a limited overhead, we concluded that AODV was the most suitable routing protocol for our scenario. As several studies proved that AODV can be outperformed by proactive protocols with a large number of nodes, its on-demand mechanism allows here a faster response to routing needs. Our mobility pattern and our emulation system certainly affected the measures, but we found similar results to those exposed in [30].

## 5    Conclusion and Future Work

In this paper, we introduce a hybrid experimental system which can be used for different types of Ad-Hoc Networks and to evaluate different types of network protocols. This evaluation framework is composed of a new set of tools to evaluate ad-hoc protocols thanks to virtual machines. Applied to UAANETs, we have been able to prove that, considering our realistic mobility scenario, AODV is a more suitable protocol than OLSR and DSR. Concerning further studies, the fact that we used an ideal physical model has certainly an impact over our results. It could be interesting to introduce a more realistic physical model to the simulation, and consequently adapt the experimental test protocol. As the Linux system used in our experimental test protocol is different from the real Delair-Tech embedded system, we would like to introduce a real system to the tests. These results could also be compared to results obtained with a real test bed, composed of multiple real UAVs. For further researches we decided to make available to download by the community the different tools we created for this experimental test protocol. This set of tools is available at the following link: http://www.recherche.enac.fr/resco/doku.php?id=emulationtestbed.

We hope that the tools we designed and shared online with the research community will be reused and extended for additionnal studies. Indeed, we think this work could help the design, the evaluation and the validation of future UAANET systems.

# References

1. Staub, T., Gantenbein, R., Braun, T.: VirtualMesh: An emulation framework for wireless mesh networks in OMNeT++. In: Proceedings of the 2nd International Conference on Simulation Tools and Techniques. ICST (Institute for Computer Sciences, Social-Informatics and Telecommunications Engineering) (2009)
2. Hyland, M.T., et al.: Simulation-based performance evaluation of mobile ad hoc routing protocols in a swarm of unmanned aerial vehicles. In: 21st International Conference on Advanced Information Networking and Applications Workshops, AINAW 2007, vol. 2. IEEE (2007)
3. Hyland, M.T.: Performance evaluation of ad hoc routing protocols in a swarm of autonomous unmanned aerial vehicles. No. AFIT/GCS/ENG/07-07. Air Force Inst of tech Wright-Patterson Afb Oh School of Engineering and Management (2007)
4. Bekmezci, I., Sahingoz, O.K., Temel, A.: Flying ad-hoc networks (FANETs): A survey. Ad Hoc Networks 11(3), 1254–1270 (2013)
5. Chaumette, S., et al.: CARUS, an operational retasking application for a swarm of autonomous UAVs: First return on experience. In: Military Communications Conference, MILCOM 2011. IEEE (2011)
6. Rosati, S., et al.: Dynamic Routing for Flying Ad Hoc Networks. arXiv preprint arXiv:1406.4399 (2014)
7. Daniel, K., et al.: AirShield: A system-of-systems MUAV remote sensing architecture for disaster response. In: 2009 3rd Annual IEEE Systems Conference. IEEE (2009)
8. Cameron, S., et al.: SUAAVE: Combining aerial robots and wireless networking. In: 25th Bristol International UAV Systems Conference (2010)
9. Xu, Z., et al.: Analyzing two connectivities in UAV-ground mobile ad hoc networks. In: 2011 IEEE International Conference on Computer Science and Automation Engineering (CSAE), vol. 2. IEEE (2011)
10. Bouachir, O., et al.: A Mobility Model For UAV Ad hoc Network. In: ICUAS 2014 Proceedings (2014)
11. Sahingoz, O.K.: Networking models in flying Ad-hoc networks (FANETs): Concepts and challenges. Journal of Intelligent - Robotic Systems 74(-2), 513–527 (2014)
12. Mauve, M., Widmer, J., Hartenstein, H.: A survey on position-based routing in mobile ad hoc networks. IEEE Network 15(6), 30–39 (2001)

13. Clausen, T., et al.: Optimized link state routing protocol (OLSR) (2003)
14. Alshbatat, A.l., Dong, L.: Cross layer design for mobile ad-hoc unmanned aerial vehicle communication networks. In: 2010 International Conference on Networking, Sensing and Control (ICNSC). IEEE (2010)
15. Paul, A.B., Sukumar, N.: Modified optimized link state routing (M-OLSR) for wireless mesh networks. In: International Conference on Information Technology, ICIT 2008. IEEE (2008)
16. Belhassen, M., Belghith, A., Abid, M.A.: Performance evaluation of a cartography enhanced OLSR for mobile multi-hop ad hoc networks. In: Wireless Advanced (WiAd 2011). IEEE (2011)
17. Perkins, C.E., Bhagwat, P.: Highly dynamic destination-sequenced distance-vector routing (DSDV) for mobile computers. In: ACM SIGCOMM Computer Communication Review, vol. 24(4). ACM (1994)
18. Open-mesh, http://www.open-esh.org/projects/open-mesh/wiki (visited on April 08, 2014)
19. Perkins, C.E., Belding-Royer, E., Das, S.: Ad hoc on demand distance vector (AODV) routing (RFC 3561). In: IETF MANET Working Group (August 2003)
20. Aggarwal, A., et al.: AODVSEC: A novel approach to secure Ad Hoc on-Demand Distance Vector (AODV) routing protocol from insider attacks in MANETs. arXiv preprint arXiv:1208.1959 (2012)
21. Royer, E.M.: Multicast ad hoc on-demand distance vector (MAODV) routing. IETF Internet Draft, draft-ietf-manet-maodv-00. txt (2000)
22. Maltz, D., Johnson, D., Hu, Y.: The Dynamic Source Routing Protocol (DSR) for Mobile Ad Hoc Networks for IPv4. RFC 4728 (February 2007), http://www.ietf.org/rfc/rfc4728.txt
23. Bose, P., et al.: Routing with guaranteed delivery in ad hoc wireless networks. Wireless Networks 7(6), 609–616 (2001)
24. Bondy, J.A., Murty, U.S.R.: Graph theory with applications, vol. 6. Macmillan, London (1976)
25. Brad, K., Kung, H.-T.: GPSR: Greedy perimeter stateless routing for wireless networks. In: Proceedings of the 6th Annual International Conference on Mobile Computing and Networking, pp. 243–254. ACM (2000)
26. Lin, L., et al.: A novel geographic position mobility oriented routing strategy for UAVs. Journal of Computational Information Systems 8(2), 709–716 (2012)
27. Lidowski, R.L., Mullins, B.E., Baldwin, R.O.: A novel communications protocol using geographic routing for swarming uavs performing a search mission. In: IEEE International Conference on Pervasive Computing and Communications, PerCom 2009. IEEE (2009)
28. Lin, L., et al.: A geographic mobility prediction routing protocol for Ad Hoc UAV Network. In: 2012 IEEE Globecom Workshops (GC Workshops). IEEE (2012)
29. Shirani, R.: Reactive-greedy-reactive in unmanned aeronautical ad-hoc networks: A combinational routing mechanism. Diss. Carleton University Ottawa (2011)
30. Performance of mobile ad hoc networking routing protocols in realistic scenarios. In: Military Communications Conference, MILCOM 2003, vol. 2, pp. 1268–1273. IEEE (2003), doi:10.1109/MILCOM, 2003.1290408
31. OMNeT++, http://www.omnetpp.org/ (visited on July 29, 2014)
32. ORACLE VM Virtualbox, https://www.virtualbox.org/ (visited on July 28, 2014)

33. Jorg, W., et al.: Position-based Routing in Ad Hoc Wireless Networks. In: Ilyas, M., Dorf, R.C. (eds.) The Handbook of Ad Hoc Wireless Networks, pp. 219–232. CRC Press, Inc., FL (2003), http://dl.acm.org/citation.cfm?id=989711.989724 ISBN: 0-8493-1332-5

34. OLSRd, an adhoc wireless mesh routing protocol, http://www.olsr.org/ (visited on July 29, 2014)

35. AODV-UU, http://aodvuu.sourceforge.net/ (visited on July 29, 2014)

36. Song, A.: PicoNet II - A Wireless Ad-hoc Network For Mobile Handheld Devices. PhD thesis. University of Queensland (October 2001)

37. Forsmann, J.H., Hiromoto, R.E., Svoboda, J.: A time-slotted on-demand routing protocol for mobile ad hoc unmanned vehicle systems. In: Defense and Security Symposium. International Society for Optics and Photonics (2007)

# Author Index